Advance prai~~s~~
by J~~e~~

"The introduction does its job. I can't wait to read the whole book!!!"

Kathleen McLain, Real Estate Agent

"I am loving your writing. You are very talented and funny. I want to go visit Australia!!! I want my husband and my daughter to read it next."

Audrey Ziegler, Graphic Artist

"It's solid from beginning to end. I couldn't put it down! I was in Queensland on Magnetic Island this morning. I can't wait to get back to the story."

Lisa Calvert, Entrepreneur

"Fabulous descriptions of 'Oz.' I felt like I was there with you! It makes me want to go!"

Kristin Kirman, Salon Stylist

"Just got the book and read the first few pages. WOW. WOW. WOW. Can't wait to dig in."

Caroline Rolman, College Student

"Descriptive, inviting, intriguing, educational, and enlightening. You have an easy to read style and have done a wizard-like job of telling your story of 'Oz.'"

Gary Greenfield, Business Consultant

"This book is a wonderful adventure through Australia, a trip into the back country that most of us can only dream about. An American in Oz touched my heart and soul."

Katie Graves, Advertising Specialist

An American
in
Oz

Discovering the Island Continent of AUSTRALIA

Jennifer Monahan

INFINITY
PUBLISHING

Copyright © 2010 by Jennifer Monahan

COVER PHOTO: "Road to Kata Tjuta" The image was captured by the author on January 9, 2000 in the Uluru-KataTjuta National Park – A World Heritage Area, deep in the heart of the outback.

ISBN 0-7414-5811-X

Printed in the United States of America

Published January 2010

INFINITY PUBLISHING
1094 New DeHaven Street, Suite 100
West Conshohocken, PA 19428-2713
Toll-free (877) BUY BOOK
Local Phone (610) 941-9999
Fax (610) 941-9959
Info@buybooksontheweb.com
www.buybooksontheweb.com

Dedicated to
my parents, Meredith and Eleanor,
my husband, Patrick,
and my sister, Lisa.

Your support and encouragement
mean the world to me.

The Origin of *Oz*

"Oz" is a playful spelling
of the abbreviated letters for
Australia - AUS (pronounced "awz").

And the spelling of the sound "awz"
was inspired by the classic
American children's tale
The Wonderful Wizard of Oz
written by L. Frank Baum in 1899,
published in the summer of 1900.

To receive your free ebook* version of
The Wonderful Wizard of Oz by L. Frank Baum
go to: www.jennifermonahan.com/uploads/Wizard.pdf

*Ebooks are electronic books, not physical books. An ebook is a digital
file (PDF) that is downloaded off the Internet and saved onto your
computer's hard drive. It can then be read on the computer or printed on
your home printer and put into a folder or binder to be read like a book.

CONTENTS

Author's Note: the book is written from an end of the day perspective. *Italics* reflect current moment thoughts and place descriptions.

Every effort has been made to make accurate and truthful statements about the places, people, animals, plants and things of Australia. A few names have been changed for privacy purposes.

The journey begins with the flight in from the east.
Travel with the author by plane, train, and automobile
through a country comparable in size to the
continental United States.

Map Source: CIA Maps and Publications (2000)
Travel route graphics courtesy of Audrey Ziegler

To view a full color version of the map, go to:
www.jennifermonahan.com/uploads/OzBook_Map.PNG

INTRODUCTION

*"What lies behind us and what lies before us
are tiny matters compared to what lies within us."*
Ralph Waldo Emerson

The first question most people ask when I tell them I went to Australia for two months is, "When did you go?" The second most popular question is, "How were you able to go?" "It was December 1999," I answer, "My boyfriend and I were there to celebrate the new millennium."

At the time, Jeff and I were sharing a house in Florida and sharing all expenses equally. I was self-employed, neither one of us had children, and I intentionally chose a career that was flexible. Working as a freelance bookkeeper, I was able to set up my own schedule and select jobs that fit into that schedule. To make sure there was always enough time and money to travel, financial obligations and day-to-day responsibilities were kept to a minimum. The rent was reasonable, utility costs were low, I ate meals at home, took lunch to work everyday, my car was paid for, and I chose activities that were free such as swimming, biking, and long beach walks. Total monthly expenses were $1000, and I was earning twice that amount each and every month.

But it wasn't always that way.

Four years earlier, I was married, owned a home with a mortgage, had three cats, a few birds, paid one car payment after another, and worked fifty to sixty hours a week as a U.S. Postal Service clerk. I also played the role of landlord. There was a small cottage in the back of the house that my husband and I rented out and managed ourselves. Life was full, routine, and somewhat complicated.

In 1995, all that changed when my marriage ended. It was a mutual and amicable decision. We gave the birds away and divided our possessions fifty/fifty except for the cats, of course. My husband agreed to take full custody, and I got visiting rights. Fortunately, and by choice, neither one of us had any children, so it made things a little bit easier. After eleven years of marriage, and at the age of 37, I began a new chapter in my life.

Setting up a simple and minimalist lifestyle after the divorce, or "correction" as I like to call it, was intentional. I realized I could live anywhere, do anything, and take a job transfer if I wanted to. It was time for something new and different in my life. For the past twelve years, I had been working for the U.S. Postal Service doing everything I knew to climb the professional ladder and rise above full-time clerk. I *really* wanted to be a Postmaster. I wanted my own little office in a quaint little Florida town somewhere, anywhere, and any town would do.

In order to get ahead, I took several home-study postal management courses on my own time and volunteered for every assignment that came my way. I was the model employee saying, "Yes," to jobs no one else wanted. But after two unsuccessful Postmaster interviews (they were few and far between), I was led to believe that the lack of a college degree was holding me back.

Young, bored, and anxious to get on with life, I had quit college in my junior year as a Business Administration major. Thanks to the encouragement of my Postmaster, I decided to return to school at the age of 33. It was hard working full-time, managing a household, a rental property, and taking two and three college courses a semester. I'll admit, when classes first started I did a lot of whining, especially about the fact that I would be 35 when graduation came around. Fortunately, everything was brought into perspective when a very wise friend of mine said, "Jennifer, you're going to be 35 anyway. You might as well be 35 with a degree." That was exactly what I needed to hear. I buckled down and got through as quickly as possible.

In the same week as my birthday, I graduated and gave myself the gift of closure. I had finally finished what I started seventeen years earlier, and it felt great. A new level of self-confidence and self-reliance emerged, but the joys of holding that diploma were short lived when I continued to interview unsuccessfully for the coveted job of Postmaster. It seemed as if the decision makers were filling the vacancies with employees who had less experience then I had, and there was no making sense of it all. After seven years of hitting my head on the proverbial glass ceiling, I got frustrated and finally got the hint. The change I was looking for was not within my current employment. Once I got honest with myself, I realized there was another path to take, and it was time to let go of the old. I knew it like I know I am right-handed. I just didn't know exactly what the new path would look like.

I searched for a way out of my quiet desperation by going to the library and borrowing all kinds of books and cassette tapes on life and how to change my life. I turned my car into a "university on wheels" and listened to the teachings of Wayne Dyer, Marianne Williamson and Deepak Chopra whenever I drove anywhere. Wearing headphones while sorting the early morning mail before the doors opened to the public, I listened to countless hours of self-improvement tapes to broaden my way of thinking and see new possibilities for my life. I knew the answers were available, and I was determined to find them. I searched the classified ads for jobs and business opportunities trying to find one that appealed to me. Preparing for the transition, I continued to reduce my monthly expenses by subscribing to newsletters such as *The Tightwad Gazette* by Amy Dacycyn.

It was a challenge figuring out what my next career was going to be, but I finally got an answer. It had been right in front of me all along, and when I finally saw it, I was astonished at how blind I had been. I once heard that we can get the message in a whisper, we can get it in a nudge, or we can get it in the smackdown. I was one of those who had to get it in the smackdown.

Over the past nine years, I was constantly learning about money and the financial side of life simply because I was interested. Financial publications of all types were scattered throughout the house. The one book that affected me the most was called *Your Money or Your Life* by Rubin, Dominguez, and Tilford. It forever transformed the way I looked at work, money, and my relationship between the two. How best to manage, invest, and spend our well earned dollars, and come out ahead at the end of the day, was fascinating to me. Genuine interest led to creating small business deductions and investment portfolios in the stock market and real estate. Occasionally, I was inspired to attend one of those free seminars that accounting and law firms offer so I could learn more about wills, trusts and estate planning for myself and my parents in case there were questions later on in life. Accounting was also an extension of my job with the Postal Service. At the end of each business day, I was the one who counted the money and filed the daily sales reports to our main office. For seven years, I was the one who balanced the books and submitted the quarterly and annual financial reports to postal headquarters.

The core reason I chose Business Administration as a major (after stumbling through the first two years undecided) was because I saw that everything in life is a business. Whether it's a college student's budget or a seven-figure one, success is measured in how well the money's managed and the business (or life) is run. The day I woke up to my calling was the day I asked the questions, "What am I already good at? What do I already know? What service can I offer outside of the Postal Service?" Over the years, I had learned a marketable skill and had something of value to offer the community. I decided to become my own boss as a freelance bookkeeper.

Strangely enough, all the while I was learning what I could about finances, I was clueless to the fact that I was in training to work in the private sector. For years, *intuition, imagination* and *inspiration*, my "smarter-self" as I call the three i's, were setting me up and leading me into a solution to the restlessness I was feeling in a career that had once served me so well for so long. The routine of the job was starting to get to me, but I loved the regular paycheck every two weeks. I loved the benefits of great health insurance, paid vacations, paid sick leave, and the satisfaction of steady employment. I enjoyed working with the public, and along with thirty of the most dedicated people I know, we delivered something of value every single day. And then one day, everything changed.

The defining moment, the moment I *knew* it was time to leave the Postal Service, came when a customer walked up to the counter and asked, "How much does a postcard stamp cost?" It was an entirely reasonable question, but I lost it. My eyes filled with tears and my throat suddenly tightened. I had answered that question a gazillion times, and in that moment, the words simply wouldn't come. Unable to speak and on the verge of a full blown meltdown, I did my best to hide my temporary moment of insanity and gently pushed the stamp in front of the customer so she could read the amount for herself. She told me how many she wanted, I handed her the stamps, and I barely got through the sale. Seconds later, I closed my window (that's postal jargon for sales counter), took a ten-minute break, and did what I had to do to recompose myself and return to duty. Afterall, the mail must go through. I rallied and tried to convince myself I could stay, but the nudges to leave were getting stronger and more frequent.

Despite all efforts made by my "smarter-self" to push me out of misery and into joy sooner than later, I remained stubborn and chanted the words, "I don't know where to start." I was so wrapped up in the question of "How am I going to find my first bookkeeping job?" that I never made a move. But the universe works in mysterious ways, wanting more for us than we do for ourselves at times, and the first client actually came to me. It was a typical work day just like any other. A month after the postcard stamp meltdown, I was watching a customer put away the roll of stamps she had just purchased when she looked up and asked, "Jennifer, do you know anyone who does bookkeeping?" Out of habit, I began searching my memory for someone I knew. A split second later, I woke up and thought, "It's me! This is it. This is my way out." I gave the woman my phone number, and within days we were working together. She only needed assistance seven hours a week. After a month working both jobs and thoroughly enjoying the new one, I gave my two months notice of resignation to the Postmaster.

Talk about self-imposed agony. I convinced myself that I gave the extra long heads-up so management would have time to find someone to replace me and I would have time to train a fellow employee to do all those one-of-a-kind jobs I had volunteered to do over the years. It turned out that four weeks notice was plenty, and it was clear that I was painfully pulling away.

There were dozens of sleepless nights in those last months on the job. I journaled, I cried, I questioned everything about leaving. Common sense told me to stay, and it was a loud, almost angry, voice. For a long time I believed safety and security could only be found in a 9-5 job. It was the truth for me until the day I changed inside and no longer saw it that way. I knew deep down it was time to move beyond the predictable and trust my *intuition*, take action on *inspiration*, and believe in the strength and joy of *imagination*. Those are the aspects of ourselves that lead to real and lasting happiness.

I read *Feel the Fear and Do It Anyway* by Susan Jeffers to muster up the courage and go through with my plan. I listened to the quiet calm voice within gently encouraging me to take the first really big leap of faith of my life. There was a quote I read often that described exactly what I was going through. Anais Nin, a French born American author, said, *"And the day came when the risk to remain tight in a bud grew more painful than the risk that it took to blossom."* It reassured me that I was doing the right thing.

My sister, Lisa, and friends closest to me helped me through the roughest part of that transition. They knew what I was going through and knew I could make it out on my own. Their words of encouragement often came when I was at my lowest and needed to hear them the most. My family and friends believed in me in those moments I didn't believe in myself. We all need people like that in our lives. It's absolutely essential in the pursuit and *attainment* of our own personal happiness.

On Friday, March 27th, 1998, I removed "the golden handcuffs," the shackles that bind many government employees tied to the belief that a government job is the only place to find safety and security. At exactly 5:00 p.m., I punched that old timecard for the last time and walked out feeling as if a huge weight had been lifted off my shoulders. I was ready to see what the world had to offer beyond the four walls of the post office.

It took three months to reach the point where I was earning more than enough to pay my bills. I finally had proof that I could leave the post office and thrive in the aftermath. It turns out, word had spread within the community that I was working as a freelance bookkeeper, and the phone rang each time I was ready to add another client into the mix. The initial seven hours a week with one client grew to thirty-five hours a week and five clients. I was living my desire; to work when I wanted to and take time off when I needed it most.

One year later, I had saved enough money to go to Australia.

The "No Plan" Plan

It was the summer of 1999 when Jeff and I were discussing what to do at the turn of the millennium. We asked ourselves, "Where do we want to be on December 31st?" We both had the sense that it was important to make it memorable. We wanted to be somewhere other than our own backyard.

Jeff told me he had always wanted to snorkel the Great Barrier Reef off the coast of Queensland in the northeast portion of Australia. I love to swim and had snorkeled a few times in the Florida Keys. It sounded like a great idea, but Australia, the reef, too, for that matter, seemed so big and so far away, it was a concept difficult for me to grasp at first. Looking back, I have no idea why Australia appeared so unreachable. For five years prior to that conversation, I had taken vacations on my own and with girlfriends to Taiwan, the Solomon Islands, New Zealand and South Korea. New Zealand is so close to Australia that many Americans visit both countries on the same trip, but my trip to New Zealand was limited. I wasn't able to do both. Up until that initial discussion about Australia, one week had been the longest amount of time I ever stayed in any one country due to the constraints of a postal job.

"How long should we go for?" I asked Jeff once I got past the initial shock, came to my senses, and realized I could go anywhere I wanted to if I put my mind to it. After we talked about it, we decided we needed at least a month. The time change alone would take several days to get used to and there were dozens of interesting places to visit. "Ayers Rock would be a great place to be on New Year's Eve," I said. And then I remembered one of my clients had a son named David living in Queensland who held an open invitation for me and Jeff to visit his organic tree farm near the Great Barrier Reef. In the past, I never took the invitation seriously, and now it was becoming a reality. The mental itinerary was filling up fast.

A few weeks later, Jeff asked me, "Do you think you can take two months away from your job?" Now that was a stretch. My first concern was that the work would pile up so high my clients would have to replace me. A great inconvenience, and would it be a permanent replacement? There were no guarantees, no contracts, and no unions assuring I would have a job when I got back. The only way to find out how each client felt about my absence was to ask them. Four said, "Yes, we can wait until you get back," and the fifth agreed to take on temporary assistance. I simply had to trust that they would all welcome my return and work would resume as usual.

In planning our trip, Jeff and I came up with three known points of interest we wanted to cover in a country nearly the same size as the continental United States. They were:

1. Swim the Ningaloo Reef on the west coast near Exmouth, Western Australia

2. Celebrate New Year's Eve at Ayers Rock in the Northern Territory, located in the center of Australia

3. Head northeast to swim the Great Barrier Reef and visit David's organic tree farm in Queensland

That was it. We had two months to cover four weeks worth of traveling, so there was plenty of time to explore the country further. We realized there were a lot of unknowns, and for some reason, we were not concerned with filling in the blanks. We were going to "wing it," figure it out as we went along, allow Australia to show us the way, and that was something neither one of us had ever done before.

To learn more about a country I knew very little about, I went to the local library and took out three videos so I could "see" Australia. One video in particular stood apart from the others. It was about the Indian Pacific Railway, a train that runs from Sydney to Perth, from the Pacific Ocean to the

Indian Ocean, and back again. It's the same distance one would travel if going from Savannah, Georgia to Los Angeles, California.

Since the Ningaloo Reef was on the west coast and we were flying into Sydney on the east coast, we decided it would be a great idea to take the train immediately upon our arrival and enjoy the three-day ride to Perth, as we acclimated to the new time zone, a time zone exactly opposite to ours at home. We could get to the west coast and get over jet lag all at the same time. So we booked our train reservation well in advance of the trip and had one reservation in place. My need to know everything ahead of time was somewhat satisfied. The second arrangement to cover (other than the required plane reservations) was to become card carrying members of Hostelling International. We were on a budget and knew we would be staying in youth hostels along the way.

By October 1999, all the plans we were going to make were made. We didn't know how we were going to get to the Ningaloo Reef once we got off the train. We didn't know how we were going to get to Ayers Rock by December 31st, and we didn't know how we were going to get to David's tree farm deep in the rainforest of Queensland. The "how" was none of our business, yet.

Hours of planning went into the packing stage of our preparations. It may have been winter in Florida, but it was summer in Australia, and we were going to experience a wide range of weather conditions. We also planned to camp along the way, possibly in the outback, so we packed our gear, tent and all. We packed everything we thought we might need for the next two months.

A few weeks before leaving the 'States, Jeff bought a current issue of the *Lonely Planet Australia Travel Guide*. Since we really didn't know what we were doing, a guide book seemed like a good idea. I bought a small travel journal so I could record every experience of every day. I knew this was going to be an extraordinary two months, and I wanted to remember as much of it as possible. I also knew, deep down to my core, that I was about to take the *second* biggest leap of faith of my life....

..... and down the yellow brick road I went.

PART ONE

Arrival Sydney and the Train to Perth

*"The journey of a thousand miles must begin
with a single step."*
Lao Tzu, Chinese Philosopher

Day 1, Wednesday December 8, 1999

December 7th never happened, not in my lifetime anyway. The travel agent told us we would cross the International Date Line as we flew over the Pacific Ocean and that we would miss a day, but I really couldn't grasp the concept. We left Florida on December 6th and arrived in Australia on December 8th. I thought I might see an extra long day, an extra long sunset, experience something unusual that would mark this strange phenomenon, but nothing out of the ordinary ever happened. I decided to flip my mental calendar ahead and leave the lost day in a category called "I'll figure it out later."

The entire trip was twenty-eight hours door-to-door real time. The first leg was eight hours from Florida to California, then six hours waiting for our connecting flight at the Los Angeles airport, and another fourteen hours flying from Los Angeles to Sydney overnight. It was not part of the trip I was looking forward to. I did my best to sleep sitting up in coach class and managed to get some rest, if I could call it that. To prepare us for our 8:00 a.m. arrival, the Qantas crew gave everyone warm face towels and cold drinks. It was a welcome touch, and I did feel better afterwards.

The final landing approach into Sydney did the trick to transform the long journey into a distant memory. As the plane banked its last turn, I could see the world famous Sydney Opera House. That was proof enough we had indeed traveled half way around the world and our adventure was about to begin.

With our luggage collected, paperwork in order, passports checked, and permission to stay in the country for three months at most, clearing customs went smoothly. Jeff and I made our way to the airport terminal exit to public transportation where countless vans and taxi cabs were waiting, and that's where we stood for the first time on Australian soil. At mid-morning, the sun was already high and bright in the sky.

It may be December, but it's summertime in "the land down under." South of the equator, the seasons are opposite to ours in the 'States. In addition to the reversed seasons, north has become south and south is north as far as the weather is concerned. As we head south, the temperatures will get cooler, and as we head north it will get hotter. I can easily accept a warm December since I've been living in the tropics for the past fifteen years, but the north/south thing is definitely going to be a challenge.

Standing among the other travelers, I noticed that a majority of the crowd was able to get their gear into one backpack. Jeff and I had managed to fill a green army duffle bag, a full-size frame backpack, one more rolling duffle bag and two small backpacks or "daypacks." We were prepared for every conceivable temperature, had brought a full set of camping gear, including the all-important coffee pot, several kinds of footwear, and far too many clothes. I thought, "Oh my gosh, how embarrassing," and then immediately justified my position with, "I'm probably going to need it all. I want to be prepared for anything."

Overhearing the conversations from those around us who were also waiting for a ride, we quickly learned the ins-and-outs of shuttle buses. A shuttle or mini-van would take us to our first destination, downtown Sydney, at a fraction of the cost of a taxi. We came prepared. Before leaving Florida we traded US dollars for AU dollars and our pockets were filled with enough closely guarded cash ($250 AU/$163 US) to get us through the first few days until we figured out the banking system and the best way to pay for food and transportation.

A shuttle with room for seven passengers pulled up, and after a short discussion with the driver, we figured out he was going in our direction. We loaded our stuff into the back of the van, fortunately the other passengers packed light, and we were on our way. It was really bizarre watching the driver confidently drive on the left side of the road, sailing past cars on his right, as he steered from the "passenger" side of the car….culture shock, pure and simple.

The ride was relatively quick from the airport to the train station (our train to Perth was leaving from this station the following day), and we were suddenly faced with our first major decision: Where were we going to stay the night? For some reason, we hadn't made any hotel reservations for our first night in Sydney. In hindsight, it would have been a good idea to have thought that one through a little better, but we didn't, and we had some work to do. So we wouldn't look like complete idiots, we had the driver drop us off at a point near the Pacific Railway Station, and then we acted as if we knew what we were doing. "Fake it till you make it" was our motto.

We got out of the shuttle, paid the driver, and trekked with our gear in tow to the first hotel we could see. Two blocks away was the Pacific International Inn at 717 George Street, Sydney. Fortunately, they had a room available and we checked in. Already relieved to have a place to put our bags, Jeff and I had a conversation about what we should send back home and what we really wanted to keep. In a matter of minutes, we made the executive decision to make no changes at all and deal with it.

Within our first hour in Sydney we discovered the Youth Hostel Association (YHA) next to the station. For curiosity's sake, we took the short walk over and asked if they had any vacancies. The young woman at the desk said they had been booked for well over a month, and I immediately felt grateful for the room at the newly remodeled Pacific International Inn.

I did some mental comparisons of the two accommodations and decided the extra cost and comfort was worth it. We've got a beautiful room, and a continental breakfast will be waiting for us in the morning. I further rationalized that we just spent the past 28 hours traveling and this was no time to cut corners.

It was still morning and as tired as we were, Jeff and I knew it would be best if we could stay awake as long as possible to acclimate to the new time zone. We headed back to the hotel and took a seat at the hotel's street side café. After ordering a veggie wrap, I took a deep breath, slowed myself down, and took a good look at my surroundings. I watched the traffic through the reflection of the hotel's large pane windows, and for a brief moment, felt a sense of normalcy as I saw the cars pass by on the "right" side of the road. Knowing it was only an illusion, I looked at Jeff and said, "We're in Australia. We did it. We're really here!" He smiled back and said, "Yes, we are."

Ready to pay our bill and wanting to do the right thing, we asked our server how gratuities work. She said, "Tipping is optional, and quite often, if a tip is given, it's only in the small amount needed to round up the bill to the nearest dollar. The hourly wage for servers is similar to any other job. We don't rely on tips as our primary source of income." We learned that while some servers will outright refuse the larger gratuities offered them, others gladly accept the bonus with a smile.

The café wasn't busy, so Jeff and I chose to stay and pass the time by watching more of the traffic and people go by.

We soon met Joe, a Czechoslovakian, who came to sit at the next table. He was our first acquaintance, and a colorful character at that. His strong European accent, sturdy build, and thick wavy grayish/black hair was distinctive and easy to remember. I guessed him to be in his sixties, and he seemed to be a regular at this particular café. From the way he talked, he was definitely a local. We thoroughly enjoyed his company, the stories he told about his homeland, and how he got to Sydney. We told him we had just arrived, talked about the United States, about Australia, and then mentioned that one of our bags, the army duffle, had been ripped in transit and needed repair. When I said we would probably come back to stay at the same hotel at the end of our trip, he gave us his phone number and said, "Call me. I will certainly remember you. I'll recognize your accent." I thought, "Your accent? I have an accent? No, *he's* the one with the accent!" In that instant, I realized that I had become the foreigner. For the first time, that I was aware of, I was going to be the one who stood out and sounded "funny" or "different" every time I spoke.

As we were leaving and saying our good-byes, Joe told us where we could get the duffle bag repaired. He directed us to a small tailor's shop tucked inside the Queen Victoria Building and Imperial Mall (QVB), a short walk to 455 George Street. (Built in 1898, the QVB is a gorgeous mall with Romanesque-style domes.)

Among the wide variety of stores selling the finest Aboriginal art, Australian gemstones, local crafts, and, of course, outback clothing were Internet cafés, bars and restaurants. The small tailor's shop was right where Joe said it would be, and the tailor took the bag with a promise that it would be done in ninety minutes. Jeff and I made a beeline to a nearby Espresso Café to get a strong cup of coffee and biscotti. Maybe that would help us stay awake. Taking in our new surroundings, it wasn't long before we noticed that Sydney was a multi-cultural city and extremely metropolitan with a very young population. After fifteen years in south

Florida, affectionately known as "God's waiting room," I was enjoying the change of pace.

Right on schedule, the bag was ready. The mall was so unique we decided to stay and take a longer look before heading back to the hotel. I wanted to window shop, check things out, and possibly get a jump on my souvenir shopping. The architecture alone was fascinating, and I realized that if it hadn't been for Joe and the torn bag, we would have missed the experience entirely. Until this morning, I had never heard of the QVB.

Sydney bars open at 10:00 a.m., sometimes earlier, and while it was barely noon, we could see, peeking through the doors, how full they already were. Apparently, Aussie's (pronounced aw-zees) take their pubs and their free time seriously. Listening to the conversations among the crowd we noticed that some of their favorite phrases were, "No worries, mate," "Not a problem," and "Not a drama." Aussies seem to have a healthy mix of work and play, and I sensed an overall feeling of happiness in the air.

Live music was playing at the open square in front of the mall. I saw a young man with dreadlocks and an African woman playing drums. They both moved beautifully to the beat of the music and looked as if they had been performing together for years. Many of the women standing around had long braids and wore colorful African print clothing. It was wonderful to see such diversity and originality throughout the crowd, and I had fun watching everyone else having fun.

In the same area of the mall, Jeff and I noticed a second group had gathered around the brick square. In the center was a man dressed in a donkey suit walking on all fours kicking up his heals, throwing his head around, and doing the best donkey impression I had ever seen. A basket for tips was placed on the ground in front of him. He was entertaining and gave a wonderful performance, but it wasn't long before jet lag overruled our fun. With map in hand we decided to head back, this time taking a different route to the hotel. Around the corner from the QVB, we stumbled on Chinatown and the Pacific Herbal Clinic on Pitt Street where eastern medicines were sold. As we passed the beautiful old stone buildings, Jeff said it reminded him of Philadelphia, Pennsylvania.

It's easy to assume that Sydney is the capital of Australia, just like Washington, D.C. is the capital of the United States, but it isn't. Had I given it much thought, I probably would've come to the same conclusion. Before coming here, I really didn't know what Sydney was to its country. With a short lesson in geography, I learned that Canberra (pronounced canbur-uh), to the south, is the nation's capital, the central seat of government, and Sydney is a state capital, the capital of New South Wales. There are six states in all (New South Wales, Victoria, Queensland, South Australia, Western Australia, and Tasmania) compared to our fifty states back home, and there are also two major territories (Northern Territory and Australian Capital Territory). Technically there are several more territories, but they aren't always listed for some reason. What the difference is between a state and a territory I have yet to figure out. All I know is we are going to do our best to see as much of Australia as possible. With our three known destinations (Ningaloo Reef, Ayers Rock, and the Great Barrier Reef) and a train ride taking us coast-to-coast, we are sure to see at least five of those eight regions.

The walk through downtown did us both a lot of good, but we were still out-of-sorts. The little bit of sleep we managed to get on the plane wasn't nearly enough to get us through the day. At 2:30 p.m. Sydney time, we decided to take a nap for a couple of hours to recharge.

The plan is to wake up in time for dinner and then stay up as late as we can. Sydney is fourteen hours ahead of Florida, and it will most likely take more than one good night's sleep to adjust. Tomorrow morning we have a train to catch. There will be trails to hike, big rocks to see, and coral reefs to swim. With two months vacation ahead of us,

the longest amount of time I have ever devoted to fun, we are
standing at the entrance of one very large playground! And
right now, all I want to do is sleep.

Day 2, Thursday   December 9, 1999

The "short" afternoon nap ended up lasting nine hours. We
missed dinner, but despite the long sleep, we somehow
managed to rest comfortably through the night. Apparently,
our bodies were smarter than our brains. By morning, we
were both feeling better, and that was all that mattered.

Our second day in Sydney began promptly at 6:30 a.m.
After a leisurely breakfast, we packed up our stuff, checked
out of the hotel, and made our way to the train station to
catch the 11:30 train to Perth. As we walked the two blocks
with three pieces of luggage dragging behind us and a
daypack on each of our backs, I came to the conclusion that
we brought enough clothing and gear to camp out for six
months. Every other traveler I continued to see knew how to
pack far better than I did, and I took notes of what each was
carrying and how.

I realize that on some level I came prepared for Y2K,
short for Year 2000. News of potential disaster to the world's
computer infrastructure when the clock strikes midnight on
December 31ˢᵗ has been fed to the public for a very long
time. I honestly don't know what to think. Some believe there
will be a total computer melt-down when the year changes
from '99 to '00 due to programming issues with a two-digit
year instead of four-digits. Who am I to question such logic?
My secret emergency plan, if things do indeed go as badly as
some say it will, is for me and Jeff to buy enough food, coffee
and water to hold us for a few weeks. We'll simply camp out
until the world rights itself again. If things are still a mess
after a few weeks, we'll move on to Plan B...whatever that
looks like. I haven't said a word to Jeff. He's convinced

everything's going to be fine and it will be business as usual on January 1ˢᵗ. My deepest hope is that Jeff is right.

Once at the Indian Pacific Railway Station, it was easy to figure out where to go and what to do next. Everything was written in plain English and posted very clearly. With tickets in hand, we found our way to our designated train, our home on wheels for the next sixty-five hours.

As we boarded the train, we met our first fellow passenger, Michael, a Lebanese-born opal miner from Adelaide. (Adelaide, the state capital of South Australia, sits in the same position in Australia as New Orleans sits in the United States.) Michael said he moved there with his parents when he was five years old, and he spoke fondly of the transition from one country to the other. He told us he had hundreds of raw opals at home, and if only he had a few on him, he would have given us one. I totally believed him and wondered if it was our American accent that initiated the kindness or were Aussies this way with everyone? Michael's instruction, if we happened to pick up any raw opals along our travels, was to keep the stones in water. Opals are extremely fragile and must stay wet until processed. That was my first lesson in Opal Etiquette 101.

The second person we met was Elton the conductor. With great enthusiasm he informed us that it was our train that was rear-ended by another train last week in "the accident." He spoke as if we had heard the news already. Of course, we hadn't. Quite understandably, news like that doesn't generally make it to the 'States, but he had no way of knowing we had just arrived. The second bit of news relating to our specific journey explained the reason we were not going to leave the station on time. Lightning had hit one of the train signals down the line, and no trains were moving until the signal was repaired. The outage caused a three-and-a-half hour delay moving our departure back to 2:55 p.m. Elton assured us that we would make up the time with shorter stops in each town along the way. It was in that

moment I saw a universal commitment to excellence among
train conductors everywhere. It reminded me of home.

Elton gave us directions to our "Holiday Class" cabin,
which translated to "a berth of our own." When he saw how
much luggage we had he kindly remarked that there wasn't
going to be enough room for the seven of us and suggested
we check the larger items. Confident we could tuck a bag
here and a bag there, Jeff and I took matters into our own
hands and proceeded to bump and drag our way through the
winding halls of the train. Standing at the doorway of our
cabin, it became clear what Elton was talking about.

*Permanently fixed inside the cabin are two cushioned
armchairs facing one another that convert to an upper and a
lower bed, similar to a set of bunk beds. We have a sink,
towels, miniature closet, mirror, reading lamps, and
foldaway table. When the beds are in place, the standing
room only section disappears. It's an efficient use of space
and not much bigger than the average American closet. The
showers and toilets are conveniently located down the hall
and to the right at the other end of the carriage or "railroad
car" as I know them to be called. Jeff and I will share the
bathroom facilities with all the other passengers in our
section of the train for the next three days.*

*The Indian Pacific Railway journey from Sydney to Perth
(2700 miles) will be the equivalent of traveling from
Savannah, Georgia to Los Angeles, California. The ocean-
to-ocean adventure will take the better part of three days, 65
hours to be exact, and move us through several time zones.
Along the way, Jeff and I will continue to adjust our body
clocks to the current time while we keep the trip moving
forward. That's the plan anyway.*

With plenty of time to regroup and repack, we dug into
the three larger bags and took out only what was essential for
the next few days. Content to have our luggage out of sight
and out of mind, we headed out and back onto the train
platform so we could hand over the excess stuff. I could only

imagine what the clerk was thinking when she saw us coming. To be honest, I didn't want to know. The gentle grin on her face spoke volumes.

When it was finally time for our journey to begin, we headed for the Nullarbor Lounge, a carriage designated for the three S's: sitting, socializing and sightseeing. At 2:55, right on the dot, the train pulled out of the station. In a matter of minutes the hypnotic sound of the wheels on the track began to do its magic in helping us unwind from the day's events. For the second time since landing in Oz, I took a long deep breath and relaxed into the knowing of where we would be and what we would be doing for the next three days. We were finally on our way.

With a third carriage to explore, the dining car, we took the short walk to Café Matilda, popped our heads in, and then turned around to walk back through the other two carriages for an overall assessment of our new surroundings. There was plenty of room to stretch our legs, eat our meals and visit with the other travelers. I decided it was going to be a great trip.

Back in the Nullarbor Lounge, we enjoyed the train's journey through the Blue Mountains, and I understood why this part of New South Wales came highly recommended in all the travel guides as a sight to see. It was one beautiful landscape after another. Throughout the late afternoon and into the evening, we saw a countryside filled with quaint little towns and farms west of Sydney. There were lambs, pigs, and cows, all familiar farm animals in a land far from home.

I've only been in Australia for thirty-eight hours, and already, I am positively smitten.

Day 3, Friday   December 10, 1999

I woke up at 6:20 a.m., looked out the cabin window, and saw my first wild kangaroo. There it was sitting peacefully under a tree 50 yards out from the railway tracks. I did my best to hide my enthusiasm and allow Jeff to continue sleeping. I was sure there would be more 'roos to see when he woke up. All through the night the train had taken us farther away from the city and deep into the southern outback. The desert landscape was bright orange, and the trees, with their twisted odd shapes framed against the desert sky, looked as if they had been drawn by Dr. Seuss himself. It was all very surreal.

The remainder of the morning was gorgeous as we continued to leave civilization far behind. I sat contentedly for hours in our cabin, watching the kangaroos and emus outside the window. An occasional horse, sheep, cow, farm house, and even a vineyard appeared throughout the countryside. The views were so picturesque I wanted to get out and stay a while.

We arrived at our first official stop at 11:45 a.m. in a town called Broken Hill on the far western edge of New South Wales. With Sydney on the far eastern edge, we had crossed our first state and were about to begin our journey into state number two, South Australia.

Broken Hill is positioned in Australia right about where Jackson, Mississippi is positioned in the United States. This outback town is famous for silver, lead, and zinc, and the minerals are shipped all over the world. Unlike Jackson, Mississippi, Broken Hill stays cool through the summer months due to the arctic breezes off the South Pole. I continue to chant, "South is north and north is south as far as the weather is concerned." I have some unlearning to do if I am going to keep things straight in my head.

While the train was in the station at Broken Hill, and with a few Australian dollars in my pocket, I jumped onto the platform and rushed into the depot in search of quality snacks to add to our stash. Jeff stayed behind, probably to make sure the train didn't leave without me. My heart was pounding with excitement knowing I had less than fifteen minutes to find my way around and get the job done. I managed to find some homemade chocolates a woman was selling in the ticket booth lobby, and I was back onboard with minutes to spare. What a girl won't do for chocolate.

With everyone accounted for, including all new passengers, we left the station earlier than scheduled and recouped some of the time lost at the start of our journey. The conductor wasn't kidding when he said we would move right along. I put the chocolates away, and we headed for Café Matilda (probably named after the famous Australian song *Waltzing Matilda*) to eat our third meal on the train. Due to the limited seating during peak dining hours, we asked to share a booth with an Australian couple named Peter and Patty. They told us they hadn't been on a train in over forty years and were enjoying the change of pace from their usual routine of traveling by plane or car. They were thrilled to be doing something different and were very pleasant company.

I noticed I was feeling much better than the day before. The gentle rocking of the train and clickety-clack rhythm of the rail helped me get the deep sleep my body required. I was glad to have some normalcy back into my life. This was my first overnight train ride, and I asked myself, "What took me so long to try this mode of transportation?" It's definitely the way to go. The food? Well, that's another story. The menu reflects the usual American diner assortment of hot dogs, hamburgers, grilled cheese sandwiches, French fries, chips, and sodas. With a captive audience, I expected the kitchen to offer a bit more variety, possibly along the lines of some local delicacies such as kangaroo tail or emu stew, but they didn't, and to tell you the truth, that was alright with me. As a vegetarian, I wouldn't have tried it anyway. The only true disappointment was the coffee station. It consisted of a hot water dispenser, instant coffee, sugar and non-dairy creamer.

That was a bit of a bummer. Fortunately, we had thought ahead in the food department. Knowing we were going to be dining in one place for three days, and due to my dietary restrictions, we had bought dried fruit and trail mix at the QVB mall in Sydney. The assortment of snacks added variety to a limited menu, and I was grateful for a bit of foresight. Jeff is a meat and potatoes guy and had more to choose from.

Later on in the day, we met a couple from England who gave us a few tips on traveling around Perth, the capital city of Western Australia. The couple strongly recommended that we visit a nearby vacation destination called Rottnest Island, a favorite among Aussies. I wrote it down in my notepad. Maybe it will fit into our plans as the days unfold. We were reminded that it's December, summertime in the south, and told that the island would be packed with tourists, but it was worth a visit if only for the day. The couple explained how unbearably hot and humid it is up north the closer one gets to the equator towards Indonesia and Papua New Guinea, and that Australians take their holidays in the south this time of year.

Darwin, one of the cities Jeff and I considered exploring on the northern coast of Australia, was experiencing temperatures well over one hundred degrees. We began to rethink our recent plans to see that part of the country and left it open for discussion. I decided that everything was going to be upside down for awhile as I wrapped my mind around this new way of thinking. The days were going to get longer and brighter as we moved through December and January, and Oz had officially become the land of opposites.

We were told that when we left New South Wales and crossed the border into South Australia we entered the second of three time zones that span the Australian continent. I decided that another hour added to the mix was not going to make a bit of difference. I changed my travel clock and got on with the day.

At 5:30 p.m., we rolled into Adelaide, the capital of South Australia. This was Michael's stop, the young opal miner we met at the start of our journey. I imagined he would be home soon and glad of it. We hadn't seen him since the train left the station, so I assume he was assigned to a different carriage, but I will always remember what he looked like. He was the spitting image of the actor who played the mummy in *The Mummy* starring Brendan Fraser. Michael was big and strong and very handsome. Surely, he must do well in the opal fields and equally as well with the ladies.

The train stopped in Adelaide for two-and-a-half hours, and we took advantage of the bus tour set up by the Indian Pacific Railway. I wanted to see as much of a city known as "The Festival City" and "The City of Roses" as I could in the short time given. It was a beautiful ride, and Jeff and I enjoyed it very much.

Adelaide is one of the oldest and largest cities in Australia. In 1895, Mark Twain was among its many visitors. He said he was thoroughly captivated by this beautiful city and saw Australia as "a very fortunate country to have such beauty within its boundaries." The "City of Roses" comes from the fact that there are over 45,000 rose bushes growing throughout the city. Adelaide is also home to a beautiful mix of architectures, dozens of statues, a Mediterranean climate, rolling hills, and acres of parklands all scattered throughout the city. The entire area is well thought out and was obviously planned with a vision. It reminds me of Portland, Oregon, and I definitely want to go back one day. Some of the best Australian wines come from this area, and opals are mined in the fields just north of the city. We saw huge selections of both local "gems" in the shops throughout Adelaide.

Back on the train, we ate dinner (again) at the Café Matilda and met a young couple named Jaime and Laura who came aboard in Broken Hill. They said their original travel plans were to drive from Sydney to Perth, nearly three thousand miles, but all that changed when they wrecked their car in Broken Hill. They didn't give us any details about the accident or how they disposed of the car, and we didn't ask. Instead, I silently made up a story that they hit a kangaroo and were too embarrassed to tell us about it.

I have been reading about how dangerous it is to drive in the outback after dark and to watch for kangaroos crossing in the night. Kangaroos migrate in the cool of the evening, especially in the summer months (which it is even though it's December), and they tend to jump into the headlights of oncoming cars. While we have deer and rabbits that do the same, the outback has kangaroos, and if it's a "big red," the largest of the breed, that jumps into the road…that's a lot of damage to the 'roo, the passengers, and the car.

I learned an outback joke. Here goes:

"You've heard of a kangaroo, right?"
"Right"
"Then what's a Wasaroo?"
"A kangaroo that didn't make it to the other side of the road."

It's eight-thirty in the evening, long after dinner, and the sun has finally set. I just realized that we haven't seen any kangaroos since this morning. They don't tend to come out in the heat of the day, but I haven't seen any this evening either. Maybe there will be more tomorrow.

Day 4, Saturday   December 11, 1999

My kangaroo count was low this morning. South Australia is the driest state on the driest continent on earth, not much can survive in the southern outback. The earth was colored in deep red, orange and purple hues. An occasional splash of green was thrown in for good measure. The wispy shrubbery, I figured out, is called spinifex. Eucalyptus trees were growing in seemingly impossible odds, and the spinifex reminded me of the sage bushes we have in the West with their dry twisted branches. Wild galahs (pronounced gah-*lah*), also known as pink cockatoos, appeared in the trees today. After my initial excitement, I realized they are as common as crows. The beautiful pink heads and the bright red coloring under their wings made a nice contrast to the outback landscape passing by.

Instead of giving in to the lulling sound of the train on the tracks and take a nap whenever the mood struck, I stayed awake from sunrise to sunset and finally got a good long night's sleep last night. It wasn't helping me get through the jet lag to sleep whenever I wanted to. It was actually making things worse. Ugh. Live and learn. I decided to keep the cabin chairs set up as seats throughout the day rather than collapsed into sleeping bunks with an open invitation to lie down. Whenever I retreated to our berth to write or sit quietly with my thoughts, the seats were a constant reminder to stay awake.

At 9:30 a.m., the train stopped in a small town called Cook, situated in the middle of nowhere. The sign posted nearby read "Population 3 or 4." If there was a road to this town, I didn't see it, and if it did exist, it was a really, really long and lonely ride from who knows where. The area around Cook was what I imagined the outback to look like with its super flat terrain, no trees, and dry as a bone. There were a few homes scattered around and, surprisingly, one hospital. The sign at the hospital read,

If you're crook come to Cook.
Our hospital needs your help – get sick!

("Crook" means sick in Australian slang)

In addition to the unusual signs, within 50 feet of the railway tracks were two old jail cells. The single cells looked more like outhouses than anything else. With a population of three or four, and supposedly, a hospital to run, who has time to get into trouble? Something told me that the train pulling into the station was the only activity that town ever truly saw.

It was during our stop in Cook that I had another revelation, an *aha!* moment concerning our train. Up until that point in the journey, I hadn't questioned what was in the other boxcars that we had no access to, and I decided to find out. As I walked up and down the red desert floor, I took a good look at the long line of cars. Some were filled with automobiles just like our auto trains back home. There were several large container cars obviously transporting cargo, and half a dozen other boxcars that will forever remain a mystery. But I wasn't concerned with those. What interested me were the extra passenger carriages, the ones with berths so large a person could stand up when the beds were down and may have included a private bath. Dining cars where the food was surely an improvement over hot dogs, hamburgers and grilled cheese sandwiches, where tables were draped with linens, silverware and real china plates, and a different menu was presented at each meal. Today I learned about "First-Class." *Now that's the way to see the outback.*

After a short stop, most likely to deliver mail, water, and various supplies, the train slowly pulled out of Cook. Throughout the rest of the day and night we continued deeper into the Nullarbor Plain.

The name "Nullarbor" translated means "no trees." Looking at the map, there wasn't much at all between Tarcoola, South Australia, the eastern edge of the southern outback, and Kalgoorlie, Western Australia, at the western edge of the desert. I was beginning to believe Cook's sole existence was to give us an interesting place to stretch our legs. The Nullarbor Plain is also where the Indian Pacific Railway holds the record for the longest stretch of perfectly straight track in the world at 478 km long (296.36 miles). Elementary math teaches us that the shortest distance between two points is a straight line, and with absolutely nothing, and I mean nothing, in the way, those railway surveyors did their job well.

I've noticed that Jeff has been adjusting to the time change quite nicely. Throughout the day, he could be found in the Nullarbor Lounge and much preferred it to the cramped quarters of our berth. He enjoys hanging out with the younger passengers telling stories and learning Australian slang (also known as 'strine or "stroin"). I would go back and forth between the quiet of our cabin and the social scene. Each time I visited the group Jeff was ready with a new story or phrase. One 'strine phrase was particularly memorable. Jeff and the others were in tears of laughter when he said to me, "Okay, okay, here's one....I'm going to 'have a slash.'" "Have a slash?" I asked, "What's 'have a slash?" My mind was racing with crazy thoughts. Jeff answered, "It means 'take a piss!'" Australians sure have a strange way of expressing themselves, but I'm sure they say the same about us.

Tonight, I saw an *amazing* sunset. The clouds turned from white to watermelon, and the horizon was an exquisite blend of peach and cantelope. A camera couldn't possibly do it justice, so I didn't even try to capture it through the window of a moving train. It was one of those, "You've just gotta be here" moments.

After a long day of traveling it was dark and late into the evening when the train took a three-hour stopover in Kalgoorlie, our last official stop before Perth.

Kalgoorlie sits halfway into the state of Western Australia, right about where Phoenix, Arizona sits on our map at home. Western Australia is the largest of the six states, the largest in the world for that matter, and takes up nearly one third of the entire island continent of Australia. It makes Texas look like Rhode Island. Okay, maybe not that small, but Western Australia is BIG, really, really BIG. Oddly enough, as big as it is, it is the least populated state of them all, due to the fact that most of the land is uninhabitable to the average person, plant, or animal.

Kalgoorlie is an active gold mining town known as the "Golden Mile," complete with "Hay Street Hookers" walking the streets and barmaids wearing nothing but lingerie called "skimpies." The town looks like a staged Hollywood set in a Wild West movie except this is the real deal. It's said that the richest square mile of gold in the world is here, and from what I can tell, they're still mining it to this day.

Kalgoorlie is also where I saw my first Aborigines, Australia's first residents. They have dark, almost black skin, distinct facial features, and there is no mistaking them. More than 50,000 years ago Aborigines migrated from the northwest. Thousands continue the ways of their ancestors, living on the land and going "walkabout," a barefoot journey into the harsh environment along "songlines" or tracks that stretch for hundreds of miles through the outback. Gone for months on end, the Aborigines have mastered the art of traveling light wearing little more than a loin cloth and carrying only a few necessities.

Today, many Aborigines have chosen to move into the cities and assimilate into modern day culture with great success. And there are those who seem stuck in between the two worlds.

As Jeff and I walked through town, we were approached by several Aborigines begging us for money hoping to get a sympathetic handout from the daily delivery of tourists. It was a reminder of the streets in New York City, San Francisco, or any town for that matter, where we have our own asking for a handout.

After peering into the bars, doing our best to avoid the red light districts, and seeing just enough to bring the brochures to life, we found our way back to the train in plenty of time to settle in before departure. Tonight's feature presentation in the Nullarbor Lounge was the movie *Notting Hill* starring Hugh Grant and Julia Roberts. I had seen it before, but after four days traveling and a recent bout of sensory overload, a good Hollywood movie was the ideal end to a very bizarre day.

This is our last night on the train. Tomorrow, we'll be in Perth.

Day 5, Sunday   December 12, 1999

I woke up with a bright sun at 4:30 a.m. I thought, *geez that's early*, until I realized my watch was wrong. Yesterday, when we crossed the border from South Australia into Western Australia, somewhere between Cook and Kalgoorlie, we traveled into the third and final time zone, and I missed the memo to change the clocks. It was really 5:30 a.m. Once I figured out what was going on, I felt better about getting up "so early." Perception is everything.

During breakfast, it dawned on me that Jeff and I were only a few hours away from reaching the other side of Oz, and I felt the first pangs of nervousness at the thought of stepping off the train. We weren't arriving cold the way we arrived in Sydney, without knowing where we would sleep our first night. We thought ahead this time and, while still in Sydney, made reservations with the Britannia YHA (Youth Hostel Association) on William Street for our first two nights in Perth. I, for one, wanted to ease into our "no plan" plan with as much grace as possible. But it was still a big wide world "out there." It wasn't clear in my mind what we were going to do after our two days were up, but two days should be enough time to figure out how to get to the Ningaloo Reef in the north, our first of three known destinations.

In the final hours on the train, the scenery outside the windows was growing more beautiful with every passing mile. We were finally out of the deepest portions of the outback and surrounded by lush green fields dotted with sheep. Galahs filled the trees more so than we'd seen in the past. While the outback had a beauty all its own, I was thoroughly enjoying the changes ahead. It was clear we were edging closer to the coastline of the Indian Ocean. The excitement I felt towards our next adventure began to overrule any fears I had for the countless unknowns before us.

We arrived in Perth right on schedule at 9:30 a.m., easily making up the three-and-a-half hour delay as the conductor had promised. The Britannia YHA shuttle bus, our own personal van, was waiting for us at the public transportation dock outside the train station. The young driver standing by was a welcome sight. We loaded all of our stuff and rode the short distance to the hostel. Once we were settled into our room we headed out into the city.

My first impression of Perth was, *"Wow!"* I had no idea how absolutely beautiful it was going to be. It was as if I had discovered something rare and unique, except for the fact that millions of people had gone before me.

Perth is situated along the banks of the Swan River, a river named after the abundance of black swans. In comparison to the 'States, Perth sits on the continent of Australia where Los Angeles sits back home. The climate here is touted as "The best of all the other capital cities" because there are more sunny days in the year than cloudy ones and the humidity is low. That's a perfect blend by most people's standards in any part of the world. It's been called "The Dallas of Australia," and I did not make that up. They really call it that. So the next logical question becomes, "Is everything bigger here in southwest Western Australia?" We'll see.

Jeff and I found our way to a shopping center, ate sandwiches with freshly made bread, and came back to the hostel to lie down for a 4:00 p.m. nap—Perth time. Our nap turned into a long sleep and we woke up at 2:30 in the morning, a major mistake in my opinion. Just when I thought I was on local time and it was safe to rest awhile, I was, once again, wrong.

I've noticed that I am sleeping more than what is considered normal, and I believe it's because I'm more stressed than I care to admit. I've been stressed about what is ahead, stressed about being so far from home, stressed about how this is the longest stretch of time Jeff and I have ever spent together, and are we going to get along? There is stress to my body to make the necessary change to the longitude and latitude in addition to all of the time changes. Whatever the excuses and reasons are, I am getting really frustrated because this is supposed to be a vacation. Relax already.

I know enough to admit that I do "check out" and go to sleep when I get overloaded with too many decisions and too much change. Ever since we landed in Sydney and started walking through the city, I've had to keep reminding myself to look the right way so I don't walk into traffic. Now there's a habit that absolutely must be changed immediately. It's critical that I look both ways and remember which direction the traffic is coming from each and every time I cross the street. People have died looking in one direction as a bus seemingly appears out of nowhere. Splat! It can happen in an instant. It's a very serious problem Westerners must be concerned with. We may see the oncoming vehicle, but the mind can play tricks and tell us from past programming that the vehicle is going away from us when it is actually coming towards us. It takes being fully and completely present to cross the street safely in countries where they drive on the opposite side of the road. Okay, I'll get off my soapbox now.

Two thousand seven hundred miles down, roughly 4,000 more to go. We don't specifically know what we're going to do tomorrow, or should I say "today"? It's 3 a.m. Do I try to get back to sleep or stay awake as long as humanly possible? I have got to figure this out.

PART TWO

Western Australia
Kangaroos, Reefs, and One Really Big Party

*"We don't accomplish anything in this world alone.
Whatever happens is the result of the whole tapestry of one's
life and all the weavings of individual threads from one
another that creates something."*

Sandra Day O'Connor
Retired Supreme Court Justice of the United States

Day 6, Monday   December 13, 1999

I could smell the coffee brewing in the hostel kitchen first
thing this morning. After three days of bad instant coffee, it
didn't take me long to find the source of that great aroma.

By 8:00 a.m., the hostel was buzzing with activity. I had
been looking forward to settling into the trip, of really *being*
in Australia, and this was an excellent place to begin. Kids
representing every corner of the world were gathered in the
common area of the hostel, and it was a real melting pot of
cultures. As many as five different languages could be heard
throughout the hostel, and it was definitely "a whole new
experience," as my mom would say. It was fun to listen in on
the conversations to get a sense of what a few of the travelers
would be doing that day. There was a lot of sharing of food,

drink, space, and stories. The excitement over being strangers in a strange land was palpable.

While I was bringing a cup of coffee back to our room, Jeff headed for the pay phones to inquire about renting a car from Perth to Exmouth, so we could get to the Ningaloo Reef. He came back with more information about our friends, Laura and Jaime, than he had answers concerning car rentals. Laura and Jaime, the young couple we met on the train, had given us their hotel information before Jeff and I went our way and they went theirs at the train station in Perth. Jeff said we were all to meet in our hostel's lobby after breakfast.

With the Britannia YHA in the downtown section of Perth, Jeff and I decided to take a walk around town, get some fresh air, and stretch our legs. It was a bright sunny morning, and the temperature was a perfect 78 degrees. We discovered a café next to the post office and took care of the two items on our morning's agenda with one fell swoop. I mailed three picture postcards I had written on the train, and ten minutes later we were sitting down to a delicious breakfast. The organic granola with fresh peaches was a welcome change after three days of diner food.

Back at the hostel we met Laura and Jaime, and then the four of us walked to one of the shopping areas in Perth. Target, the familiar discount store back in the 'States, was there, but I found out later it wasn't the same Target. Same name, different company. I found a pair of Teva-like sandals, perfect for everyday walking, and then shopped for a wide-brimmed beige linen sun hat. I expected it would be an easy hunt, but they didn't have what I was looking for.

The four of us walked for miles, taking in the sights and sounds of the city, and we ended up at Laura and Jaime's hotel on the banks of the Swan River. The view from their room was far more spectacular than the view from ours. Ours was so "memorable" I couldn't describe it if I was given three options to choose from and one was the real deal. With access to a phone, Jeff decided to put a second effort into our car rental search. Our friends gave us permission to make as many local and toll-free calls as we wanted. It was time to get answers to the questions we had about heading north in a car of our own.

It turned out that our sense of distance was off. We finally looked at a map to see what all the fuss was about; why there were so many rules and why it was so expensive. We discovered two things: A—It *is* a long way from Perth to Exmouth, the equivalent of driving from Los Angeles to Eureka, California, about nine hours, and B—There's not much civilization between the two points. If the rental car were to break down in the middle of nowhere, that would be a bummer of a deal. With every phone call Jeff made, the rules and regulations got more and more complicated, and the price exceeded our naïve expectations.

We had considered a visit to Broome, a city north of Exmouth, as our second alternative to Darwin, but with Laura and Jaime's help, we got realistic. After a lengthy discussion, Jeff and I decided to drop any notions of traveling too far north. Not only was the distance an issue, but the extreme heat turned out to be the first of several good reasons to cancel. We did the math and saw that two months had its limits. If we were to snorkel the Ningaloo Reef, travel to Ayers Rock for New Year's Eve, make it to Queensland to swim the Great Barrier Reef, *and* enjoy each adventure, we would need to keep a fair amount of time between each point of interest. Our agenda had countless unknowns written all over it. We still didn't know how we were going to get to Ayers Rock in the center of Australia, and we were a long way from figuring out how we were going to get from Ayers Rock to Queensland on the east coast. There was no need to complicate things by adding an intentional side trip. What we needed was room for the "how's" to emerge.

After a late lunch by the pool, we said good-bye to our friends for the last time and headed back to our room for a nap. Reality checks can be exhausting.

When Jeff and I came to our senses, we agreed that we couldn't possibly see *all* the cool spots in Australia on one trip. Two months was a lot, but not enough to cover a country the size of the continental United States and still enjoy it. Our focus shifted toward finding the best way to get to the Ningaloo Reef. We came to the conclusion that flying was the way to go. The more we thought it through the more it made sense and, most importantly, the more it *felt* right. A sense of relief washed over the both of us. The struggle was over. Our next phone call was going to be to the airlines, and that particular call was going to wait until tomorrow. At 7:00 p.m., we ate an extra-large pizza and called it a day.

Despite all the frustrations around the rental car debacle, I am still able to enjoy the capital city of Western Australia. My general observation of Perth, now that I have had a whole entire day to make my assessment, is once again, "Wow!" The parks are gorgeous, the skyscrapers are a work of art, the restaurants represent a wide variety of cuisines from around the world, the people in the city dress with style, and it's all so wonderfully different from home.

I may be a bit on edge in our "no plan" plan, but hour-by-hour I am relaxing into my new role as "the foreigner."

Day 7, Tuesday   December 14, 1999

We both slept in this morning. *I am officially on Perth time.*

At breakfast, we began the day with our sights solely on Exmouth and booking a plane ride north. By the end of breakfast, we realized we weren't ready to go. We were feeling a pull to stay in the area and take the advice from the English couple to visit Rottnest Island. With Darwin and Broome officially cancelled, we had a lot more time on our hands. The decision to see Rottnest Island was upgraded to "brilliant" when the YHA staff gave it two thumbs up.

Since there was a possibility that we would stay overnight on the island, Jeff and I checked out of the room and moved our extra gear into the hostel's storage room for a small fee. The two small daypacks were filled with basic necessities, and the framed backpack held the snorkel gear. With a much lighter load, we walked down the hill to the Barrack Street Jetty. That's where the hostel staff said we could find a boat along the banks of the Swan River that would take us over to the island. Arriving ten minutes before Oceanic Cruises was scheduled to depart at 10:00 a.m., and without a ferry schedule in hand, we were pleasantly surprised with the timing. I got a sense that we were on to something. By staying open to inspired ideas, maybe things were going to work out better than if we had everything planned ahead of time. Just when I was beating myself up for coming all this way so ill-prepared, I decided to start paying attention and notice, really take in, what was happening as a result of not planning so much.

On our way to Rottnest Island, there were a few short stops to take additional passengers onboard. With the boat nearly full, the captain docked at a small pier in Fremantle, a town next to Perth, for a 30-minute layover. That's where all passengers were asked to disembark and then told a second larger boat would arrive to take us the rest of the way.

Jeff and I could see a lunch stand, complete with outdoor picnic tables, right across the street from the dock. We were hungry, and not knowing what was available on the ride over, we decided to eat while we had the chance. We got a couple of sandwiches, sodas, and some fries, and we were finished in time to board the second boat.

The sun was shining through a bright clear blue sky, and the temperatures were in the low 80's. Along the way, and still close to land, we saw several dolphins swim up to the boat to take a closer look at us before riding the surf of the boat's wake for a good 15 minutes. Through a loudspeaker, the captain talked about the surrounding lands and how the Aborigines have been instrumental in preserving the sacred sites of their ancestors.

Perth and Fremantle are growing fast. Development is as strong as in any highly populated city on the coast. Some of

*the homes are stunning. As big as they are, they manage to
fit nicely into the landscape. And then there are homes that
look as if the architect and owner were trying too hard to
make something special, but they missed the mark.*

*The terrain and climate remind me of southern
California. This may be the only place where Australia and
the United States line up spot-for-spot, no flipping required.
Slightly warmer in the summer and cooler in the winter,
Perth and San Diego enjoy gorgeous weather year round.
Maybe it has something to do with those ocean breezes.*

It only took 25 minutes to cruise the 13 miles from
Fremantle to Rottnest Island. Due to high winds on the open
waters, the ride was a rough one. I was getting queasier by
the second, turning pale, and was about to lose my lunch
when the crew docked the boat. I was saved without a
moment to spare. Once on dry land, all systems returned to
normal. That was close.

Looking around, the first thing I noticed was a
lighthouse, and that's when I made a connection that made
my knees go weak. It wasn't fear, and it wasn't nausea. It
had everything to do with the sudden realization that a wish I
once wished had just come true.

Eighteen months ago, I saw an independent Australian
film on television called *Under the Lighthouse Dancing*. The
movie was based on a true love story that took place on an
island many years ago. Naomi Watts is in it, and the beauty
of the film's location made such an impression on me that I
watched the long trailer of credits at the end to find out
where it was filmed. It was Rottnest Island, Australia. I made
a note to one day, someday visit that island if only I knew
where it was. As a dream destination, I kept it only to
myself.

The mention of Rottnest on the train didn't jog my
memory and neither did all the conversations we had leading
up to our arrival. The island could have been along the east
coast or off the northern tip of Australia, near Darwin, for all
I knew. I had yet to look it up. Rottnest was a distant

thought, and it wasn't until I saw the lighthouse that everything clicked.

It was noon when we arrived, and given my recent *aha!*, we knew we were going to stay at least one night. Rottnest gives a beautiful first impression with its clear sparkling waters, rolling landscape, and wide open spaces. It appeared the residents had a tight control over land development. Not an easy battle to win, that's for sure.

We were prepared to do whatever it took to find a room and stay for longer than a day. Information related to lodging, restaurants, tours, equipment rentals, whatever we wanted, needed—and didn't know we wanted or needed—was located right on the dock. Everything was clearly posted and easy to understand. It was our own vagueness we had to deal with.

We didn't have a clue what kind of accommodations were still available, so we grabbed a few brochures and headed for the "main settlement" in the heart of Rottnest. Most of the hotels were a short distance from the dock, but at each location we heard the "no room at the inn" message. "We've been booked solid for months," they told us. Determined to find a vacancy, we kept looking despite the fact it was high season and the island was crowded with tourists. And there we were, two more additions to the ever-rising count.

Our last remaining stop before taking the island bus deeper inland was Rottnest Lodge. As luck would have it, there were four rooms available. Before we were told how much the room would cost, Jeff and I, together, said, "We'll take it." Guessing there had been a last minute cancellation, we immediately booked the room for two nights. The desk clerk confirmed that December through March is Western Australia's summer holiday peak and the island was nearly filled to capacity.

Rottnest Lodge is much like what I would expect to find in the Bahamas. The architecture, large tropical plants and beautiful courtyards have a distinctive island feel. Each room opens into a garden area and the lodge has a very relaxed and casual atmosphere. We were so excited to have a room at high season that we gladly paid the $155 AU ($100 US) per night and quickly unpacked our bags before setting off to find the free bus.

One of the unique aspects of Rottnest Island is the fact that there are no personal vehicles on the island. Two buses, one that runs for free and one that charges $5 AU ($3 US), make continuous loops throughout the island. The free route is limited, but it takes us everywhere we want to go. The $5 a day bus has a much longer route and, from what I could tell from the brochure, traverses the entire island. A third option for getting around is to "hire a push bike" or "rent a bicycle" as we say in the 'States. With all of our snorkel gear, wet suits included, Jeff and I chose the bus; though it is a beautiful island to ride a bike around. The paved roads are more like extra wide bike paths with only the occasional bus and service vehicle to watch out for.

The free bus took us to Kingstown, Phillip Port, a remote part of the island where we took our very first swim in Oz. We found a beautiful secluded beach where huge rocks stretched across the sand and out towards the sea. It reminded me of a scene from the movie *The Planet of the Apes*. The water was freezing by my standards, and I was glad we carried our wet suits all the way from Florida. There was no chance I would have gone in the water without the extra protection from the cold.

The reason the water is so cold is because it comes from Antarctica, the icy continent at the South Pole. Swimming off the coast of Rottnest Island is like swimming off the coast of Maine where the water never ever gets warm. Australia's southern most reef, Pocillopora Reef, is here. I had no idea coral could survive in such cold temperatures.

While snorkeling the waters at Phillip Port, we saw plenty of fish, a small shipwreck, and our first bits of coral. Some of the locals walking by along the beach told us there was better snorkeling in other areas of the island, which explained why that particular beach was virtually empty, but we were more interested in staying away from the crowds. Besides, it was still a good swim to us. In Florida, the visibility is quite poor along much of the coastline. Today's swim was a major improvement over what we were used to.

It was a very pleasant afternoon as we sat on the beach and watched the ferries and sailboats go by. Some little creatures were scurrying in the bush 50 yards off the beach, and that's when we saw our first two quokkas, the small local residents that give Rottnest Island its name.

Like the kangaroo, quokkas are marsupial. About the size of a raccoon or large rabbit, quokkas are also nocturnal. They're unique to this area and can be found on a few other islands nearby. This island in particular was named by the Dutch explorer, Willem De Vlamingh, when he discovered this patch of land in 1696. The hills were crawling with the furry critters, and upon mistaking them for rats, he called the island "Rotte nest" or "Rats Nest." Over time, the name evolved into Rottnest.

It wasn't long before we discovered the one and only downside to this beautiful island. There was no talk of it, no mention in the brochures, no warning from our British friends on the train. We had to experience it up close and personal. It was the flies, hordes and hordes of flies.

There was a constant *bzzz* all day long around our food, around our heads, and then the winged demons got on our nerves. The flies were small, they didn't bite, but they were really, r-e-a-l-l-y annoying. While walking through town we noticed that some of the tourists resorted to face nets. The locals didn't wear face nets, so we decided to blend in. We kept our time outdoors to a minimum and whenever outside, we did a lot of swatting.

By early evening, there was a drastic change in the weather. The light ocean breeze across the island was gaining strength, enough strength to challenge anything that wasn't sufficiently anchored down. It was the "Four o'clock

Fremantle Doctor" blowing into town. We didn't ask what "Fremantle Doctor" meant, but Jeff came up with a definition all his own. He said, "It's the cure for flies." Those little wings were no match against the wind, and the flies couldn't hover over a nice hot meal if their little lives depended on it.

It's our seventh full day being together all day, every day. In four years, this is a first for Jeff and me, given our day-to-day schedules. Between work and individual interests, we always had time apart whether it was a full day or partial. We're getting along well considering the stress and challenges inherent to traveling.

While we have always gotten along in the past, there's nothing like being on the other side of the world with 1,001 decisions to bring out the best and the worst in a person. It's a legitimate challenge to any relationship. What I'm noticing, so far, is we are in complete agreement regarding the decisions we've made, and we're making sound choices; no small feat under any circumstance. It's a good thing we started strong because we have seven more weeks ahead of us.

It's the end of a great day, and I am looking forward to tomorrow, a full day on Rottnest Island.

Day 8, Wednesday   December 15, 1999

I woke up to the sounds of a zoo . . . but there is no zoo on Rottnest Island. Among the thousands of birds singing and *screeching* at 5:00 a.m., I recognized the crows and peacocks as the most vocal. Jeff, being the night person that he is, was able to sleep despite all the noise.

An hour after sunrise, a pheasant flanked by three young male peacocks came to our door. The whole bunch of them stared through the screen and sent the not-so-subtle message of "Got any food? Got any food for me?" I didn't see any warnings to the contrary, so I quietly grabbed the leftover bread from last night's dinner and stepped outside to share the bounty. It may have been frowned upon, encouraging such bold behavior, but I fed them anyway.

From our motel room I could see a hill that looked as if it might offer a great view once I climbed to the top. Jeff was still sound asleep, I was anxious to explore the island, so I headed off alone. Unfortunately, the warm summer air blowing over the cold waters of the Indian Ocean created a sea fog, the kind San Francisco is famous for, and I could see about as far as I could throw. It was a disappointment, but the beauty of standing in the fresh air before the flies woke up made the trek worthwhile.

On the way back, I noticed a pop-top on the ground. It was the old-fashioned kind, the kind with the large ring that pulls completely off the can. It reminded me of my past and all those beers I drank when I lived in Utah in the early 1980's. I stood staring at the pop-top and then at the ground around me and at the pop-top again. Suddenly, like in one of those movie moments where the camera zooms in for a critical focus, I felt as if I was being transported back to the 'States, back to the trails I had hiked a hundred times before. As quickly as I left, *woo oomph*, I was back on Rottnest Island. It took me a few seconds to get my bearings and remember where I was. Wanting to capture the moment, I bent down, picked the pop-top up off the ground, gave it a good close look, brushed the dirt away, and put the metal ring in my pocket.

By the time I got back to the lodge with my treasure trash, Jeff was awake, dressed and ready for breakfast. We took our scones and coffee to a table by the pool, and as we ate, I told Jeff all about my morning. It was still too cold for the flies to get up to speed, and we were grateful we could eat in peace. The sun burned away the thick cloudy haze and another bright day emerged. Once breakfast was over, the conversation shifted to answering the all important question of, "Where shall we snorkel next?"

Taking the same bus we took yesterday, this time on a different route, we headed for a reef in Little Salmon Bay on Parker Point. The locals assured us the visibility would be better there than where we had snorkeled yesterday. From the moment we arrived, we could tell they were right. The water was exceptionally clear. The sunlight streaming through to the ocean's floor intensified the colors of the fish and coral, and there was a greater variety of both.

As I was snorkeling, I noticed there were sign posts planted throughout the coral beds. Jeff said it was an underwater self-guided tour through the reef, and tours like that were rare, maybe only six in the world. I also noticed I was getting a bit stressed trying to figure out the names of the fish and what kind of coral was in the reef. That kind of stress has no place on a vacation, so I decided to let go of my need-to-know-everything. I was already taking in massive amounts of information required on a moment-to-moment basis to navigate my way through a foreign land. I decided it was time to simply be with my surroundings. The fish and coral were just as beautiful without a name as they were with one.

Halfway through the tour the cold water got the best of me despite my wearing a wetsuit, and I made the reluctant decision to get out. As beautiful as the swim was, my thin tropical blood couldn't take the chill for more than an hour. Once on land, I was content to sit in the sun and warm up, as I waited for Jeff to finish the tour. Forty-five minutes later, he walked out of the ocean with a big grin on his face. He talked the whole way back to the bus stop, telling me all about the fish, shells, and coral he had seen.

As we sat on the bench waiting for our ride, four quokkas approached and sat patiently nearby expecting a handout. They seemed friendly, and I bent over to pet one of them. It went well. I still have all five fingers, but it was a risky thing to do. On the upside, I did heed the warnings posted all over the island that read, "Do Not Feed the Quokkas." As friendly as those rodents were, it appeared that a lot of people had ignored the signs and fed them anyway, because those "rats" of Rottnest Island were very fat and happy.

Another, less cute, wild animal on the island is a highly poisonous snake called a dugite. There are pictures of it posted in all the public areas so we can recognize one if we see it cross our path. The dugite's bite is potentially fatal to humans, and the snake blends a little too well into its environment, making it difficult to spot. We haven't seen one or stepped on one yet, and I hope we never do.

While riding the bus from the beach back to our motel room, I struck up a conversation with a woman sitting in the seat in front of me. Since we were on the island where *Under the Lighthouse Dancing* was filmed and the woman said she was a local, I asked her if she had ever heard of the movie. She answered, "Yes, I have. I was *in* it!" She went on to tell me a few behind the scenes stories of where and how the movie was filmed. She had a silent role as a party guest and said, "I was the one wearing a bright blue dress and putting up streamers for the wedding reception." She told me about one of the illusions the producers created for the film in order to save money. The wedding reception looked as if it had been filmed on the island, but it wasn't at all. That scene was filmed in a quarry in Perth. Tons of sand had to be trucked in to give the quarry a beach look, and in the end, it was cheaper than shuttling 158 extras out to the island.

The woman named several of the movie locations that were on the island: Porpoise Point, the Bathurst Lighthouse, Hennetta Rocks, and the Wedding Chapel—the chapel next door to the motel where Jeff and I are staying. When the free bus came to a stop, the woman got out and I never did see her again, nor did I get her name. I added the chance meeting to our growing list of serendipitous moments.

When Jeff and I got back to the main settlement we were drawn in to the local museum by its historic charm. Built in the 1850's as a hay store, the museum's home was a link to the past. Inside were displays of island artifacts and countless stories about the island's earliest residents. The first story that caught our attention was the one about the shipwreck we saw yesterday. Finding details of the wreck's history was as exciting as stumbling on the wreck itself.

The ship was called the *Uribe*. Built in 1868, it was an auxiliary schooner that brought supplies to Rottnest Island. The boat sank in "June or July 1942" in the very spot it lies today. We learned of several other wrecks scattered around the island, making snorkeling and diving in this area well worth the effort it takes to get there.

The more I read, the more I realized I was far more interested in history than biology, and I had room in my brain for more information after all. There was information about the chapel featured in the movie, that it was built in 1840 and originally used as a schoolhouse and meeting place by the earliest island residents. Wanting to go inside and see, firsthand, where one of the scenes from the movie was filmed, I left Jeff in the museum to continue his tour and walked the short distance over to the chapel. It was closed due to extensive renovations. There I was, standing within a stone's throw, on the safe side of the construction barrier, and no entry permitted. I thought, "I'll have to come back another day."

In addition to the shipwrecks and the chapel, we learned about the island's origins as a prison. Rottnest is similar in many ways to Alcatraz, the abandoned prison that sits on a small island off the coast of San Francisco. Escape from both Alcatraz and Rottnest was extremely difficult, some say impossible, for prisoners due to the cold, swift running currents surrounding each island. If an escapee didn't drown, he was recaptured during or shortly after his swim to the mainland.

In the 1840's, Western Australian Aborigines, native Australians that white settlers once considered a "problem," were brought out to Rottnest and kept in "The Quod." The prison houses remain to this day. Some of the crimes on record were truly misdemeanors and didn't warrant the punishment that followed prosecution. The conditions were horrific, and it wasn't until 1902 that the jail was officially closed.

With enough history lessons for one day and several postcards purchased for my photo album, we finally headed back to our room. Jeff laid down for a well deserved nap, tired from his long morning swim, and I, knowing we would be leaving the island all too soon, set off on foot to see more of Rottnest.

Having heard about the purple sunsets the area is famous for, I decided to find out what it would take to get to the other side of the island and see one for myself. There were pictures, all throughout town, filled with colors so surreal they looked like paintings, and I was determined to get a shot of my own.

After a good long look at the bus schedule, the island map, and asking the locals how to "get there from here," I figured out that the free bus didn't go the route I wanted it to after 6:00 p.m. I might have been able to take the $5 bus or hire a push bike and pedal all the way to the other side of the island, but I wasn't feeling ambitious enough to do either one. The flies were still annoying as ever, and the Fremantle Doctor had yet to arrive. I decided, instead, to walk down the hill from the main settlement to the water's edge, hoping and praying the winds would pick up. Along the way I saw dozens of quokkas foraging among the bushes. "They really are cute for being rodents," I thought.

The island was exceptionally quiet due to all the day trippers heading back to the mainland. I relished the peace and calm of an island with no cars and sparse development, and felt gratitude for being able to stay over for two nights. As I stood on the shoreline and looked out onto the water, my body relaxed and reminded me, loud and clear, that I had been on the go since 5:00 a.m. It was time to head back to the lodge.

We're only in our second week, the millennium is sixteen days away, and any expectations I had for the trip have already been exceeded. Rottnest Island is everything I imagined and more. Whatever happens from this point on is hereby considered a bonus.

Day 9, Thursday   December 16, 1999

Again, I was wide awake at sunrise. Jeff was still sleeping when I left for an early morning walk down to The Basin, a popular place to swim because the water is clear, shallow and inviting. Last night, we made plans to take an early ferry to the mainland. One last morning walk on the beach was the only thing on my mind.

There was the ever present *bzzz* around my head, and I thought, "Paradise and Pests. If the island wasn't so beautiful, I would have to seriously reconsider this as a dream destination, because the flies are nearly ruining it for me."

The locals tolerate the mild seasonal annoyance the same way I have grown accustomed to the bugs back home. Every warm climate has issues with bugs no matter how much effort goes into destroying them. I hardly notice the mosquitoes, no-see-ums (tiny sand fleas that are difficult to detect by the naked eye), and cockroaches. "Oh that?" I say to my out-of-town guest who is completely freaked when a roach lands on her shirt. "That's a flying cockroach. They're harmless."

Coming from a state where bug-free skies are a priority, due more to the threat of disease-carrying mosquitoes than pleasing the multitude of tourists, I don't know if Rottnest Island residents have plans to eradicate the flies—spray them out of existence the way the exterminators in Florida spray mosquitoes. The experience of being dive-bombed by a retrofitted DC-3/C-47 aircraft contracted to drop thick clouds of poison on a private residence in the middle of the day is not a pleasant one, especially when the house windows are left wide open. It's happened to me more times than I care to count. Maybe Aussies believe bugs and humans can coexist and flies are not a threat to human health. If spraying heavy doses of bug repellent is the only alternative to swatting flies, I'll swat flies any day...or maybe not. I haven't decided yet. That's a tough one.

I walked, flinging and flailing my hands in front of my face, back to the lodge with plenty of time to spare before checking out. After a leisurely breakfast, the usual scones and coffee, we gathered our things and boarded the 10:45 a.m. ferry back to Perth. It was another gorgeous day and bittersweet to be leaving the island so soon.

The return voyage was much smoother than the ride I experienced going over to the island, and I was greatly relieved. Any worries I had about getting seasick went wasted, as is the case with most worries. It's all such wasted energy. I noticed that Aussies say "No worries" at the end of almost every conversation. If I said, "Thank you," I heard, "No worries." If I said, "You've been very helpful," I heard, "No worries." If I said, "I can't find a good cup of coffee," I heard, "No worries, *it's roit ova they-ah.*"

No worries....I think those Aussies are on to something.

We arrived, full-circle, back at the Barrack Street Jetty a little more than 48 hours from when we first left the docks. For the first time in three days, Jeff and I talked about what we were going to do next. Up until that moment, we hadn't given it much thought, at least I know I hadn't. After another executive meeting, we made a call from the pay phones nearby and booked an efficiency room at the Metro Inn near the Swan River for only $54 AU ($35 US) per night. Feeling the effects of two days' worth of snorkeling and hiking, we splurged on a taxi to drive us up the hill to our next destination. It was time to get our stuff back, but before we loaded up, we decided to check our emails.

The driver left us at our neighborhood Internet café, the one that sits around the corner from the Britannia YHA. After an hour of reading and writing, Jeff ordered Chinese "take-away" (I'm still getting used to that phrase) from a nearby restaurant. We were thinking ahead towards dinner trying to make life as easy as possible at the end of the day. We learned it was better to lump errands and decisions together whenever possible.

At the YHA, we gathered our things, piled it all in a nice big heap, and called for a second taxi to take us to the Metro Inn. This time, the ride was more than a luxury, it was an absolute necessity. Twenty minutes later we checked into our room, put the food in the fridge, and did nothing for the rest of the day.

This is the first trip where I have had the benefit and convenience of email. To be able to stay in touch with friends we have met along the way and carry on a two-way conversation with friends and family back home amazes me. I look forward to each and every opportunity we get to log onto our email accounts. It's created a new dimension in travel that I never would've imagined on my own.

I still enjoy writing and mailing postcards from the places I have been. My parents have no computer and wouldn't directly hear from me otherwise. I have a few friends in the same category who are not yet online, but I'm guessing they will be getting an email address soon. However popular emailing becomes, I do hope there will always be a place for the handwritten note, a personal message with a personal touch.

Technology is designed to make our lives easier, to add to the quality of our lives. I pay attention if I've crossed the line to the point where the opposite may be happening. The thing I'm most excited about is the myriad of possibilities the Internet has created in the form of work. New options opened up for me when I left the Postal Service and began working out of my home. Maybe I can find the ultimate career of working from anywhere in the world, thanks to the Internet.

Day 10, Friday   December 17, 1999

At breakfast, Jeff and I discussed how we could get to Exmouth today. By the time we finished our second cup of coffee, we had changed our minds.

There was a possibility, being that far north, we would fly directly on to Ayers Rock in the Northern Territory, never to see Perth again. We felt rushed and tense in the thought of leaving and a peaceful calm in the decision to stay. It was as if we knew we'd be missing something if we forced a flight out too soon. We decided to take the easy path and stay put.

In the past, all of my vacations were a constant whirlwind of activity, planned out to the finest detail. I was always on a mission to see and do as much as possible in the short period of time allotted to the trip. Invariably, I was left exhausted to the point where going back to work seemed more like a vacation than the vacation did. When the monotony of the job returned, it was time to repeat the process. If we do this trip the way I have done so many in the past, it will mean insanity for both of us. The "less is more" concept is starting to sink in, and Perth is calling us to slow down.

Since taking the cruise through Fremantle, we had heard that "Freo," as the locals call it, is another "must see" destination. Jeff and I decided if the locals had plenty to say about it, it was worth a visit.

We extended our stay at the Metro Inn for one more night and made plane reservations with Ansett Airways, Australia's domestic air carrier, to fly north to Exmouth early tomorrow morning. Another twenty-four hour delay won't jeopardize our goal to snorkel the Ningaloo Reef *and* get to Ayers Rock by December 31st.

With our immediate needs taken care of, we headed out the door and walked the short distance to public transportation, a commuter train called Transperth. The schedule, routes, and payment were easy to figure out. In no time at all we were in Fremantle. For the fourth day in a row, we were standing on the shores of the Indian Ocean.

Fremantle turned out to be a beautiful historic town loaded with character and plenty to do and see. We asked around for the best place to eat and were directed to a vegetarian restaurant on High Street called Hara Café. It was exactly what we were looking for. Tucked amongst the shops and pubs on a side street in the heart of downtown, Hara Café served up a fresh, delicious, and affordable Indian meal. Without our helpful guides, the odds of finding this gem on our own were slim to none.

After lunch, we walked through town and found the Fremantle Prison. Built by convict labor and opened in 1855, it was an active maximum security site until 1991. Hard to believe eight short years ago inmates lived in such miserable conditions. The stone prison cells were cramped and cold in the winter and cramped and hot in the summer. Prisoners rebelled against the scorching temperatures in the summer (January) of 1988 and made demands for better treatment. They held officers hostage and set fire to the prison, causing millions of dollars in damage before order was restored two days later. Authorities got the message and finally shut the prison down.

There was a chapel room for prisoners seeking redemption and salvation. It most likely served as a brief escape from their cramped quarters as well. The tour guide pointed to the Ten Commandments posted high on the wall. The Sixth Commandment, "Thou shalt not kill," had been changed to "Thou shalt not commit murder," because the death penalty was carried out in the nearby prison gallows. There had to be a distinction between right and wrong when it came to taking a man's life, and the subtle change in language gave prison officials a clear conscience when hanging murderers on death row. Death row inmates were expected to understand the difference between two similar acts. When we toured the gallows on the main floor of the prison, a noose—ready for the next execution—dangled from the rafters.

One of the prison's most moving exhibits was a beautiful set of drawings left behind by one of the inmates. The prisoner had drawn on the walls of his cell. Out of those drawings a story emerged about the artist himself and gave depth and meaning to a seemingly empty shell. Now a part of history and preserved under clear thick plastic, the drawings represent a less violent side of Fremantle Prison. Officials realized that inmates were calmer and easier to control when the creative process wasn't stifled.

The tour was filled with stories that brought the prison experience alive. We learned how Australia's first settlers (after the Aborigines) were Great Britain's throwaways and prison guards, and the entire continent was viewed as one gigantic correctional facility, from which no one would ever escape. In the late 1700's, Great Britain sailed the first of its convict ships past Brazil, past the southern tip of Africa, and into what is now known as Sydney Harbor. That was where the "criminal class" was turned into slave labor and became Australia's construction crew. They worked their way from Sydney to Fremantle leaving behind the convict legacy Australia is famous for.

This unsavory group did not mix well with the native Aborigines, and it was a brutal beginning. Some historians claim that the United States had a similar start. In addition to the "White man versus Indian" conflicts America is well known for, there is evidence to support the idea that England's first ships to the New World were filled with outcasts and rebel rousers. Maybe our settlers weren't as "bad" as the baddest that arrived on the shores of Sydney, but they were definitely nonconformists and independent thinkers. It takes a tremendous amount of courage and a little bit of crazy to go into the unknown. The outcast/rebel theme sounds like a viable one to me. And that's all I'm going to say about that.

After a few hours in the Fremantle Prison, we walked freely through the long series of gates that once held countless men behind bars. I was instantly reminded of the privileges we enjoy on a daily basis, often take for granted, and occasionally complain about. I've heard it said, "Perception and attitude is everything." It really is.

Jeff and I continued our walk through town and found another good Indian restaurant half a block away from the Hara Café. While eating an early dinner, we asked our server where we should go to see "the best of the best" in Fremantle sunsets. We were directed to a local gathering spot that reminded me of Mallory Square in Key West, Florida where the crowds gather at the end of the day. There weren't any magicians, fire eaters, or jugglers—the sort of entertainment Key West is famous for, but the feeling of being on the edge of the world was the same. We didn't see the elusive purple hues the Indian Ocean is capable of delivering, but it was a colorful sky and a beautiful end to a day filled with freedom.

We rode Transperth back to Perth, recounting the day's events, positively hooked on Fremantle. By the time we got back to the Metro Inn, we decided to stay "just one more day." There's a grand opening scheduled for a brand new submarine exhibit tomorrow that looks really interesting.

Before heading up to our room, Jeff asked the front desk clerk to add an extra night, and I called Ansett Airways to alert them of our change in plans. The airline reservationist graciously moved our booking ahead twenty-four hours without a single fee or advanced credit card payment. "No worries, mate," she said, "It's all taken care of."

Jeff and I will fly out the day after tomorrow.
I love this place.

Day 11, Saturday   December 18, 1999

Today marks our seventh day in the great state of Western Australia. Hindsight is alright when looking back on good experiences, and it's been a long time since I've been in agreement with choices of the past. Four years ago, in an unhappy marriage, struggling to find answers, and wondering why my life wasn't working out very well made hindsight a difficult reality to accept. I wasn't good at listening to and following my gut instincts, but this trip is beginning changing all of that.

First thing this morning, we walked from the motel to the Transperth train station which was six blocks away. Jeff and I decided to see another area of downtown Perth, the business district, so this time, we took the train to the main station. We each enjoyed a nice hot bowl of oatmeal and a cup of espresso before continuing on to Fremantle for the second day in a row.

Transperth runs on the honor system, and I have never seen anything like it. Tickets are sold self-service from vending machines, and there are no turnstiles to validate tickets and count passengers like the subways in New York and Washington, D.C. Anyone can walk on at anytime. Since it is a train and not a subway, all the stations are above ground, super clean, and open to the elements. Once everyone is on board and the train is in motion, official ticket collectors stroll up and down the isles on a random basis. It's anybody's guess when they will appear. If someone wants to beat the system and attempt to ride for free, they may get away with it, but the fares are very reasonable. I get the feeling that most riders play by the rules. It doesn't seem worth the hassle and expense of getting caught.

The best part of riding the train is that it keeps me off the streets. I am still challenged to remember to look in the right direction when I cross the road to avoid getting run over. Forget about a sudden 'roo crossing, even the best of drivers would have a hard time avoiding a sudden woman crossing. Add in the nervous anticipation I feel about driving our own vehicle, and I am happy to take public transportation whenever possible.

Before we got to Fremantle, Jeff and I made an unscheduled departure from the train when we saw a Blockbuster Video store in a shopping center within sight of one of our stops. I was thrilled to see a familiar "face," and Jeff kindly indulged my whim to look for the movie *Under the Lighthouse Dancing*. Since I couldn't find it for sale on the island, I thought I had a good chance of finding it for sale in a town near the island, but no luck. We hopped on the next train and rode into Fremantle. My search for the movie continued.

Upon our arrival, we headed straight for the submarine tour we saw advertised yesterday, but before we got there we took a second detour into an Internet café. After an hour of cyberspace socializing, we finally reached the shipyard. It turns out that during WWII, Fremantle was a place of refuge and a very active base for our own United States Navy submarines operating in the southern hemisphere.

The tour of the "unknown sub," as I have called it since I didn't make note of any details, was impressive and began with the challenge of climbing down the boat's ladder into the cramped spaces below. Today was not a good day to wear a sundress. *What was I thinking?* The well-made display boards inside the sub explained what each section was. And the experience of walking, often ducking, through the tight quarters to see firsthand how a submariner lived made an impression on me.

How do they do it? How do they live for days, weeks, possibly months on end hundreds of feet underwater isolated from daylight, fresh air, and the everyday luxuries we often take for granted, such as a walk in the park? I learned that submariners are known as the "silent service" and they are a rare breed indeed. They experience a level of courage and trust between one another that most of us will never know or begin to understand.

A friendly staff of volunteers kept us moving along. Passing through the main control room, I noticed a computer keyboard at one of the stations. It looked as if it was waiting for a command. The empty chair was too much to resist, so I sat down to pretend I was a submariner. As I *ever so lightly* placed my fingers on the keys, one of the tour guides yelled out, "DON'T TOUCH THE KEYBOARD! THE SHIP IS LIVE!" I immediately jumped back and was informed that if I had given the right keys the right amount of pressure I may have launched a torpedo right there on the docks. Whether it was for real or an Aussie joke, I'll never know, but they sounded dead serious. I felt like a two-year-old who just *had* to touch everything, and I was in big trouble. How embarrassing. Jeff and I quickly moved along and said our good-byes to the volunteers. They, in turn, were probably glad to see that "crazy American" go.

We wasted no time in heading back into downtown Fremantle where we found "The Market"—a large indoor flea market that closed daily at 5:00 p.m. sharp. With a few hours to spare, it was time to do some souvenir shopping. Like any good partner to a shopaholic, Jeff patiently sat outside on a park bench while I made the rounds in search of the elusive Aussie hat. Luck was on my side, and I finally found one. There it was, the beige wide-brimmed linen sun hat I had been looking for since we arrived in Sydney eleven days ago. I didn't care if it was made in Taiwan. As far as I was concerned, I had officially become *Australian*.

While inside the market I also found one of my favorite foods, stuffed grape leaves. I bought ten of them. They make the perfect snack and carry well. Once I was done shopping, proudly wearing my new hat, Jeff and I headed back to the Hara Café to enjoy another healthy meal. I am totally convinced that this wonderful little restaurant, located at 33 High Street, is one of Fremantle's best-kept secrets. I added it to my revisit list because delicious vegetarian restaurants are few and far between.

At 6:00 p.m., we could hear live jazz music playing two doors down from the café. It was refreshing to be in such a lively, bohemian atmosphere. The crowds were young, the dress was casual and colorful, and the historic charm of the city all came together to create a character all its own. As we walked the short distance to watch the sunset at The Roundhouse, Fremantle's oldest landmark, the music followed us all the way there.

Tonight's sunset was a bit different than last night's. I suppose sunsets are like snowflakes—no two are exactly the same. This time the sun squished like a hard boiled egg when it hit the horizon, and the illusion was a first for me. While the colors were not as vibrant as last night, it scored a "10" for uniqueness.

If only I could swim far enough, I could reach the shores of South Africa from here.

Day 12, Sunday   December 19, 1999

There was no rushing around this morning. With little more on our agenda than to pack for our late afternoon flight to Exmouth, we lounged. I didn't realize how much we have been going, going, going until we came to a screeching halt.

Last night, I asked for a late check out so we could leisurely prepare for our 3:15 p.m. departure. To pass the time, we swam in the pool, read in the shade, and at 11:00 a.m. a storm rolled in. It was as if nature was saying, "You're doing too much. Go inside and take a nap." The cool air, cloudy skies and relaxing sounds of the rain were a welcome change, and I took the pace down another notch. With all the sunny weather we have had over the past week we were able to make the most of each experience. When it was time to move on we got a good day's rest. *I believe we are on to something. Our "no plan" plan is unfolding nicely.*

We flew SkyWest, a partner of Ansett Airways. Our plane held forty-six passengers, and the flight was a bit bumpy due to the lingering storms. It was one thing to be able to weather the storm from our motel room earlier in the day and quite another to be *in* the storm. Fortunately, it didn't take long to get out of the clouds, and in no time at all we were making our descent for a stopover into Geraldton, a town one third of the way up the coast. After a quick change of passengers we were back in the air for the remaining three-hour flight to Exmouth.

The Exmouth Airport was small and sat 15 miles outside of town. Along with the other passengers, Jeff and I, with all of our gear in tow, boarded the awaiting airport shuttle bus. Before leaving Perth, we decided that finding a room this far north was going to be easy, since it was off-season, and we didn't make any reservations.

The reason the airport is so far from town is because it was originally built during World War II and used as a United States Navy Air Patrol Base from 1942 to 1944. The mission to protect the surrounding waters and coastline known as Exmouth Gulf was called "Operation Potshot," and I am certain there are United States servicemen alive today who remember it well.

Considered one of the newest towns in Australia, Exmouth was established in 1967 to support operations at a Navy station called Naval Communications Station Harold E. Holt. Built by the US government, the station is a city unto itself with a gym, indoor basketball court, bowling alley, tennis courts, a movie theater, football/softball field, and swimming pool. These days, the facilities are enjoyed by local residents and guests visiting the area. Exmouth, known as the gateway to one of the best kept diving secrets in the world, the Ningaloo Reef, has transformed into a tourist destination.

Many of the street names throughout town honor Australian, British, and American servicemen who served during World War II. The homes here are extremely modest,

*basically the equivalent of a box, and built for function only.
I get the feeling we are seeing Exmouth in the early stages of
growth, just like seeing California long before the real estate
boom set in. It may be hot here, but the reef alone is worth
the trip. Whale sharks, giant, docile plankton-eaters swim in
these waters from March through June. It's one of the few
areas in Australia where they can be found. Unfortunately,
we won't be able to see them, but giant, docile plankton-
eating manta rays are here, and so are the sea turtles. We
will do our best to find both.*

It was dark when the shuttle dropped us off at the Potshot
Resort. Our lack of planning worked against us this time
around and we had a hard time deciding where to stay. One-
by-one we watched all the other passengers get off the bus at
various locations. It was clear they knew what they were
doing and we didn't. We didn't know where we were, hadn't
done our homework, and because of all of our stuff, we
hesitated to get off the shuttle and commit to walking any
more than we had to. The shuttle didn't stop at every
accommodation. Sometimes it stopped at the end of an
empty road, and it was important that we knew where we
were headed before we stepped out. We were sure we'd
figure something out and decided not to ask for help. Instead,
we floundered on our own and had a lousy time of it.

As far as we could tell, we were on the only public
transportation available. Calling a cab, if we could find a pay
phone, was not a guarantee either. After a few false starts,
thinking we knew where we were going to stay, changing
our minds, and at one point getting off the bus only to get
back on again, the driver was losing his patience with us. We
finally asked him to take us back to the place that appealed to
us the most, the Potshot. It was not one of our finer
moments, and the ride ended on a very stressful note.

Fortunately, the kitchen was open late, and we were able
to get a hot meal at the pool bar. Menu selections included
American fare prepared with an Asian influence, and the
food was very good and satisfying. If I had been a drinker, I

would have ordered a shot of whiskey as well. Make that a double.

It's 9:00 pm. I'm so glad this day is over.

Day 13, Monday   December 20, 1999

Assuming we were going to stay in Exmouth for a few days and take daily excursions out to the reef, our number one goal this morning was to move to a different motel. The staff at the Potshot Resort was professional and friendly. The lobby, restaurant and public areas were clean and presentable, but our room was far from ideal. It felt dirty and musty, and we had a rough night sleeping. The conditions may have had something to do with Cyclone Vance, a storm that hit the area in March 1999. Part of the resort was destroyed. Jeff and I could have spoken up and asked for an upgrade, but we didn't.

Throughout our travels, we've noticed that a regular cup of coffee, especially in these remote regions, continues to be the same quality offered on the train. Here it is, day thirteen of the trip, and we have finally come to the conclusion that if there isn't a high-end cappuccino maker or espresso machine around, our morning jolt consists of instant granules, dissolved in hot water, contained in a plastic foam cup. And the creamer is generally a non-dairy powder. Yuck.

Soon into our search for better accommodations, we changed our plans entirely. Making calls and asking countless questions about the area and how to navigate our way to the Ningaloo Reef, we learned that it was best to head south. We also learned that renting a vehicle in Exmouth was much easier than renting one in Perth. We found a reasonably priced white/two-door/right-hand-drive/manual shift Suzuki jeep at the Exmouth Cape Tourist Village. It reminded me of the postal jeeps I used to drive when I worked for the U.S. Postal Service, and I was excited that it would be ours for a few days. Jeff and I were told we could take the jeep as far as we wanted for as many days as we wanted, but there was a catch. We were allotted X-number of "free" kilometers (km) and we had a lot of ground to cover. Beyond the set amount, we were going to be charged an additional price per km. Jeff and I made an agreement to pay attention to the distances and keep within our budget.

With our very own set of wheels, our Florida Driver's Licenses making us totally legal (How cool is that?), and all of our stuff jammed into the back of the jeep, we headed for Cape Range National Park and the Ningaloo Reef. The jeep's "air conditioning" only worked when the windows were down. In other words, there was none. The only thing that was going to keep us the slightest bit cool was through the scientific formula of "refrigeration by evaporation," the wind against our perspiration. We knew what we were up against and were in for a true outback experience.

Before leaving the city limits we stopped at the local grocery store to pack a few basics such as bread, peanut butter and jelly, fruit, an assortment of snacks, and twelve gallons of bottled water. The store was about the size of a large convenience store, and had everything we needed. Our guide book, *Lonely Planet*, warned us, the jeep rental staff warned us, and all the local brochures sent the same message, "There is no water in the park. Be sure to bring your own."

On the store shelves, I spotted Vegemite, an Aussie staple. It's a product mentioned in the popular song *Down Under* recorded by the Australian band, Men at Work. Feeling a bit silly in the moment, I picked up a jar of the brown stuff and sang the chorus, "I come from a land down under...." Jeff gave me "the look" along with a pleasant half smile. After I finished singing (rather poorly I might add) we had a discussion about whether or not we should try the yeast-filled paste. I had heard Vegemite wasn't very good, a bit "salty," and that it was an "acquired taste," so Jeff and I agreed to leave it on the shelf. We decided peanut butter was in the same category and bought the biggest jar available.

The change in temperatures from Perth to Exmouth is the equivalent of flying from Oregon to southern California in the summer, only it's hotter here, ridiculously hot, even for me, the Floridian. It may reach as high as 40-50 degrees Celsius (Australian measurements) which translates well into the triple digits, nearly 120 degrees Fahrenheit (USA measurements). That's more than hot, that's scary hot, but we're going anyway. No wonder it's off-season.

I'm still doing my best to remember to flip the country upside down. Add in the adjustment of driving on the left side of the road, the sun coming up way too early, and the new sights and sounds of Western Australia, it's all a bit overwhelming at times, but in a good way.

Flying to Exmouth brought us back into kangaroo and emu territory and, because the town is quiet this time of year, wildlife can be seen within city limits. This morning, a mother emu and her two babies walked right up onto the motel's front lawn, a mere twenty steps from the front door. Jeff and I were in the lobby when we turned to see the group take a drink from the puddles made by the lawn sprinkler. The motel's receptionist said the emus often come into town for water because the surrounding desert is so dry.

Once the little emu family got their fill, Jeff and I watched them take a leisurely stroll straight down the center of the road, following the double yellow line. It was one thing to see emus in the Nullarbor Plain sitting under the trees with the kangaroos, and another thing entirely to watch them strut down a paved road, heads held high, as if they owned the place.

The barren roads of Exmouth gave us an ideal place to get used to driving on the "wrong" side of the road from the "passenger" side of the vehicle. When it was my turn to take the wheel, I felt as if I was learning how to drive all over again. The manual three-speed transmission meant that I had to use my left hand to shift gears and steer with my right. While all this was going on I had to unlearn a few American rules of the road, so I could learn a few Australian ones. The most adventurous part of the unlearning/new learning occurred at every intersection. It was all I could do to remember which lane to end up in once I had completed my turn. After a mile or so, I gladly switched places with Jeff and we headed out of town to Cape Range National Park.

The drive south turned out to be a simple and easy one through the coastal deserts. I can only guess that the world's tourist industry hasn't picked up on this area yet—probably because it's so remote—because very few people were on the roads. I figured, like any beautiful place, it's simply a matter of time before more people discover this area and make the effort to get here despite the heat.

The Ningaloo Reef stretches 67 miles throughout the Indian Ocean weaving its way in and out, up and down Western Australia's shoreline like a sea snake. Cape Range National Park, the land that borders the reef, offers plenty of access. In many places throughout the park, the coral beds are only a short swim from the beach, no boat required. More than five hundred species of fish can be found in these waters, and the coral is said to be spectacular. These were all the reasons we were excited about coming here and why this reef in particular made it on our short list.

Upon our arrival at Cape Range National Park, we headed for the Milyering Visitor's Center. It's a small, very modest building with an impressive display of local wildlife and sea life inside, extremely well done. A kangaroo and her baby, also known as a "joey," were lounging on the brick pavers under the eaves of the building. They were doing their best to keep cool in the soaring temperatures. For me, seeing a kangaroo up close and personal was more bizarre than seeing the emu family walk down the road back in Exmouth. Just like the emus, I had only seen kangaroos from a distance, and there I was standing 10 feet away from the strange looking marsupials. I took pictures of the mom and baby, no zoom required, and then looked around for more unusual sightings. That's when I noticed, 20 yards out, a dozen kangaroos, and they were watching my every move.

Once my eyes adjusted and I knew what to look for, the 'roos began to take shape one after another throughout the desert landscape. They are known as "big reds," the largest of the breed, and they blend extremely well into the red sand of the desert. They looked harmless enough, but we were warned to keep our distance.

For the most part, kangaroos are similar to grazing deer. Both species have adapted to the effects of humans moving into their territories and have a reputation for being more of a pest than a threat. But like any wild animal, if a 'roo believes it's being threatened in any way, it can become aggressive and territorial. Keeping a safe distance, I admired them from afar. I didn't trust the ones lounging under the eaves either. A full out 'roo attack would look something like a kick-boxing match, and I would be the one left bruised and battered.

In addition to a potentially irate kangaroo, another wildlife concern was snakes. Just like on Rottnest Island, we were warned about the venomous reptiles that have the potential to kill with a single bite. We were given clear descriptions of their markings, or lack thereof, and told to take great care when walking, especially with sandals, through the desert sands and the low lying bush to avoid stepping on anything that moved.

Another health concern was dehydration and sun exposure, the dangers of too much sun. The locals call this part of Australia "Melanoma Country." Great. Nice to know. We've been slathering on the sunscreen and drinking water every chance we get. The usual precautions were suggested; wear hats and long sleeve shirts, stay in the shade whenever possible, and use a high level SPF sunscreen. We got the message and have been doing our part. My Aussie hat went from being a novelty to a necessity, and I wear it every chance I get.

Driving past the visitor's center and 60 miles deeper into the park we headed for Yardie Creek & Gorge. Yardie Creek is a campground, beach, and river bed all rolled into one. Wide enough for boats, the creek follows a gorge flanked by beautiful red rock walls, and eventually spills out into the Indian Ocean. Boaters love Yardie Creek, but since this location is so remote (and it is summer) there were very few people around. We practically had the place to ourselves.

We took our first swim out to the Ningaloo Reef, but soon discovered that it was too far out for our comfort at that particular point. The surf was rough and the water temperature was cold. My third ocean swim wearing a wetsuit, and I found out what a fair weather snorkeler I really am. All I managed to do was get tossed around in the waves, and the experience was over as fast as it began. Jeff made a grander attempt at finding the reef and eventually gave up, due to the rough seas as well. We both knew we'd find a better place to snorkel and called it a day as far as reef explorations were concerned. On the upside, the campground was beautiful, and we had only begun to scout the area.

After dusk, the kangaroos were on the move, and with our newly trained eyes we could see the "big reds" scattered throughout the desert. Jeff and I sat 50 yards away from the beach and, keeping our sights on the ocean's horizon, could see the 'roos hopping along the shoreline. I expected to see them in the outback, but a kangaroo on the beach? No way.

It was after sunset when we pitched the tent, the same tent we carried all the way from Florida. Once camp was in order, we took a short hike above the gorge. The air was cooling quickly, and it felt great be out in the open and relieved of the heat. We followed a trail and counted kangaroos along the way. Occasionally I would mistake the smaller 'roos for rabbits. I believe I was trying to find some sense of normalcy in a very bizarre situation. The moon was rising, and we could see that it was a day or two from being full. Strangely enough, the later it got, the brighter it got as the moon lit our path all the way back to the tent.

Hours later, we were still wide awake; the moon's energy affecting us like a double shot of espresso. It was midnight when we decided to take another walk along the beach. We were told at the visitor's center that this was sea turtle nesting season and after sundown the turtles were coming ashore to lay their eggs in the sand. Our search turned up empty.

We'll keep looking. They're bound to be here somewhere.

Day 14, Tuesday   December 21, 1999

It was nice sleeping under the stars, and I was feeling good about our decision to camp out. Considering how hot it was during the day yesterday, the nighttime conditions were a pleasant surprise. Temperatures dropped significantly after the sun went down, and without a tent to block the steady ocean breezes, we would have been slightly chilled through the night.

Come morning, the cycle repeated itself. Temperatures rose quickly, and by 7:00 a.m., late morning by my standards, we were forced out of the tent by the blazing heat. As soon as we stepped into the fresh air, flies starting buzzing our faces. We hadn't noticed them yesterday. Maybe our excitement to be among the kangaroos overrode the annoyance.

To keep my sanity, I sat in the jeep, ate my apple in peace, and watched the kangaroos hop in and out of sight while Jeff took a swim. That early in the day, the cold water didn't seem to faze him. I, on the other hand, required the heat of high noon before I would get in the ocean. It was cool in the shade of the jeep even though the jeep was parked in the sun. All it took was cracking the windows enough to allow the air to pass through. If it wasn't for those sea breezes, we would have been doomed to a miserable trip.

No where on earth have I ever seen the desert meet the sea the way it does at Yardie Creek. While I've never been to coastal Africa, the movies are filled with scenes similar to this one, so I decided this is what Africa must look like. For a brief moment, I imagined I was on safari. The kangaroos were the large game animals, and I was cruising along the desert bush searching for wild game. It was a short stretch of the imagination because I really was in a jeep, the Australian accents of everyone we meet sound British and a bit South African to me, and the air is hotter than anything I have ever experienced. Yep, this was as close to Africa as I have ever been geographically and otherwise.

After a hearty lunch of peanut butter and jelly sandwiches, we took a walk along the beach. With fewer clouds in the sky, the sun was the strongest yet, causing temperatures to rise above 100 degrees. Finally, the cold water was going to work in my favor, and I knew I wouldn't need a wetsuit. To protect myself from the intense rays of the sun, I wore an oversized t-shirt and slathered on the sunscreen. What a difference a day makes.

The deep blue-green water was calm, the fish were plentiful and colorful, and there was coral everywhere. The reef had finally lived up to its reputation. I still didn't know exactly what I was looking at, and it didn't matter. I was thoroughly enjoying the swim.

For some reason, I had no fear of sharks or any other under water creatures for that matter. I've been swimming in the Gulf of Mexico for so long without incident that I've been lulled into a false belief that open waters are safe. Jeff and I have been warned of the local dangers, especially sharks, and told not to touch the coral or any creatures amongst the coral. "I can do that. I can keep to myself," I thought. The reef itself was sharp, and there were spiky sea creatures lurking in the crevices that could send a snorkeler to the emergency room if the two came in contact. A deep respect for the sea was definitely in order.

Sea turtles have risen to the top of my "must see" list, and we are determined to find them. I've been asking nearly everyone I see if they know where the turtles are. "Yes, they are here," they say, "It's all about being in the right place at the right time." Jeff said he noticed fresh turtle tracks in the sand earlier this morning, so we know they are close.

After a morning of snorkeling, we packed up the tent and drove back to the Milyering Visitor Center to touch base with civilization and make plans for our second night in the park. We met a nice couple from Holland, Jeroen (Yur-oon) and Ottine (O-teen), who were on an extended holiday as well. The common ground of being somewhere so remote gave us all an instant connection. We talked about where we were from and where we thought the best snorkeling was. Jeff and I learned that this was Jeroen and Ottine's last day in the area before heading out. We didn't ask where they were going. We were all on an adventure that could change course at any time.

Adjacent to the visitor's center, near the beach, we saw sixteen kangaroos all sitting under a series of four naturally formed overhangs that gave the 'roos plenty of shade. Beyond the rock ledges was the ocean. The "big reds" were moving ever so slightly as they did their best to stay in the shade. One of the kangaroos had a joey in her pouch. The mom looked at me with a watchful eye, and that's when I noticed that every single kangaroo in the group was doing the same: frozen like rabbits anticipating *my* next move. I walked away, and they never left their post.

While in the park we saw several interesting creatures. First, there was a strange bird walking down the middle of the road. It looked a lot like a Secretary Bird, a bird most commonly found in Africa. It was three-feet tall, had extra long legs and was really beautiful. I later identified it as an Australian bustard (not to be confused with the South African bustard), commonly known as a bush turkey. Jeff and I were also fortunate enough to see a four-foot long prehistoric-looking lizard, called a goanna, cross the road ahead of us. It moved in slow motion and with strong authority. They're known to be elusive, and sightings are rare. The reduced traffic may have lured the giant lizard out of hiding.

Hours passed like minutes, and we were thoroughly enjoying our stay in the park. Surviving on peanut butter and jelly sandwiches, it was food-for-fuel only in the dining department. There were no full-meal concessions available, and that was alright by us. Our priority was the adventure of Ningaloo Reef, and our focus was still on the turtles. The ranger at the visitor center told us to head to the northwest end of the cape. Due to the impending full moon, egg-laying activity along the shoreline was escalating. "You'll see them," she said, "They're everywhere."

We drove several miles north to a stretch of coastline famous for late night turtle nesting. Having asked enough questions, we finally knew which beach to go to. It was still a few hours before sunset, so we took a side trip up to the Vlaming Head Lighthouse at the top of the hill. It looked like an excellent vantage point to watch the sun drop down into the ocean. Despite the strong winds blowing hard across the hill, we stayed until the last bit of light disappeared over the horizon. The evening's colors were gorgeous, and it was another sunset worth mentioning. Afterwards, we drove down the hill and headed straight for the turtle beaches a short distance down the road.

In the beach parking lot and before Jeff brought the jeep to a stop, he shouted out, "There's one! It's huge!" As we scrambled to get out of the vehicle, we could see the sand flying high in the air as the mom-to-be dug fast and furiously to lay her eggs. Standing with one foot on the sand and one still on the parking lot we spotted a second turtle coming up and out of the surf 50 feet down the beach. As if on queue, and maybe they were, another one crawled out of the surf, and then another. They looked like big shiny beetles in the moonlight laboriously inch-by-inch dragging their massive bodies across the sand. Jeff and I could see turtle tracks all up and down the beach, hundreds of them. We realized there was no reason to go any further. We had front row seats to one of nature's most amazing shows.

There were more females off shore, their heads bobbing in the surf like heavy coconuts, waiting for their "moment." When it came their turn, they rode the waves onto the beach pulling the last bit of support they could from the sea before beginning the difficult passage across dry land. Gravity had become their biggest obstacle.

The turtles didn't have to travel far up on shore to reach a safe nesting spot, but moving at a pace of one foot every ten minutes, it took them awhile to get where they were going and start digging. The hole had to be deep enough to give the babies a fighting chance to survive long enough to hatch and crawl to the sea. Predators were waiting to dig up a shallow nest and eat the soft rubbery eggs before they hardened. After the hole was dug, another hour's labor was underway laying the ping-pong ball sized eggs in the hole that had been dug, and then there was the arduous task of filling the hole with sand once the eggs were in place. As if that wasn't enough, the giant sea turtle spent another hour lumbering back to sea.

Every stage of the mother turtle's struggle could be seen from that one vantage point. Sand was flying in all directions, turtles were coming and going, all in slow motion of course, and we knew we were in the right place at the right time. We had hit the turtle jackpot, and it was spectacular, a spectacular end to a spectacular day.

The cool desert night breezes have brought favorable camping conditions. We're still within the park's boundaries, and have set up our tent at Ned's Camp. I'm sure we'll sleep well tonight.

Day 15, Wednesday   December 22, 1999

Unlike yesterday's rude awakening, Jeff and I awoke in the shade. Thanks to Jeff's brilliant idea to pitch the tent next to a group of tall trees, we were able to get an extra hour of sleep. He made a victory pot of coffee over an open fire, and we both enjoyed a warm drink in the cool morning air. It was heaven....for another 30 minutes. When the sun rose higher than the trees the party was over. The flies and the heat were back.

To prepare for our first swim of the day, we packed up and loaded all of our stuff into the back of the jeep, slathered on the sunscreen, and headed for Turquoise Bay, otherwise known as "The best snorkeling in Western Australia." Now there's a claim to live up to.

Immediately upon our arrival at Turquoise Bay, I declared, on the spot, that it was absolutely positively one of the most beautiful beaches I had ever seen. The wide, shallow, white sandy bottom of the ocean floor created a gradual descent from the beach into crystal clear, turquoise blue waters. Adding to the perfection was the Ningaloo Reef waiting in the depths ahead. The bay truly lived up to its name.

To make our swim easy, Jeff and I walked 50 yards south along the shoreline before entering the water. The method behind the madness was to allow the current to take us back to the parking lot. We could float along enjoying the sights beneath the waterline and make progress all at the same time. While on the walk I looked for shells and found several good specimens to add to my collection at home. There was a perfect cowry, three beautiful baby pink conchs, each a half-an-inch long, a few limpets, and a miscellaneous assortment of tiny shells I never did identify. I was careful to pick up only the empty ones. If a shell is occupied by a hermit crab or any other type of critter, I will leave it on the beach every time.

As I walked into the cool waters of the bay it was like walking into a huge wading pool. Carrying my fins, all I had to do was shuffle out until the water got deep enough to swim in. Waist deep, I crouched down, pulled the mask over my eyes, slipped the fins on my feet, and off I went. The mask was holding up well, no leaks, and as I slowly kicked my way through the coral I knew right away this was going to be one of the trip's highlights. The coral and fish were exceptional. One coral head in particular stood out. Nature has the wildest imagination when it comes to shape and color, and that bit of coral piqued my curiosity. I asked Jeff if he knew what it was. He said, "It's a stag horn. Those bright blue tips are considered rare in this part of the world." I have no idea how he knew that, but it sounded good to me.

In addition to the extraordinary variety of coral and fish, a young, three-foot long green sea turtle appeared out of nowhere and cruised in beneath us. It moved quickly. Jeff and I did our best to keep up, and with my underwater disposable camera I managed to get two pictures of my first swim with a wild sea turtle. That experience was immediately placed at the top of my "best day ever" list. *Is it possible to have "the best day ever" several times over? Yes, it is.*

After the morning snorkel at Turquoise Bay, Jeff and I left the park to return to civilization, real civilization, back to Exmouth. The peanut butter jar was nearly empty and we were down to two gallons of water. The park's visitor center sold chips, ice cream and sodas; and while it gave us choices above and beyond what we had brought with us, it wasn't enough to keep us in the park longer than three days. We never did see any fresh water showers, so we were getting a bit "ripe" as they say in the camping circles. The swimming helped somewhat, but there's no substitute for a fresh water rinse. The reasons to leave were fast outweighing the reasons to stay. On the drive out we saw another goanna walking down the road, and it was equally as thrilling the second time around. What an odd creature that was.

Other than the occasional wild animal, the drive north to Exmouth was a lonely one. The cars we saw were few and far between. We noticed that each time a car passed, the driver waved. We caught on that it was a courtesy to acknowledge the other guy in the middle of nowhere. After the third car, we got faster at waving back and felt like a couple of locals.

Seventeen kilometers before reaching Exmouth, we pulled into the Lighthouse Caravan Park to check things out and break up the drive. Lighthouse Caravan Park is a privately owned campground either within or along side the borders of Cape Range National Park. Unlike Ned's Camp and Yardie Creek Campground, Lighthouse Caravan Park offered a whole lot more in the way of amenities. In addition to the tent and camper van sites, there were chalets, cabins and bungalows, a swimming pool, toddler pool, tennis court, seasonal café, tackle store, fish cleaning facility, showers, snorkel rentals and sales, kitchens available for camper use, a laundromat, petrol station, and barbeque grills for guest use. The small shop on the premises offered ice-cream, cool drinks, ice, bait, bread, milk and basic necessities. And on the front steps of this local general store is where we met Kara, the step-daughter of the owner of the park.

The second Kara heard our accents she was eager to talk to us about America. She was all teenager as she told us how *badly* she *really* wanted to see our country. Kara asked question after question about life in the 'States, and we happily answered. We learned that American movies and music videos have made quite an impression on Australians. I had no idea what a huge impact we have on other cultures, and it was a real eye-opener for me.

Just for fun, I asked Kara to teach me how to say the word "no" in Australian. It's spelled the same, for sure, but it sounds entirely different from the way we say it in America. I was fascinated by the way Aussies have managed to fit so many vowels into a two letter word. It goes something like, "no-ee-ay-oh," but I wanted to hear it from a true Aussie. After a few miserable attempts, I gave up before Kara was forced to cut the lesson short. It did not go well. Since arriving in Oz, I've heard two-year-olds say "no" better than I could.

After an hour, it was time to head down the road and get back to Exmouth. We arrived early enough to cash a few traveler's checks, restock the fruit cooler, and we passed, again, on the Vegemite. We also discovered ice coffee, the kind that comes in milk cartons, and we drank more than our share. It's really good stuff.

Next stop: Coral Bay. There was still enough daylight to make it there before dark.

Like Fremantle, Coral Bay came highly recommended by the locals, so we decided to check it out. One hundred and fifty kilometers (93 miles) south of Exmouth, it was a two-hour drive. The sights along the way consisted of dry desert sands dotted with shrubbery, a farm or two, and the occasional kangaroo and emu sitting in the shade. Termite mounds were common, and I counted one camel farm. In those two hours, we passed a total of five cars and every single driver waved. I felt a sense of belonging each time I waved back, and I liked it. There was no where else in the world I wanted to be. Everything was perfect....except for the heat... and the flies.

Without air conditioning the drive was rough. Salt was stuck to my sweaty, filthy skin, and my hair was tangled, greasy, and two days overdue for a good washing. Forget the reef and wildlife, I was focused solely on the fresh water shower that lay ahead.

The road came to an end at the town of Coral Bay, population: 120...give or take a few. There was no going any further. We had reached our destination and knew we had stumbled into paradise when we saw the oasis in front of the Ningaloo Reef Resort. There it was—a beautiful motel with a pool, palm trees, and the greenest grass we'd seen since Perth. The front desk clerk gave us the good news that a room was available, complete with our own private bathroom, an efficiency kitchen, and hot and cold running water.

Christmas, or "Chrissy" as they call it here because Aussies love shortening their words, was only three days out, and the resort could have easily been booked solid. We were taking our chances to find a room in such a small town. I was worried (When will I learn?) that we were going to have to camp a third night in a row in the nearby campground, or worse yet, drive all the way back to Exmouth, but everything worked out. We checked in, unloaded all of our stuff out of the jeep and into our room, and took the long-awaited showers. Once we were presentable, we stepped out to explore the three blocks that made up Coral Bay.

Within minutes we found the only Internet café around. It was inside Fins Café in the only shopping center in town that also happened to be right next door to our motel. I spent an hour-and-a-half and $14 US on e-mails. It was great to catch up and tell my family where I was. Fins Café had only one computer, and it was installed a month ago. The owners said the investment had already paid for itself, and I imagined they wished they had a few more.

Jazz was playing in the background when we arrived and roughly segued into classic American '50's music. The familiar songs caused me to react the same way I reacted to the pop-top I found on Rottnest Island except the confusion felt stronger this time. Music is a powerful medium for triggering past thoughts and experiences, and in my confusion I thought, "Am I home? In the Florida Keys? Where exactly am I?" It was a weird sensation, and it took me a few seconds to get my bearings back.

We were so grateful to finally have a menu in our hands and pleasantly surprised to find a wide selection of flavors to choose from. There was fish, steak, grilled vegetables, a wide variety of grains, and freshly made deserts. We were a captive audience, far from any major city, yet the Aussies made the extra effort to have a good meal available to us on the edge of nowhere. It was our first real meal in days, and a welcome change from camp food.

As evening set in, the moon rose bigger and brighter than the day before. I thought about the turtles and their struggle to lay eggs on dry land. There was probably another wave of females dragging themselves out of the surf and onto the beach at that very moment. Long after dark, the far away sun reflected light off the moon. It was so bright that Jeff and I decided to take a walk on the sand dunes behind the motel. We didn't need a flashlight or "torch" as they call it here. The white sand's glow offered us more than enough light to find our way. The effect was identical to moonlight on snow, the conditions that make it possible to cross-country ski or snowshoe at midnight in the back country; always a memorable experience.

Back at the resort, Jeff and I sat on the lawn chairs and looked out onto the bay. It was peaceful and quiet in those final evening hours, and the view was stunning.

The Ningaloo Reef, Australia's only fringing coral reef, is once again at our doorstep. I am really looking forward to tomorrow's swim.

Day 16, Thursday   December 23, 1999

Last night, we went to bed with one plan in mind, to spend one night at the Ningaloo Reef Resort and see what happens the next day. By the time morning came around, we knew we were going to stay a second night. How many more was yet to be determined. We were living in the moment, going with the flow, taking one day at a time, and I liked it.

Before heading to the beach, we slathered on the sunscreen and made the all important stop at the front office to extend our reservation. The desk clerk said, "Good on you, mate! The cleaning girls will love ya." I laughed at the expression *and* with relief that we could stay. Two days before Christmas, there were no guarantees of anything.

Curious about the oasis out front, I asked the clerk how they got the grounds so green. She told us that they watered the lawn regularly with salt water. I figured it must be a hardy breed of grass to stand up to those conditions. The salt water irrigation also explained the sulfur smell in the steam of the shower. The water piped into our rooms must have been treated to the point where it left no salt residue that I could detect, and the showers were refreshing. It may not have been what we were used to back home, but it certainly wasn't anything to complain about. Life was good in Coral Bay, and I was happy for every convenience available.

Jeff and I took the two-minute walk down to the bay with hopes of catching a glimpse of the huge plankton-eating, docile manta ray somewhere along our swim. Pictures of those amazing creatures were posted all over town, so they must be near. Again, we hiked south along the beach and then swam north along the coastline allowing the current to work in our favor. It was a nice snorkel/drift back to the motel, making our way through and around the coral. The first thing I noticed was that the water was much deeper than at Turquoise Bay, and there was a lot more coral to see. The second thing I noticed in the overall scheme of things was the uncanny progression of beauty and complexity within each particular reef. Every snorkel experience we've had has surpassed the previous one.

The day's swim was filled with schools of tiny florescent blue fish, a blue I didn't know existed on a fish. We didn't see any manta rays, but it was still an extraordinary morning, and we only got out of the water because we were hungry. Knowing the food was going to be good, I looked forward to another delicious meal at Fin's Café. After we ate, we explored the tiny seaside town of Coral Bay.

The day ended up being a lazy one, something we really needed, and after our walk we took it easy. We had been going, going, going, again without realizing it, and I was tired.

Before heading back to our room for a well deserved nap, I bought a few souvenirs. I found a yin/yang necklace on a leather string, sold by a street vendor; five postcards; and three Australia magnets, all small items so as not to bulk up our already bulky load. On our way through town, we saw Jeroen and Ottine, the couple we met yesterday at the visitor's center. It turned out Coral Bay was their next stop, too. They were the second couple we recognized since leaving Cape Range National Park, and it was great to see familiar faces.

Talking with Jeroen and Ottine, we learned about their hometown of Amsterdam, Holland (The Netherlands), a hip place to live, famous for tulips and wooden shoes. A handsome couple, they're both tall, slender, and well tanned. Ottine had curly dark brown hair that she kept pulled back, allowing a few curls to dangle over her brow, and Jeroen had long thick, wavy, dark brown hair that he also kept tight in a pony tail.

Dutch is their native language, and they both spoke very clear English. We shared travel stories and tips. They told us of their plans to drive to Perth in the coming days in a car they bought in Sydney, four weeks ago. We told them about our plans to be at Ayers Rock on New Year's Eve. We parted ways, and assumed we would run into each other again. The odds were in our favor that we would.

Jeff and I, thoroughly enjoying our time in Coral Bay, decided to stay a third night, which meant we would be in Coral Bay Christmas morning. I had been wondering what Christmas was going to look like, and the picture was coming together slowly but surely. When I went to see the desk clerk about extending our reservation out through the 25th, she said, "Good thing you came in today. You got the last room available." Yep, the travel gods were taking very good care of us.

With the afternoon free and the next 48 hours taken care of, I sat down to write my postcards. When they were done, Jeff and I discussed the logistics of getting to Ayers Rock. There were several unknowns, and it was time they were addressed. The big party was eight days away, and we didn't have a single reservation. Either ignorance really is bliss and everything would work out or we were setting ourselves up for a huge disappointment if we were to discover that every room was reserved and all planes were booked solid.

We knew flying was our only option if we were going to make it in time. With all other modes of transportation ruled out, we decided to reserve our seats on a flight departing on December 30th from Perth to Alice Springs, the town closest to Ayers Rock. We would figure out how to get from Alice Springs to Ayers Rock later.

I immediately called the airlines, and the agent said we got the last two seats. *Whew!* That was a relief. Our next biggest question to answer was, "When will we head back to Exmouth, return the jeep, and fly south to Perth?" For some reason, we weren't worried about a flight from Exmouth to

Perth. Why? I had no idea. Maybe it was too early in the trip to work out that particular unknown. I took a good long nap and hoped for more clarity. Jeff didn't seem too concerned about the details, either.

Later in the evening, as expected, we saw Jeroen and Ottine wandering through town, and we all sat down for dinner at one of the other restaurants. (I believe there are three restaurants in all, but I didn't catch the names.) We enjoyed another good meal, Italian this time, and our new friends were great company. Jeroen, in his mid-30's, has traveled a lot. He was a graphic artist working freelance, which offered him extensive time off. Ottine worked as a temp in a mental institution (I imagined she had plenty of stories to tell) which gave her the freedom to keep up with their travel schedule as well. They were very serious about each other and talked about getting married when they got home.

It was nice to hang out with another couple similar in age on a similar adventure on the edge of nowhere. It was 9:00 p.m. when we parted ways, fully expecting to see one another again.

Our room, the meals, and souvenirs are reasonably priced, especially for a beach front hideaway. Our exchange rate is strong, and Australians are not in the practice of charging a premium for peak holidays. That is a welcome discovery. Our ocean view room at the Ningaloo Reef Resort in Coral Bay is only $110 AU ($72 US). Granted, it is not a five-star hotel, but the location and hospitality are first-rate.

I have shifted my internal gears down another notch and am deeper in the groove of being in Australia playing the role of a traveler. Having time to allow the day to unfold instead of holding to a tight agenda is refreshing, but it does take getting used to. There are five-and-a-half weeks ahead of us. That's plenty of time to master the art of travel. I hope.

The moon is full. The food is delicious. We have a nice room. Jeff and I continue to get along and enjoy each others' company, and we're meeting new friends along the way.

Living in the moment is not one of my strong suits. I'm still a work in progress, but I'm learning the benefits of "Now." We're making just enough plans to keep our trip moving along smoothly, and that's all that matters. Take care of today and tomorrow is taken care of—there's a mantra I can live with.

Day 17, Friday   December 24, 1999

It's Christmas Eve, and Jeff and I went on a true "outback adventure." From an aerial map showing the full length of Ningaloo Reef, we saw where the coral beds weaved in and out, up and down the coastline. Twenty-five miles south of Coral Bay, the beds came in close to shore in a remote section of the desert. There was a road leading into the area giving us an opportunity to explore a portion of the reef rarely seen by others.

With a bit of detective work, asking the locals for information, we learned that the property in question was a ranch the size of Delaware (unconfirmed, but quite possible) called Warroora Station—a sheep farmer's homestead. We also learned that the homestead was open to visitors. Without calling ahead, we hopped into our jeep for the ninety-minute ride through the desert and followed the long dusty road up to the main house. Standing at the front door, we gave three solid knocks. Astrid and Murray Horack were there to greet us. It must have been a slow day on the farm for them to be home at any given hour of the day.

I never did get it straight whether they were caretakers or owners of the homestead, but it didn't matter. Originally from Amsterdam, the Horack's informed us that the admission price to the wide open spaces of their "sheep station" was $5 AU ($3 US) each. Jeff handed them an Australian $10 bill and we were in. Astrid pointed one way to the shoreline, while her husband, Murray, pointed us in an entirely different direction. They laughed when they realized what they had done and assured us that both trails would take us to the reef. The station's western border stretched 51 km (31.68 miles) along the Ningaloo Reef coastline. With a mental toss of the coin, Jeff and I chose to take Murray's route, which meant we headed north.

Down the road, with the farm house long out of sight, we got stuck in the sand. I took the wheel, Jeff pushed the jeep out of the rut, and we were on our way again. The road wasn't really a road. It was more like a trail, and the trail got worse the farther we drove. We knew it would be a long walk back if the jeep were to get permanently bogged down in the sand, so we decided to turn back and ask for Astrid's route.

We made it back to the house and headed out for round two. This time we drove south to the "tip" of the property and, like the first trail, it was a long rough ride over and around several small sand dunes. Jeff did exceptionally well navigating our little jeep through the ruts, hills, and valleys of the desert outback sheep station. We took our time, played it safe, and made it to the shoreline. The successful ride gave us confidence that we would make it all the way back, and there was enough water and snacks packed in the jeep to ensure our survival until the Horack's found us if worse came to worse. They were the only two people on the planet who had a clue where we were.

The wind was blowing hard across the ocean creating whitecaps and a choppy surf. If we had any sense at all, it would have been wise to abort the trip upon arrival, but we didn't. We were on an adventure and decided to stick to our plans and go for a swim. It had taken us three hours to find that reef, and we weren't about to let a few waves get in our way.

High atop the banks of the Indian Ocean was a huge sand dune Murray called a "sand blow out." It was one of the landmarks that signaled we were in the right place. Murray explained that the small mountain of sand was slowly encroaching onto and into their water supply, and they were concerned they might have to dig another well in order to keep a constant flow of water. Digging another well was a huge and expensive undertaking, something they didn't want to do unless they absolutely had to. They monitored the encroachment on a regular basis and hoped for the best. It was an eerie sight and reminded us of the threats to the shores in Florida, where erosion has destroyed countless homes and businesses built too close to the water's edge.

The tides were moving south to north, so we set our sights on a sandy beach a short distance up the coast and, once again, let the currents do the work to get us where we wanted to go. Underwater visibility was extremely poor due to the choppy surf making it nearly impossible to see the reef. What we did get from the swim made the trip entirely worthwhile—we found out where the *big boys* hang out... big turtles, that is.

I didn't see them at first. Like the kangaroos, they blended well into their environment. The cloudy, murky water didn't help, either, and added to the illusion of invisibility. It wasn't until the turtles started to move about that we could see we were surrounded. They were giants, dozens of them, the same size as the turtles we saw the other night laying eggs on the beach. It was the mother load of all mother loads.

Unlike the calm and casual younger turtle we saw at Turquoise Bay, these turtles were panicked by our presence and swam away as fast as possible. For all we knew, we may have been the first humans they had seen in a very long time, and they didn't want anything to do with us. I saw a group of six resting quietly on the bottom until we got too close for comfort and stirred them up. They paddled every which way. Though I felt bad for disturbing them, I was thrilled by the experience.

Several minutes went by before I realized how long it had been since I took a good look at the beach to be sure I wasn't drifting out to sea. It was definitely rough, but no rougher than a brisk day on the Gulf of Mexico. I felt strong and in control of the situation. To make certain I was alright, I lifted my head up out of the water and was relieved to see land straight ahead and a manageable distance away. I knew Jeff was to my left, and I took an extra long look to be sure he was okay, too. All was well…until I looked to my right.

Three feet away I saw a strange dark brown object breaking the surface. "Shark!" was my first terrifying thought, and two seconds later, the object registered as a turtle. It had surfaced, taken a breath, and looked around at exactly the same time I did. The second we made eye contact, we both silently screamed, *"Ahhh!"* It took off one way, I ducked under the water and went the other. I don't know who was startled more, me or the turtle.

While the reef turned out to be a huge disappointment because we couldn't actually see it, the turtle encounter more than made up for it. Miraculously, Jeff and I made it back to the homestead alive and without getting the jeep stuck in the sand. All in all, it was a crazy thing to do, but given the outcome it was a risk worth taking. Exhausted, hot, full of dust, sweat, and salt, we sat outside on the patio and told Murray and Astrid about our day. While driving through their property, we had seen a total of four foxes running along that back road. I was not expecting to see foxes in Australia, so I asked the young couple what the story was. Astrid explained that a fox is a sheep herder's nightmare.

Foxes are not native to Australia. They were brought over to the island continent by the British years ago to participate in the popular sport of foxhunting. The hounds obviously let a few get away, and these misplaced carnivores have multiplied to the point where they are out of control and causing serious problems to the natural order of things. I don't know where dingoes, the wild dogs of the outback, fit into all of this, but I do know that the outback has enough of its own challenges without adding to the list.

Jeff and I must have been quite a sight because our hosts offered us the use of their outdoor shower if we wanted to "clean up." Jeff and I gladly accepted. The cool fresh water was manna from heaven, rinsing the salt and sand off our skin. Afterwards, Astrid and Murray told us more about life on a sheep station, the sheep shearing season, and even their wedding.

The homestead was powered by solar energy with the option of an occasional energy boost from a nearby generator when needed. Phone service was available through a satellite relay, and water was pumped in by windmill. With Y2K only a week away, Astrid and Murray would be totally unaware of any blips or power failures. They lived "off the grid" for the most part, though they did order their food by fax machine. Once a week, a mail contract driver, in addition to delivering the mail, delivered their groceries. Now there's an efficient use of service. As a matter of fact, while Jeff and I were swimming with the turtles, Astrid was taking inventory of her most recent grocery and mail delivery. I imagined it was a welcome sight to see the mailman drive in every seven days.

There was a small open-air bar just off the patio. A blackboard displaying the "Quote of the Moment" hung prominently on one of the posts. On that particular day the quote read, *"The money I save won't buy my youth again,"* by Ian Moss. I was reminded of how fortunate I was to be able to take a trip of this magnitude while I was young enough to enjoy it. At 41, I was holding my own, swimming, hiking, and camping in remote sections of Oz.

While still at the homestead, Murray and Astrid went into more detail about their wedding three months ago. Astrid seemed truly happy to have company and someone to talk to, and I, for one, was in no hurry to leave. She invited us into her home to take a look around and explained that the house was filled with beautiful antique furniture from the day they moved in. Some of the pieces were large and gave the homestead a character all its own. She showed me photos of how she and her husband turned their backyard into a paradise for their wedding reception, and I was reminded of the Rottnest Island movie *Under the Lighthouse Dancing*, where the beach, or rock quarry, was transformed as well.

The couple's wedding photographer worked for a local newspaper called *The Western Australian*, and the couple's picture and story ended up on the front page. They were thrilled to make headline news, and Astrid pointed to the original article that was proudly framed and hanging on the homestead's living room wall. Murray also told us about his uncle, Neil McLeod, who was a local celebrity in Exmouth. Murray said, "Neil has a reputation for giving fantastic tours." I made a mental note to give his uncle a call if we had the time to see more of the area.

With the homestead bordering on 51 km of Indian Ocean coastline, that has got to add up to thousands of acres of land, maybe more. But measuring in acres is not how they do it here. Australian homesteads are measured in hectares. One hectare is equal to 2.471 acres, and an outback sheep and cattle station can measure in the millions of hectares. However big Warroora Station is, it's bigger than I can comprehend.

At any given time, the Murray's have as many as 25,000 sheep. The sheep are sheared once a year in November, the beginning of summer, and it's a major event. In addition to the harvesting of wool, it's also the time of year when the older sheep are separated out and sold off for slaughter.

The bunk houses, where the professional sheep shearers stay, can be seen scattered around the property near the house. For the most part, shearers are a nomadic group and get their work done in record time before moving on to the next homestead. This is serious business, and it's a proud Aussie worth his weight in gold who can sheer the fastest. It's both a highly professional and highly competitive line of work. Formal competitions can be found throughout Australia. Official shearing organizations are lobbying hard to make sheep shearing part of the Olympic Games because at the competitive level it is considered a sport.

Sheering season just ended and the sheep, most of them neatly trimmed, were scattered back out into the fields. We could see a few rebels that slipped away from the herd and didn't get clipped. Murray said, "There are always a few that avoid capture. When a sheep misses two and three seasons in a row, the heat of the sun is extremely rough on them. They may have avoided capture, but it often costs them their lives. Many won't make it through the summer."

We said our good-byes and made it back to Coral Bay with plenty of time to spare before our 7:30 p.m. Christmas Eve dinner reservation at Fin's Café. Emails were my first priority, and I had 30 minutes to read and answer as many of the five messages I had waiting before we sat down to eat. Five was a lot for me.

Our meal was delicious, and the restaurant made the evening special with a festive atmosphere, Christmas lights and all. As we were eating chocolate cake for dessert, Jeroen and Ottine walked by, so we invited them to join us at our table. They each ordered an espresso, and we ended up swapping stories of the day.

At the same time we were being tossed around in the surf, they were out on a manta ray tour with a spotter plane to find the "gentle giants." The first ray the plane spotted was a relatively small one. Knowing its location, the boat cruised in to give the snorkelers an experience of a lifetime. Soon after that encounter, the plane spotted another larger ray, one that had a twenty-foot wingspan. The boat motored over to the second location where the guide gave the signal for the swimmers to jump in. Jeroen and Ottine said the ray was so huge that every snorkeler was able to swim a few feet above it. Describing his experience, Jeroen was visibly moved. He said all ten snorkelers came back with a sense that they were above the center of the ray. It was that big. After hearing about their story, Jeff and I decided we would stay one more night, Christmas night, and take a manta ray tour on Sunday. It was on our agenda, but we had cancelled the idea until our friends convinced us otherwise. It sounded too good to pass up. We would check with the office tomorrow to see if our room was still available.

Day 18, Saturday   December 25, 1999   Merry Christmas!

This is in no way, by any stretch of the imagination, a typical Christmas for me. Looking back, I haven't had a normal Christmas since I returned to the single life four years ago. There is no tree, no ritual of any kind, and no piles of brightly wrapped gifts in the living room. There is no living room. I'm in a motel, and, while I may be a long way from home, I know in my heart that my family is thinking of me, as I am thinking of them.

This is the second Christmas I have enjoyed since leaving the post office, and it is especially sweet to be in Australia during two of the busiest months in Florida. Between the Christmas rush and the heavy influx of winter residents and tourists, a trip like this would have been impossible two short years ago.

Jeff and I were both up early, an easy thing to do when the sun is high and bright at 4:45 a.m. *I'm beginning to think the clocks are all wrong here.* Since yesterday's reef swim was more about turtles than fish and coral, we were both excited to swim the reef at our doorstep again.

The resort was unusually quiet, and we seemed to be the only two people awake as we grabbed our snorkel gear and walked out of our room and headed straight for the bay. When we got to the water, there were fish over two feet long swimming in the shallowest parts. They scattered in all directions the second our feet touched the water.

Our plans were to swim to a sandy point positioned a tenth-of-a-mile up the beach to a spot where the land took a sharp curve to the west. The resort staff said they had seen the rays there recently. We decided to try our luck to see a manta ray without the aide of a boat, and walked straight out into the sea.

The coral was beautiful, and the morning sun warmed my back as I headed for the point ahead. There was a greater distance to cover this time, and half way into the swim I grew tired. I felt as if I had been swimming and swimming, but I wasn't getting any closer to shore.

I had a brief moment of panic that I would get too weak and the current would get the best of me. I feared I would be swept out towards Madagascar, never to be seen again, so I conserved my energy and took a turn towards the shoreline south of the point. I wanted to be absolutely sure I wasn't drifting. The reef and rays were no longer of interest to me. I wanted out. What began as a leisurely swim up the coastline turned into one of the most challenging moments of my life. Every ten minutes I stopped to tread water so I could build my strength back up. When I felt I could go on, I started swimming again. I kept checking on Jeff, who appeared to be doing alright on his own route to the point, and I was relieved that he was okay. As I got closer to shore and the water got shallower, I grabbed onto every rock I could to propel myself forward. They were jagged and sharp, and I had to be extremely careful to avoid getting cut, but they meant survival to me. I had something to hold onto. When I finally made it past the rocks and onto the shore, I sat exhausted and shaking, thinking of what could have gone so terribly wrong.

Ten minutes later, Jeff made it to the point, and I never did tell him what happened. I was too tired and embarrassed, and he didn't ask any questions. We walked the long walk back to the motel, in silence. It was still morning when we returned to our room, and the only thing I wanted to do was lie down. Between our drive to the sheep station yesterday and the morning's fiasco, that was enough activity for awhile. Jeff was unusually quiet, too, and we never did talk about the morning's events or why we were giving each other the silent treatment. That was our relationship, keep quiet until the storm blew over, and it always did.

Jeff went to the office to see about extending our stay one more night, but it was closed. We came to the conclusion that our room was available. If there was no one there to check us out, there was no one there to check anyone in. It was another lucky break, and I relaxed.

At 1:00 p.m., we went to Fin's to get a bite to eat, and to our surprise, it was closed, too. The whole town of Coral Bay had shut down for Christmas, something unheard of back home, and we were on our own to fend for ourselves. I dug into our supplies and found a can of lentil soup we had bought back in Exmouth. That, along with the Italian bread leftover from last night's meal, was enough to keep the hunger away. I heated the soup on the stove in our room. There was nothing gourmet about it, but I felt pretty good about the fact that we had something decent to eat under the circumstances.

I slept most of the day, and by evening we had both recovered gracefully from the morning's upset. Jeff never did say what was bothering him and neither did I. In our silence we ended up enjoying a simple, peaceful, and very restful Christmas, listening to the sounds of the surrounding holiday parties. Music and laughter filled the air, and the day ended far better than it began.

Earlier in the evening, while I was taking my second nap of the day, Jeff said he went for a walk south along the shore. He told me he saw Santa Claus cruise by in an inflatable skiff, waving to everyone on the beach. That must have been quite a sight.

Day 19, Sunday   December 26, 1999

The day after Christmas is called "Boxing Day" in Australia. New Zealand, Canada, and the United Kingdom all share the same holiday, and it's directly linked to Christmas. The term "Boxing Day" comes from a tradition started centuries ago when employers would box gifts for their workers the day after Christmas. It is now a popular shopping holiday full of after-Christmas sales just like we have back home.

Four nights at the Ningaloo Reef Resort, it was our longest continuous stay yet, at one accommodation. We packed our bags, loaded up the jeep, and then walked over to the front desk to pay for our last night's stay and check out. The staff was delighted to hear of our change in plans, and we thanked them for their hospitality as we said our good-byes. Next stop: Fin's Café for a good breakfast and a real cup of coffee.

With no solid plans from that point on, it was time to hold another one of our executive meetings and figure out what to do next. Well rested and recharged, we decided to make a second attempt at seeing giant manta rays before leaving the area. Yesterday's setback was not going to get the better of us. We asked our server how to book a charter boat tour, and he told us that every morning the boats were anchored, ready and waiting, to take people out in the bay in front of the resort. Oddly enough, I hadn't noticed the boats before. No worries (love that expression), it was still early. We had plenty of time to walk down to the shoreline after breakfast to see if we could catch a ride out into the wide open seas.

As we lingered at the outdoor café, we saw Jeroen and Ottine gassing up their car. We waved to each other, and when they were done they came over to our table to say good-bye. They told us their month long vacation was ending in a few days, and the reason they were headed down to Perth was to sell the car and fly the rest of the way back to Holland. If they couldn't sell the car in Perth, they were going to drive all the way back to Sydney, across the Nullarbor Plain, to what they considered a stronger used-car market in the east. They wanted a good price and were willing to do whatever it took to get it.

We told them of our plans to fly south to Perth in three days, so we could catch a connecting flight on December 30th to the town of Alice Springs, the gateway to Ayers Rock. We thought arriving the day before the millennium would give us plenty of time to settle in before the big party. It was a plan that required several critical pieces to fall into place, such as transportation from Alice Springs to Ayers Rock and a place to stay once we arrived...if we could find a place to stay on the biggest night of the millennium. It was also a very expensive plan starting with $1200 AU ($780 US) for both of us to fly from Perth to Alice Springs—the equivalent of flying from Los Angeles, California to Lincoln, Nebraska. We noticed that we were not entirely committed to this scenario, but we didn't know what else to do. Flying all the way appeared to be our best option, because there was so much ground to cover.

To complicate matters, once we were at Ayers Rock, we didn't know how we were going to finish out the trip. Would we fly to Queensland where the Great Barrier Reef was or somehow rent a car from Point B to Point C? And then we still had to get back to Sydney. It was getting more complicated and more expensive the more we thought it through and tried to explain ourselves. There's a saying in the world of marketing, "A confused mind never buys," and we were definitely confused. It totally explained our procrastination towards setting up any firm travel arrangements.

Sitting there with our friends at Fin's Cafe, minutes to spare before we would never see them again, all four of us had a momentary flash of brilliance. Suddenly everything became clear. I don't remember who said it first, but a solution emerged creating a win/win all the way around. Jeff and I still had five weeks left in our trip; Jeroen and Ottine's journey was coming to an end; they had a car to sell; we had transportation issues. A conversation began about how we would buy their red 1983 Ford Falcon station wagon. How perfect! A couple of Americans in Oz cruising across the outback in a Ford. Now there's a scenario I could get excited about. Up until that moment, I had no idea Ford sold cars in Australia.

The four of us came up with a plan to team up and drive to Perth together. Once in Perth, Jeff and I would buy the car for $2700 AU ($1800 US), and Jeroen and Ottine would fly back to Sydney and go home. With the terms and conditions of the sale set, we shook on it. Jeff and I rationalized that with our final destination in Sydney, we'd be able to sell the car when we were done with it, too. Everything was falling into place.

Jeroen and Ottine told us they originally paid $2800 AU for the Ford, but they deducted $100 because the right front headlight and bumper had been damaged a few days ago in Exmouth. Their car hit a "big red" in the dark of the night. Exactly as the brochures warned, the 'roo suddenly jumped out of nowhere and into their path. Just before contact, Jeroen said, "The big boy gave us a stare and then *boom!* the 'roo bounced off the bumper, kept on going and disappeared into the night. I immediately turned the car around to see if it was harmed, not that there was anything we could do if it was," he admitted, "but we did check things out. The kangaroo was nowhere to be found." The damaged front end was the only remaining evidence that the crash occurred. Ottine said, "It was the biggest kangaroo we have ever seen, and it really shook us up."

Jeff and I knew that buying any used car was a gamble, but this situation was truly unique. A few days earlier we were privy to a candid assessment of the vehicle, before any of us knew the deal was coming. At dinner on Christmas Eve, Jeroen and Ottine told us how well their car was running and how it had taken them from Sydney to Coral Bay. Driving that far was the equivalent of driving from Savannah, Georgia to San Francisco, California the long way, via Los Angeles. There's nothing but desert throughout most of Australia, and few roads lead from east to west.

When we asked Jeroen where he and Ottine bought the car he told us they found it advertised in *The Sydney Morning Herald* newspaper. The Ford was a one-owner vehicle, and the original owners said they were "ready to let the old girl go." The "Mum's Taxi" sticker placed long ago in the rear window was code, in my opinion, for "This car is reliable." She appeared to have a lot of miles left in her.

Jeroen and Ottine agreed to wait in Coral Bay while Jeff and I went on our manta ray tour, the one we had yet to book. Once we got back to dry land, the plan was for the four of us to take the two cars north to Exmouth, an hour-and-a-half drive, return the rental, and spend the night in town. The following morning, with all four of us in the Ford, we'll begin our journey south to Perth. Knowing the car was all but sold, Jeroen and Ottine were happy to alter their plans by one day. Our original idea to be in Ayers Rock for New Year's Eve was looking like a "no go." Jeff and I decided to keep an open mind to see what the future had in store.

We are five days away from the turn of the millennium, and it's now anybody's guess where we will be. Since we are about to buy a car, it quickly sank in that we are going to have to cross the Nullarbor Plain in the Australian outback, again. Now there's a reality check. Do we drive the whole way? Do we look into putting the car on the Indian Pacific Railway part of the way? I admit, I am a bit freaked out about driving across a deadly desert. It doesn't matter how reliable Mum's Taxi is. All cars, even the best of them, break down occasionally.

My mind was spinning a mile a minute with the sudden change in plans. I calmed down when I remembered we had a charter boat to find and manta rays to swim with. Must re-focus.

It was 10:00 a.m. when we finally walked down to the beach and found a charter boat where our server said it would be. And yes, there was room onboard for two. Our boat, *Dominator*, belonged to a different company than the one Jeroen and Ottine had found. The captain, a gruff, but gentle man with a big smile, and in his mid-thirties, informed us that his crew did not use spotter planes. "The manta rays are all around this area. It just takes a boat to find one," he said.

Fully confident we were going to have a successful outing, Jeff and I took the captain's word for it. We left the shore with three crew members and nine other passengers. At least five different countries were represented on that small boat. Several age groups were covered as well, from children to senior citizens. Our first stop was at the point where Jeff and I had snorkeled yesterday morning. It was true. There had been sightings there recently, and the crew wanted to try their luck. With no rays in sight, we headed further out into the Indian Ocean. The crew had a particular area in mind that was generally a sure thing.

Our first encounter with sea life was with a thirteen-foot tiger shark. It had vertical stripes on the side and an extremely wide body. Its mouth looked to be the size of a drum barrel, big enough to swallow a person whole, and I was relieved to be *on* the boat at that particular moment in time. The shark cruised with us for ten minutes, and we watched its tail wave slowly back and forth, gliding seamlessly through the water. One of the crew members told us it was unusual to get such a good look.

Soon after the shark took a turn out to sea, we came upon three dolphins and experienced another, "unusually close encounter," we were told. Maybe that's a line they used with all their guests. I really didn't know. Meanwhile, we kept our eyes open for manta rays. Ten more dolphins swam by to check us out, and still no rays. After two hours, I could tell that the crew was getting as discouraged as their guests. The captain was determined to find a manta ray, so we keep searching.

Jeff and I had decided to save money going with this group, because it was the more expensive tours that used spotter planes, but the benefits of a bird's eye view of the sea became obvious. Without those planes, it was a hit-or-miss chance of zeroing in on our target. The odds were in our favor of spotting one, but they were still odds. Knowing we were getting restless and wanting to give us our money's worth, the crew decided to take us to an area known for sea turtles.

As soon as the turtles were spotted, the boat stopped, and all eleven of us jumped in the water. Finally, some action. We had been given strict instructions to leave the turtles alone because touching and feeding them was strictly prohibited. They were all around us. I swam up to a group of three to get a closer look, but despite all efforts at a stealth approach, the turtles darted away. When a sea turtle wants to make a move, it can do it with speed and grace. This must have been a young herd, because all of them were much smaller than the ones we saw swimming in the ocean near the sheep station a few days ago. After 15 minutes, everyone was back on board and back to the business of manta ray hunting. Three hours passed before we finally saw our first one.

A crew member shouted, "Black eagle ray!" It was an exciting moment. The boat engine was shut off, and we all got in the water to get a closer look. Completely startled by the mad dash of snorkelers entering the water, the ray darted off. We were called back into the boat and continued searching.

When the crew was about to give up, two *giant* manta rays were sighted. I was so anxious to swim with a ray that I was the first to jump in the water right after the guide. Once positioned above the ray, the guide raised his right arm signaling us where to swim. The manta ray was at least 20 feet across. Its dark grey backside, or topside, blended well with the dark ocean floor below; and occasionally we got a glimpse at its white underside. Its body was shaped like a flat diamond, and it moved gracefully through the water as it flapped its "wings." Cruising along several feet below the surface, it appeared unaffected by all the excitement directly overhead. Then another ray swam in next to the first. Six of us went with one, and the other six swimmers went to follow the other. Jeff said he saw a ray doing somersaults end-over-end. One of the crew members said, "That's how they stir up and gather the plankton to make feeding easier."

Time stood still, and the only thing on my mind was the awe I felt at being so close to such a magnificent creature. The moment was broken when something startled the rays. They both darted off, too fast and suddenly too far to ever catch up with. Maybe one of the swimmers got too close. Everyone climbed back in the boat to look for more.

A few minutes later the captain spotted another manta ray. Again, we followed the guide's instruction to watch for his raised hand, showing us exactly where to swim. This ray was bigger than the first two. We watched it swim up to the surface and then dive deep into the ocean again and again. At one point, I saw Jeff take a deep breath and dive fifteen feet down to get a closer look. The ray was four times his size, and with both in view, it offered an amazing contrast. Again, the ray returned to the surface and then back down to hover ten feet below. I watched as it slowly rolled over, exposing its white underside. It continued to swim upside down with the same ease and grace it did when right side up. Rolling back over right side up, I could see little "cleaner" fish clinging to the ray's body. Together they swam in perfect unison.

As captivating as the experience was, I did remember to take an occasional look back at the boat. We were all instructed to keep visual contact with our lifeline back to shore to be certain we weren't swept away by the currents. It was also important to watch for signals from the captain such as "It's time to come in," or "There's another manta ray over there." Each time I checked in I was always within safe distance and all was well....until it wasn't. I looked up just in time to see and hear the captain yelling, *"Get in the boat!"* He was frantically waving his arms with the signal to come in *"Now!"*

This was not a message of "It's time to go." I sensed there was something terribly wrong and turned the message into, "Shark!" I swam back to the boat faster than I have ever swum in my life. I saw the other snorkelers doing the same.

Two crew members, who had remained onboard, plucked each one of us up and out of the water one-by-one, as fast as we showed up. Everyone made it back safely, and my suspicion was confirmed—there was a shark swimming among us, a tiger shark.

It wasn't until I was sitting on deck that I wondered why, up until that nanosecond, I had no concern for sharks, especially after seeing one swimming in the same waters we had just jumped into? For some reason, I had not made the connection that there were no fences or boundaries of any kind between the shark waters and the manta ray waters.

The captain told us that sharks sometimes prey on manta rays and a shark can sense if a ray is stressed. He went on to say that the easiest way to stress a ray is to try to touch it. Although we were all instructed to keep a safe distance, we did see a few of the snorkelers reach down to touch one. Did those snorkelers actually "call" the shark to our waters? We will never know for sure.

As if that wasn't enough for one day, the captain announced that he wanted to take us on one more adventure, a snorkel stop at one of his favorite reefs within sight of the beach where we first started. It's a place he was obviously passionate about. As a group, we unanimously voted "Yes." When we arrived I jumped in, once again, totally oblivious to the dangers of sharks, focused solely on the pretty coral and the beautiful fish. I saw a small eagle ray and a two-foot non-threatening shark swimming among the plethora of sea life. The coral was gorgeous, and I was glad for the extra stop. Once on dry land, Jeff and I realized we had been out for a total of six-and-a-half hours. Exhausted, cooked by the sun, and very happy to be alive, it was an experience I will always remember.

We were a full two hours over our estimated time of arrival, so Jeff and I made a beeline for Fin's Café. What a relief it was to see Jeroen and Ottine patiently waiting. We told them about our day, and it turned out, their experience was entirely different, much more orderly and controlled. Jeroen and Ottine had a lot more swim time with the manta rays than we did, thanks to the spotter planes. In a strange sort of insane way, I enjoyed the excitement and life-threatening aspects of our experience. The four of us had a good laugh thanks to the happy ending.

With stories told, our focus soon turned to our drive north to Exmouth. It was important for our safety that we reached our destination before dark, before the kangaroos started migrating through the night. We had to get moving because one encounter with a 'roo was already one too many. With our jeep pre-loaded and only our snorkel gear to add to the pile, we were on the road in no time, and made it to Exmouth safely.

We found a room at the Exmouth Cape Tourist Village, the same place where we had rented our jeep six days ago. Jeff and I moved everything out of the vehicle and into our room, found a hot meal, took a hot shower, and stayed up late telling our stories over and over again to whomever would listen.

I am looking forward to my next chance to email because I have a lot to write home about.

Day 20, Monday   December 27, 1999

At 7:30 a.m., all four of us, eagerly anticipating the drive ahead, got up early to prepare for departure. The first thing on my agenda was to call the airlines and cancel our reservations from Perth to Alice Springs. "No worries," the agent said, and in an instant, our plans to be in Ayers Rock by New Year's Eve vanished.

Jeff and I returned the jeep to the rental office in the same condition we found it, shopped for snacks, and took a few minutes to explore the "library" inside the Exmouth Cape Tourist Village general store. It was a free book exchange program that consisted of one long shelf filled with dozens of used books in a wide variety of subjects both fiction and non-fiction. Travelers were encouraged to leave a book they had finished and take one for future reading. What a clever way to keep baggage light and save money at the same time.

While I was packing I realized that I had mistakenly left my passport and money in the unlocked glove box in the jeep overnight. When I remembered what I had done, I rushed out to see if everything was still there. It was, and a wave of relief washed over me. I had forgotten to do my usual "cross check" the night before to make sure all valuables were safely put away and in their proper place. I was very fortunate and vowed to be more careful in the future.

After our errands were done and the all important gallon water jugs filled, we loaded the station wagon. It all fit, every bit of our stuff, their stuff, and there was still plenty of room for the four of us. Jeroen and Ottine were a bit savvier in their packing than we were, and I was glad that *they* managed to travel light. They both piped in with well deserved sarcastic comments about "the American travelers" and made clear what they thought about our packing skills. Whether it's one month or two, the packing is the same, but we had twice as much. Once again, I made a silent vow to travel with one small backpack and a carry-on no matter where I was going.

I've often heard that physical baggage, be it excess weight or excess luggage, is an out-picturing of our mental "baggage," so I figure I have some work to do in that department. There are times in our lives when there is no place to hide.

We all agreed to take the scenic tour to Perth, to take our time and take advantage of the sights along the way. Rather than the required two days' drive, we planned to take four to cover the same distance. That should put us into town on December 30th. Jeff and I had come to terms with the fact that we were not going to be at Ayers Rock for New Year's Eve. There's no way we could drive that far in time, and it was perfectly alright with us. All the sudden changes reminded me of one of my favorite sayings, "If you want to make God laugh, tell Him your plans."

My life has taken a 180 degree turn from the one I planned out when I was 25 years old. Back then, I operated from a strong, logical, and practical approach to life, calculating financial and career goals twenty years out. I've since learned that all efforts to stay on course with too heady an idea proved futile and a tough road, at best. My heart knows what direction to take, and now that inspiration has taken a front seat, life is better than I thought it could be. I've also learned that it's alright to change course. In fact, it's more than alright. Remaining open to change is the only way life can bring in what we really want.

It was 10:00 a.m. by the time we were on our way, and the coastal beach town of Monkey Mia was our first planned destination on the long car ride south. There's not much between Exmouth and Perth, and Monkey Mia would be a welcome detour.

Monkeys are not native to Australia, so I have yet to learn the origin of the town's name. Surely a local can fill us in. What I do know is that Monkey Mia sits along the shores of Shark Bay, a protected cove, where wild dolphins swim up to land early in the morning for a free breakfast. It's a strange ritual, but twice daily the dolphins are hand fed by tourists supervised by park rangers. Since we were going to be in the "neighborhood" by outback standards, we will check it out. It takes nine hours to drive from Exmouth to Monkey Mia, and every town in between appears to be there for one purpose only, to keep travelers moving along by offering petrol and basic sustenance. Every station is a welcome sight, and they always show up when we really need one, whether it's for a cold drink, ice cream or a fill-up.

I'm doing my best to call gas "petrol," that's a new one, but I'm also getting used to a different way of measuring temperatures, distances, liquids, and land. As a result, the math part of my brain is getting a good workout. With temperatures measured in Celsius rather than Fahrenheit; land measured in hectares rather than acres; distances in kilometers rather than miles; petrol measured in litres instead of gallons, which makes the price really misleading because liters are smaller than gallons, I feel like I'm back in school for a math review. I am constantly converting numbers to keep things in perspective. For example: today the high was 38 degrees Celsius which translates to 101 degrees Fahrenheit. In my mind, 38 degrees means "cold," so I do the mental adjustments and life makes sense again.

We rolled into Denham at 6:45 p.m. Just like the rented jeep, the Ford has no air conditioning. After nine hours of wind blowing through my hair, I had had enough "fresh air" for one day. To save money, we chose to camp at the Denham Seaside Tourist Village, conveniently located on Knight Terrace, the main drag through town. Denham is a popular place to stay for people visiting Monkey Mia and is only 27 km (16.77 miles) down the road. We watched the sunset, as we pitched the tent high above the water's edge. It was a pleasant way to start the evening. After we showered the day's dirt and grime away, we drove into town for dinner. We could have walked, had we been the slightest bit motivated, but we were hungry and decided to take the easy route.

Our first stop was The Old Pearler Restaurant, also on Knight Terrace. The restaurant was described in one of the park's brochures as being located inside "The only shell block restaurant in the world." Once we arrived we could see the craftsmanship in the beautiful little building made from millions or billions (Who could possibly count?) small white coquina shells. The shells had been pressed into two-foot square blocks. Once the blocks were formed, they were stacked, one on top of the other, like concrete cinder blocks.

The restaurant was loaded with character *and* people. It's as popular in Denham, Western Australia, respectively speaking, as Joe's Stone Crab House is in Miami, Florida. Unfortunately, The Old Pearler Restaurant was too busy to take us in, so we went next door and were able to get a nice hot meal there. (I neglected to make note of the restaurant.) It wasn't long before we were back at camp and calling it a day.

I can tell the sound of the surf is going to lull me to sleep tonight. What a magnificent location for a campsite. The view is awesome. I'll add this one to the "revisit list."

Day 21, Tuesday   December 28, 1999

The sun woke us up and pushed us out of the tent with its intense heat just like it did at Cape Range National Park. Even though we've traveled nine hours south, which is like going north, the sun was still strong, and it turned our sleeping space into an oven. When we got out of the tent and into the fresh air we found it perfectly cool and breezy, a nice surprise.

Over an open fire, Jeff made enough hot java for the four of us with the coffee pot we brought from home. Our traveling partners were noticeably impressed. Anxious to see the dolphins, we agreed to skip breakfast in town and head straight to Monkey Mia. We knew we could find a bite to eat at this small beach resort, and after a fifteen-minute drive down the road we were there.

Posted on the information center's bulletin board was the dolphin feeding schedule telling us when it was time to gather along the nearby shoreline. There were two feedings a day, and they both occurred before noon. It was after 8:00 a.m. We had already missed the first one, but the second event would come around soon enough. When it was time, all four of us lined up side-by-side, with thirty other tourists, to see how the dolphins were fed. To our surprise, Jeroen was chosen by the park ranger to be one of two feeders. Then, right on cue, as if the dolphins were all wearing a watch, they appeared out of nowhere and swam right up to the shallow waters, looking for their handout. The park ranger calmly monitored the entire event, and from start to finish, it took fifteen minutes. As short lived as the experience was, I could tell it was a moment Jeroen will always remember. While he had few words to describe what it was like to feed a wild dolphin, his expression of pure joy told us all we needed to know.

Anyone who has ever seen a dolphin up close will tell you that they are filled with personality. They are extremely intelligent animals and connect well with humans. To make eye contact with a wild dolphin is an amazing experience. The local brochures explained that this daily feeding practice began in 1964 when a fishermen and his wife began throwing fish scraps overboard to the dolphins that followed their boat in from a day at sea. It wasn't long before the dolphins began swimming all the way up to the shoreline for an easy snack. Over time, tourists heard about this event, and a park was born. Today, a park ranger is there to ensure the food is carefully divided among the dolphins. It's important that the dolphins receive less than one third of their daily intake from humans, and they are on their own from noon until the following morning to encourage them to fend for themselves.

There's not much to Monkey Mia other than two cafés and a ranger station. If there was more, we missed it. Development in the area has been controlled to protect the dolphins, and the park can easily be seen in one day. Chartered catamaran sailboat tours were available, and being the full experience travelers we were fast becoming, we booked two rides on *Aristocat*. The first sail left shore in the afternoon, to check out the local sea life, and the second was a sunset cruise. On the first sail, we looked forward to catching a glimpse of a marine mammal called a dugong.

A dugong looks and behaves very much like a Florida manatee, but the differences are obvious in the color of their skin and in the shape of their tails. The dugong is brown where a manatee is grey, and the manatee's tail is flat and rounded like a giant beaver tail, while the dugong has the tail of a dolphin.

On the afternoon tour, we were fortunate to see several dugongs, and one had a small baby in tow. The baby was absolutely adorable. An hour later, things turned dark and menacing, and I could hear Steve Irwin's voice in my head with the warning of *"danger,"* thick Aussie accent and all. A tiger shark, identical to the one we saw a few days ago, came cruising by, and I got a second good look at the breed, this time from the deck of the *Aristocat*. It gave me chills, and flashbacks of our mad dash back to the boat came flooding in.

A second shark came cruising by, and it was clear how Shark Bay got its name. I never did find out what kind of shark it was. A shark is a shark. That's all I need to know. To make things really interesting, a two-foot long sea snake came slithering by, skimming the surface of the water, and I was doubly glad to be on the boat watching from a safe distance. The four of us never did make plans to go swimming, but had we been discussing it, the conversation would have ended there. The turtles and dolphins lightened up the moment, and we enjoyed another memorable day at sea without ever losing sight of the shore.

After the cruise, we drank fresh fruit smoothies at the open-air café, watched all the tourists come and go, and took each other's pictures with the three-foot tall black and white feathered pelicans sitting on the beach. Before we knew it, it was time to go out for our sunset cruise. The weather was gorgeous, it was an exceptional sunset, and we definitely got our money's worth out of the two rides.

Australian sunsets are similar to ours on the gulf coast of Florida, until there are clouds in the sky. When the clouds gather, they magnify and bring depth to the colors of the outback, and it is phenomenal. Here on the Indian Ocean, it's like a rainbow is splashed across the sky with the deepest pinks, purples, reds, oranges, and blues all swirling around in a perfect blend. Like the dolphin moment for Jeroen, there are no words to describe these sunsets and no camera can capture them. You just gotta be here.

It was another, "We're definitely not in Kansas" moment, and "Oz," once again, lived up to its name.

Back at camp, the sounds of the surf are lulling me to sleep on our last night in Denham. We'll head farther south tomorrow into denser populations as we make our way closer to Perth. The turn of the millennium is right around the corner.

Day 22, Wednesday   December 29, 1999

We got up at 6:30 a.m. and quickly packed the car to get an early start on the drive.

With New Year's Eve only two days away, we still had a lot of ground to cover. One minute there was no rush, the next, it was as if the clock was ticking much too fast. Eating toast and drinking coffee at an outdoor patio café in Denham, the four of us took turns checking the map to see what was on the way that we might have time to see, yet still make good progress. A unanimous vote was placed for a side trip to Shell Beach, where the famous Denham shell blocks came from. It was only an hour down the road, not too far out of our way, and definitely a must-see.

When we got to Shell Beach it was clear how it got its name. There were billions and trillions of small white cockleshells with a sprinkling of sand in between them all. From a distance the beach looked like white sand, but once we got closer, we could see there was virtually no sand at all. Only miles and miles of shells, or shall I say kilometers and kilometers of shells? *I'll catch on one of these days.*

Shell Beach is one of only two such beaches in the world. There's some kind of natural phenomenon that causes the over production of shells. Since shelling is one of my all time favorite things to do in life, I sat down and started looking for my own personal collection. To my left and to my right were more shells than I could possibly sift through.

Most of them were white, while the minorities were pink and blue. I made a point to collect the more colorful ones, and could have sat there for hours, but we were on a mission to keep moving. After twenty minutes, I managed to come away with a handful of free souvenirs.

The sun was miserably hot by late morning, and the question became, "When is it ever going to cool down? We're heading south!" We drove another hour to Hamelin Pool, a national park that is home to the rare and prehistoric stromatolite.

Stromatolites are living organisms, among some of the world's oldest living organisms, and they grow v-e-r-y s-l-o-w-l-y. By "oldest living organism," scientists are talking over three billion years old. It's a unique occurrence found only in a few places on our planet. (I'm beginning to sense a theme here.)

To the untrained eye, the stromatolites didn't look like much. I would've mistaken them for your average, run-of-the-mill algae growing in a large mass beneath the water's surface. But to a scientist, Hamelin Pool could easily be known as the eighth natural wonder of the world standing in the same company as the Great Barrier Reef.

The small town located at Hamelin Pool had a lot going on by the way of historical significance, but had I blinked, I would have missed it. The town was the size of Cook and probably had a population of "3 or 4." While we were there, we were told that the temperature had risen well over one hundred degrees. It was beyond oppressive. It was hotter than hot, the scary hot I had only imagined up until that point. We were driven out of the area after thirty minutes. And that was too long.

Without air conditioning in the car, the drive was insufferable until we were lucky enough to hit a rainstorm and the temperature dropped significantly. We cracked the windows just enough for cool air to come in, and it made things tolerable again. After the storm was over, we pulled into a rest area with a public cistern, another first for me. We got out and stretched our legs.

A cistern is a method of catching and storing water, oftentimes rainwater, for drinking or irrigation purposes. The sign on this particular one assured us the water was suitable for drinking, so we topped off our water jugs and moved on. One can never have too much fresh drinking water.

As we got closer to Geraldton, the city where our flight made a short layover ten days ago, we noticed the landscape changing. The terrain took on a greener hue, and there were hills and curves in the road. Up until that point, the road had been perfectly straight and flat, a long stretch of nothing with wisps of shrubbery like the portion of the train ride through the Nullarbor Plain. We decided to pass Geraldton and continued on another two hours south to cover more ground, while we still had some daylight left. Kangaroos didn't seem to be an issue anymore, but we didn't want to take any chances.

Just before sunset we found an interesting place called The Priory Lodge in Dongara, Port Denison. The Priory Lodge was built in 1881 as the Dongara Hotel and has seen a great deal of renovation since. For a while, it was a Dominican Convent, home to a nunnery, and an all-girls school before reverting back to a hotel. The current owners were investing time and money to bring the historic building back to life. The dark wide planks of the floor boards had been polished recently, and they were handsome. Our room was filled with antiques, and the ceilings were the highest I had ever seen. A pool, a pub, and a restaurant rounded out the amenities.

After checking in and before settling into our rooms, we took off for the beach to see if we could catch another exquisite sunset. By the time we arrived we were ten minutes too late for the show, but we did get to see a few remaining colors in the sky. Before returning to the lodge, we decided to eat out since it was already past 8:00 p.m. Experience has proven that Aussies close up shop early in many places, and we didn't want to count on the hotel serving a late meal. There was a good chance the kitchen would be closed by the time we got back. We walked into the first seaside restaurant we saw and were quickly seated. Right away we learned that the local delicacy was crayfish, also known as lobster because "Americans insist on calling it that," the waitress said.

Australian crayfish (spiny lobster) are as big as our lobsters back home except the claws lean on the smaller side. The two crustaceans are only a tad bit different when given a close look. Crayfish are shipped all over the world from this seaside town of about 20,000 residents, and it's a billion dollar industry. In all of Western Australia, Port Denison is considered a major city. Over 400 commercial boats fish in these waters, and I am reminded of Maine, except for the heat, of course.

A retired fisherman and his wife stopped by our table, after hearing our American accents. They said they couldn't resist saying g'day (as they say in 'strine). It was obvious the couple had been drinking because they were loud and expressed no inhibitions talking with complete strangers. Over and over they asked Jeff and me to say the word "lobster," and each time we did they laughed out loud telling us how funny we sounded. The old guy decided to try on his American accent and repeated the word "lobb-sturrr" several times over which made the four of us laugh with him. It was all in good fun and drove home the fact that we were the foreigners. The fisherman's bright red hair and tanned leather skin reminded me of a friend back home who also happened to be a fisherman. *Everyone has a twin somewhere in the world.*

Day 23, Thursday   December 30, 1999

What a nice change it was to wake up in The Priory Lodge. Space, comfort, and a roof over our heads, it's the little things in life that make it so sweet.

I would love to put my camping days behind me, but a budget's a budget, and I know there will be more open-air accommodations ahead. There's a bumper sticker that reads, "My idea of camping is when room service is late." Yep, that's me, if I am to be completely honest. Camping is cool, but luxury is the cool-est.

While the morning was pleasant, last night from 10:00 p.m. until sunup things were a bit eerie in that old nunnery. It was so quiet the silence was deafening. I got the impression the four of us were the only guests, because we didn't see another soul other than the staff. I suspect the low count had to do with the fact that the extensive renovations were completed only recently and word had yet to get out that The Priory Lodge was open for business.

After our free continental breakfast, complete with instant coffee (Where's a cappuccino machine when you need one?), we headed for Perth on the final leg of our journey with Jeroen and Ottine. We were all getting along famously, and overall, it's been a successful road trip. Jeroen remained the talker of the two, always with a story to tell. And I've enjoyed them all. Ottine has been shy and sweet with a quick wit and often jumps into the conversation when we least expect it. She gets in a real zinger every now and then, and she makes us laugh hysterically.

It was a hot drive and I was disappointed that there was still no relief despite the fact we were moving further and further towards the South Pole. We weren't in the mood for any side trips today. Instead, we took the slow and steady route stopping for the usual assortment of cold drinks, ice cream and petrol every chance we got. With little fanfare we rolled into Perth at 5:30 p.m. Finding a hotel was our first priority. The four of us decided we wanted to be in Fremantle for the millennium celebration tomorrow night, so Jeroen drove the extra 30 km (18.64 miles) to see if we could find a place to stay there instead of Perth. "Freo's a wonderful party town and will be the ideal place to bring in the new millennium!" I declared.

We noticed that droves of backpackers had descended upon the historic city, and the streets were filling up fast. It's as if the outback was calling out every traveler from the remotest regions of Western Australia, encouraging everyone to join together and celebrate the turn of the millennium in one of Australia's most beautiful locales. Jeff and I had no regrets that we changed our plans, and saw the good fortune of being in Fremantle instead of at Ayers Rock.

Amazingly enough, there was space available at the Fremantle Youth Hostel, but the rooms were set up like cabins at summer camp with bunk beds lined up against the walls. That wasn't our style, so we asked the desk attendant if he could find a YHA with two private rooms. He recommended the YHA Coolibah Hostel in Perth and called to make all the arrangements. In a matter of minutes we were set. The four of us drove back to Perth, settled into our respective rooms, and were grateful for such agreeable accommodations. The Vietnamese restaurant across the street served a delicious dinner at an affordable price.

Only 24 hours until *One Really Big Party* begins!

Day 24, Friday   December 31, 1999

It's finally December 31ˢᵗ, a day many of us have been anticipating for a very long time. Six months ago it was barely a thought to do any more than stay home and celebrate with Jeff and a few friends. If anyone had told me that I would be buying an old Ford from a Dutch couple on the west coast of Australia on New Year's Eve, I'd have bet a million dollars they were wrong, right after I told them what a wild imagination they had to suggest such a thing. But here I am doing just that. The strangest part about this day is that had I made any attempt to hatch such a plan, the "How is it going to happen?" question of all questions would have made it all seem so impossible.

With plenty of time before the festivities began, I was inspired to look into the possibility of putting the car on the Indian Pacific Railway and ride the rails to Adelaide. That would have taken us half way across the southern part of Australia. From there we could head north to the "Red Center," the heart of Australia.

I knew there were limited runs from Perth to Sydney, possibly one a week, so I called the train station to see what our options were. The operator told me that a train was currently in the station, scheduled to depart in two hours and there was room for one more vehicle. She assured me there was enough time to buy our tickets and load the car. If we chose to wait, the next opportunity wasn't for another two weeks. Waiting two weeks was *not* an option, so it was now or never. Put more succinctly, it was now or "You're driving across the red hot desert."

Was it fate that there was room for the car on the train? Would we be spending New Year's Eve on a train? Jeff and I had ten minutes to make our decision. A mad rush to the station was a viable option until I realized that we hadn't bought the car yet. It wasn't ours to put on the train. "Houston, we have a problem," as the joke goes. Jeff and I weren't going anywhere. The agreement we made with Jeroen and Ottine was to pay cash for the car, and Jeff and I had not been to the bank yet. There simply wasn't enough time to pack, make the deal, and get down to the train station in time for departure *if* we decided that was the way to go.

Yesterday I had a strong hunch to call the ticket office, but I never did. Had I called, we would've had more time to think things through and been able to make an educated decision. Feeling really frustrated and powerless over the news that our option to cross the desert by train was gone forever, fear enveloped me. The decision had been made for us, and there was no way around it. We were going to have to cross the outback by car, a 17 year old car with no air conditioning, and that was no joke. *People die out there.*

My mind was racing. I was doing my best to get a grip on the situation, and I finally took a deep breath in an attempt to calm down. I went to Jeff to explain what was happening, and I noticed that while I was talking a mile a minute about what woulda, coulda, shoulda happened, adding in "if only" this, and "if only" that, Jeff remained calm and centered. He was alright with making the long drive and couldn't understand why I was so upset. He was always much better at going with the flow than I ever was, and up until that latest upset, I was getting pretty good at it, too. The calm I saw in his eyes, and the look of "What's the big deal? It's ok, we can do it," took the edge off, and I got over my silly self. I dropped the "If only" pity party and got back to the benefits of staying right there in Perth. We had a party in Fremantle to go to, and that was more than alright. It was perfect.

At 11:00 a.m., Jeff and I walked to the bank to get the money to buy the car. Using Jeff's credit card, we took out a cash advance, and it worked the same way as it did at home: simple and easy. It was money we had budgeted for a rental car, and we rationalized that it was worth the extra fees charged to make the transaction. We knew we were going to come out ahead in the long run. As the teller gave us $2700 AU ($1800 US) in Australian $100 dollar bills (the money is very beautiful by the way), she kindly reminded us to be very careful with that much cash. She saw we were foreigners, and we appreciated her concern. On the way back to the hostel, we ordered a couple of subs and caught up on emails. It was a very productive morning.

At the YHA Coolibah Hostel, all four of us sat at one of the outdoor tables to conduct our business. We handed the cash to Jeroen, and he in turn gave us the title to our "previously owned" 1983 Ford Falcon station wagon. It felt great. With our business complete and a big night ahead of us, we took a three-hour nap to ensure we would be wide awake past midnight. From the street ads and local publications it was clear that Perth had a lot going on. There was talk of beach concerts and events all throughout the area. The roads began closing early for street parties, and for the first time in my life I was faced with more choices for fun than I could count. What a dilemma. Even the fireworks didn't wait for sundown. We could see colors bursting over the Swan River before 5:00 p.m. I could feel the collective, positive energy building as the day moved forward.

At 7:00 p.m., the four of us unanimously agreed to take the train to Cottesloe Beach, a quaint little town, a favorite among locals, on the way to Fremantle. The Transperth station was close enough to walk to. Waiting for the trains were groups of people blowing horns and wearing hats. Some celebrants dressed in formal wear, but most were casual. And there were lots of young guys with hair colored in every imaginable color. The alcohol was flowing freely, and the party had officially begun.

We got to Cottesloe Beach in time to see the sunset. Hundreds of people had gathered along the beach. Huge sand sculptures were scattered throughout, possibly the result of a contest held earlier in the day. One sculpture in particular stood apart from the others. It was in the shape of a huge hand, with all five fingers extended, reaching up out of the sand and *holding* a sandcastle. A second hand rose up to place the tip of the castle spire onto the castle that the first hand was holding. The creativity, imagination, and talent to conceptualize and then sculpt such a thing was truly amazing.

The most memorable part of being on Cottesloe Beach was the gathering of birds high up in the trees. Hundreds, probably thousands, of brightly colored loudly chirping wild budgie parrots filled the tall pines. Clearly picking up on the excitement of the evening, the birds were chirping as loud as they possibly could and drowning out the band's music. A full orchestra, amps, speakers and all, were playing on a large stage set up on the beach, and their music was muffled by the sounds of nature. In the distance, out on the ocean, kayakers had formed a line side-by-side as they watched the sunset from their own unique vantage point. It was a spectacular scene and a memorable start to what was sure to be a memorable evening. Once the sun had gone down and the colors in the sky turned to grey, we caught the next train to Fremantle.

Fremantle's train station is located next to one of the town's larger ports. As soon as we arrived, our attention was drawn to the ships docked in the harbor. The first ship we noticed was a Greenpeace boat, and it was harbored next to a ship so big I didn't know they could make ships that big. The Greenpeace craft was dwarfed by the giant Italian Navy battleship that stood, I can only guess, a good twenty stories high. The officers were on shore leave, time out from their United Nations peacekeeping mission in East Timor, an island north of Australia. I suddenly realized that both ships had arrived, along with us, at the most happening spot in Western Australia.

And then I remembered that Jeff and I had been to that dock before. Two weeks ago there was an entirely different scene taking place. A massive sheep boat was docked, and once it was filled, it was headed for Asia. We were told that sheep were being brought in day and night from the stations in the outback exactly like the one we had visited in Coral Bay. I could hear their cries and knew their final journey was not a good one. To remove the sad image from my mind, I shook it off and brought my attention back to the festivities ahead. We had a Greenpeace vessel to check out.

All four of us walked over to get a closer look. Jeroen recognized the flag flying off the mast. It was his own Dutch flag, and as we got closer we could read the full name of the ship. On the stern was painted "Greenpeace Amsterdam." Ottine and Jeroen were thrilled. There they were so far from home, and to see their flag flying made them proud. A few crew members were on deck, and Jeroen and I did our best to get their attention, but our calls were ignored. Standing within earshot, the crew turned their backs to us, obviously used to tourists like us trying to invade their privacy, their home away from home. When Jeroen and I came to our senses, we totally understood.

The Greenpeace ship was the same one I had seen on television documentaries, and it was awesome to be standing so close to it. The ship had rainbow stripes painted on the side and was called *The Rainbow Warrior*. The dove-and-olive-branch symbol was also displayed, and the large mushroom shaped fixtures (not sure what they were) on the boat were painted like large spotted mushrooms. That boat had seen things most of us will never see in our lifetimes. I said to Jeroen, "Oh, the stories the crew could tell." He agreed they would most likely send a chill up his spine and made an educated guess that the boat and crew had been south near Antarctica protecting the whales.

The enormous Italian ship next door was, well, *enormous*. Ottine, shouting up to the guard on deck, asked if we could come aboard. He said, "No way," in perfect English, but we all joked with the thought that she could have easily persuaded him to say, "Yes, of course," had she been alone. Ottine's natural beauty, slim frame, and cute smile would've been hard for any sailor to resist. He may have broken a few rules to allow her on board, especially on the eve of the most anticipated party of the millennium, but she was with us, and of course, Jeroen was, too. We moved on.

We hadn't eaten since lunch and were beyond hungry. Assuming that most places have held dinner reservations for who knows how long, we had no idea if we could find a place to sit down to eat. It was 8:30 p.m., dinner hour for a night like this, and we decided to try to find somewhere to sit despite the odds. We headed for the first restaurant we could find nearest the docks. The lights on the patio led the way. It was the Victorian Café and Restaurant on Victoria Quay Road. We noticed a few tables on the outdoor patio were empty, but they all had "Reserved" signs posted on them. To test our luck, I asked the hostess if we could be seated. The hostess asked us if we had reservations. I answered honestly and said "No, we don't." She briefly looked around at the situation, and the next thing we knew we were sitting down and ordering a delicious Indonesian meal. We were all very grateful.

Several of the entrées were printed in Dutch, and Jeroen and Ottine were more than happy to translate for us. The food was delicious, the service was gracious and professional, and the atmosphere was, of course, festive. With the Greenpeace ship still within view, we asked our server to disclose anything and everything he knew about it. He didn't have much to tell, but enthusiastically acknowledged that he knew the crew. "What an interesting place to live and work," I said, "You can really get a sense of the world's events right here in Fremantle."

Before ordering desert, we were offered a complimentary drink to toast the New Year. I chose the mimosa from the tray of assorted libations, and we all raised our glasses to friendship, prosperity, and health. Jeff and I agreed that the universal plans were working well in our favor, and all that was required was our cooperation, our saying "yes" to allow good to come into our lives.

At 10:30 p.m., we walked into the historic area of Fremantle where people everywhere were doing their best to get as drunk and happy as possible. An African band was playing in the street, Jeff and Jeroen could hear French being spoken, and we got the feeling we were in one of the biggest multi-cultural gatherings in the world. We continued to wander around, and an hour later we were ready to get out of the happy chaos. One of us came up with the idea to leave Fremantle just before midnight, and we headed back to the train station to beat the rush. It turned out that the trains were running free of charge, a gift from the city, no tickets required. We got on, four minutes before midnight, and then realized how insane that was to be on a nearly vacant train at one of the most significant moments in history simply to beat the rush.

We came to our senses and jumped off the train seconds before the doors closed and walked the short distance back into the crowd. The clock ticked midnight, horns began to blow, people started cheering, and the enormous Italian battleship let out a horn blast that was most impressive.

Hundreds of proud Italian sailors were yelling and whistling, and the magic of the evening had reached its peak. Jeroen and Ottine gave Jeff and me the Dutch greeting of three alternating kisses on the cheek. Jeff and I returned the greeting, and we all took in the significance of the moment. The year 2000 had finally arrived. Moments later, fireworks started and we climbed the steps of a nearby footbridge that took us high above the train tracks, for a better view. We watched the explosions coming from all three points: Perth, Cottesloe and Fremantle. What a show. As soon as the fireworks were over, we headed back to the train station for a ride home. Twelve-twenty a.m., and the train was packed with young, very happy people. There were a few policemen on board, all in good spirits, and were simply there to ensure order remained. They seemed to be enjoying the evening as much as everyone else.

Back in Perth, and with Y2K now history, everything appeared to be working just fine. The lights didn't go out, planes didn't fall out of the sky, and our train didn't run out of control or come to a screeching halt as they predicted it would, whoever "they" were. All was well, more than well. Things were great. Since we were twelve hours ahead of our friends and family back home, we still had time to call or email and say, "Everything's ok, have fun!" but we decided to let them figure it out on their own.

I wonder what all those people who stocked two year's provisions in case of disaster are thinking now. Are they truly happy that all is well or disappointed that they were unable to test their well-laid plans to survive amidst the chaos?

PART THREE

The Great Eastern Highway and the Southern Outback
aka: "The Middle of Nowhere"

"There are no shortcuts to any place worth going."

unknown

Day 25, Saturday   January 1, 2000

We awoke to another cool and clear morning on New Year's Day 2000. Reports were coming in from all over the world that last night was one big joyous celebration.

Rushing through the morning and anxious to get the next adventure going, the question came up, "What's the hurry?" The journey ahead to Ayers Rock and then on to northeast Queensland was the same distance as driving from Los Angeles, California to Boston, Massachusetts. No small undertaking by anyone's standards, and it was in our best interest to pace ourselves.

The Indian Pacific Railway took us coast-to-coast straight across the southern portion of Australia. With no straight point between Perth and Ayers Rock, our second planned destination, the roads will force us to stay south until we reach the half way point across the continent at Port Augusta, South Australia. The Great Eastern Highway will lead us out of Perth and run south of, and parallel to, the train tracks. Highway 1 will pick up where the Great Eastern Highway leaves off and take us the rest of the way. It'll be a unique experience in its own right with a whole different set of outback towns to visit.

Port Augusta is called the "Crossroads for Travellers." It sits on the Australia map right about where Baton Rouge, Louisiana sits on the map of the United States. There are few interstate highways throughout Australia. At this particular junction, travelers have the rare choice to head north to Alice Springs/Ayers Rock, south to Adelaide, east to Sydney or west to Perth. When Jeff and I reach Port Augusta, we'll head north to Ayers Rock, right smack in the middle of the continent, also known as "The Red Center" in the Northern Territory. After a visit to Ayers Rock, we'll continue heading north, then east towards El Arish, Queensland where David lives. From El Arish, it's a short boat ride out to the Great Barrier Reef.

I had arranged for car insurance with a phone call and a credit card yesterday. It gave me peace knowing the other driver will be covered in the event I blow it and end up in the wrong lane. It wouldn't be intentional by any means, but habits are habits, and they can be hard to change. Jeff's a lot more confident in his driving skills than I am and has announced that he will be doing most of the driving. *I wonder if insurance covers kangaroo collisions? That would've been a good question to ask the sales agent.*

With the car packed, snacks gathered, and water bottles filled, it was time to say good-bye to Jeroen and Ottine. Hugs and well wishes for a safe journey home were shared all around, and it was finally time to part ways. Jeff and I were like a couple of kids taking possession of their first set of wheels driving off the dealer's lot into the wild blue yonder. It made no difference that the car was 17 years old. It represented freedom.

Jeroen was still waving with his right hand high in the air as we took the final turn and drove out of sight. I got the feeling he was waving good-bye more to the car than he was waving good-bye to us. He had grown fond of the old girl, the one that safely carried him and his beloved across three thousand miles, give or take a few hundred. He told us it was going to be bittersweet to see "Mum's Taxi" go.

Selling the car for nearly the same price as they bought it for meant Jeroen and Ottine's only transportation costs for the entire trip by land were the price of petrol and an oil change. Jeff and I are counting on the same good fortune. As old as the car is, it has relatively low mileage (km) and is extremely comfortable to ride in, almost like a couch on wheels. I am still a bit turned around by the sight of a right-hand-drive Ford. It's a constant reminder that we are not in the US of A.

The roads were virtually empty as we headed out of the city, and it turned out to be an excellent day to practice city driving. Jeff and I came up with three good reasons for the absence of travelers:

1. Thousands were sleeping off their hangover.

2. The thousands who didn't drink were sleeping in.

3. On New Year's Day, most Australians were "On holiday."

It took 30 minutes to get out of the city and on to the Great Eastern Highway. The road led us into a dense green forest. Slowing the pace down, windows wide open, enjoying the scenery, the start of our journey was picture perfect until we heard a loud unidentifiable clicking noise. It sounded as if it was coming from the car, so Jeff pulled over to take a look under the hood. First he listened with the motor running and the gear in neutral. Then he got out of the car, and I drove slowly past him so he could get a better reference as to where the sound was coming from. He still didn't know what the problem was.

Jeff is good with cars, and knows a bit about engines, but this one had him stumped. He decided to turn the car off, let it rest a few minutes, and then turn the engine over again to see if anything had changed. The motor was silent, but the clicking noise was still there. It took a few seconds, but once the attention was off the car, we realized that the unidentified sound was coming from deep inside the woods. Things suddenly got very creepy. Jeff and I looked at each other, looked into thick dark forest, and then scrambled back into our respective seats and took off down the road. We didn't want to know what it was.

With the forest well behind us, it was time to stop and get a bite to eat. The first restaurant we came to was Café Fiume. It sat along the banks of a beautiful river filled with swans. The menu listed a typical assortment of diner/café fare, and bakery items were said to be their specialty.

There was only one other table occupied when we arrived giving our server plenty of time to talk to us about her life in Australia. It turned out she was co-owner of Café Fiume and proud of her establishment. Pointing to the black and white family photos that hung on the walls she told us how she ended up in Western Australia. There were pictures of the camps where she and her family lived when they first arrived as Dutch immigrants. Just like Michael, the opal miner from Lebanon, she migrated from the Netherlands when she was five years old. I really enjoyed talking to her and had a peaceful feeling, as if I had always known her.

After a few hours on the road, Jeff asked if I would drive. The manual three-speed, like the jeep in Exmouth, made it awkward to shift gears with my left hand instead of my right, and it took all of my concentration to get it right. Once I settled down and found my cruising position, I noticed how well the old Ford handled. I thought, "This car is really going to take us to Sydney."

Southern Cross was our next stop. Looking forward to a nice hot meal upon our arrival, it was a shock to find the town abandoned. Every business was closed due to the holiday. We were determined to find at least one restaurant open and walked right up to a café's front doors, all the while ignoring the "closed" sign hanging in plain sight. Peeking through the window we could see people inside. Jeff turned the knob hoping the sign was wrong, and to our delight, the door opened. The owner said that while they were technically closed they made the decision to feed anyone who stepped in. Sitting in our booth, Jeff and I realized it was our first dinner alone in seven days. I took a deep breath and gave a sigh of relief. The first half of the trip had been full of wild experiences with many unknowns, and I was on edge more than I cared to admit. Jeroen, Ottine, Jeff and I had a lot at stake. There was a high level of trust in place when we agreed to buy the car and drive to Perth together. "No worries," I've got to remember that one. Everything worked out beautifully.

The café wasn't the only establishment to open its doors to a couple of foreigners. The same thing happened earlier in the day when we stopped for petrol. The sign in the window read "closed," but a man came from around the corner of the building when he heard us pull in. He kindly sold us a tank-full and sent us on our way. Good thing because "Mum's Taxi" didn't have enough gas to get us to the next station, open or not. The following morning, the owner would have found two Americans camping out if he had taken the day off. Most highway gas stations in the 'States are open around the clock no matter what the holiday is. Jeff and I took our assumptions to the test when we set out on a cross-country road trip on New Year's Day. "So this is why the roads are empty," I thought, "Australian travelers know better than to drive long distances on a holiday."

Back in kangaroo country, with an hour left before sunset, our first day's drive came to a stop in the old mining town of Coolgardie, gateway to the Nullarbor Plain. There isn't much past this point, so it was important that we not go any further.

It's January 1, 2000, and we're staying in the Goldrush Lodge for the night. Built in 1881, the old hotel shows its age, but the price is right at only $30 AU ($20 US). Our room is huge, complete with fireplace and a door leading to a balcony. Looking out onto the wide streets of downtown, I feel as if I'm in an Old West movie. Any minute now a gun-toting cowboy will ride up on his horse, dismount and swagger into the saloon on the main floor. No, there are no swinging doors and saloons below, but if the walls could talk, I am sure they would have some stories to tell.

In its peak, Coolgardie, the site of Australia's richest gold strike, was home to over 50,000 people, 12 banks, 3 breweries, 2 stock exchanges, 7 newspapers, and 26 hotels. City hall and some of the other public buildings are still standing and still impressive, fit for any capital city back home. Someone had a vision for progress when Coolgardie was built, but it was progress short-lived in the grand scheme of things. One hundred years after the gold rush, Coolgardie resembles a ghost town. The gold is long gone, but the town remains a critical stopover for travelers like us.

Before going to bed, we topped off the gas tank and bought 10 gallons of water all in preparation for the longest stretch of nothing. The snack stash was replenished with bread, nuts, chips, peanut butter and jelly. Vegemite, for the time being, remains a mystery, but one snack in particular did catch my attention. Jeff and I are huge fans of the late night show called "South Park," and there on the shelf of that small convenience store was a box of "South Park Cheesy Poofs" or cheese puffs. The box read "Made in Australia," and it made my day. I bought two: one for the road and one to take home to my friend in Florida who is an even bigger fan of the show than I am. I told Jeff, "Sarah has got to see this."

There are two full days of driving before we'll see the other side of the desert, but the once dreaded passage has turned into a much anticipated adventure. My change in attitude has everything to do with staying at the Goldrush Lodge. It's in the "not knowing" of what's in store, all the experiences along the way, that has suddenly become intriguing. Jeff and I are about to "Go Outback," and had we flown over the desert or taken the train again, that would've been an opportunity missed.

Day 26, Sunday   January 2, 2000

It was an *extremely* long day of driving today, and the cool southern breezes made the trip tolerable in a car with no air conditioning. The outback towns, each with little more than a petrol station, were spaced on average 200 km (124 miles) apart. Jeff and I stopped at every single one. Whichever was needed most at the time, whether it was to "have a slash" ('strine for going to the bathroom), stretch, buy petrol or ice cream, there was always a good reason to pull over. Any sign of civilization was welcomed because other than those petrol stations, it was just a bunch of red dirt out there, at least to the untrained eye. Even the kangaroos were scarce. Studying our travel guide, I learned enough about the Aborigines to know they had a sixth sense about the desert and were experts at reading the land. I was keenly aware that they knew and understood a world most of us would never see.

Somewhere in the middle of the day and in the middle of nowhere the Australian Highway Police pulled us over for a "routine license inspection." I was driving at the time, so the officer looked at my Florida Driver's License and then asked for both of our passports, since it was obvious we weren't locals. Once he was satisfied that our paperwork was in order, he let us go. He reminded me of our highway police back home in the way he approached the vehicle and conducted himself. He was authoritative, but friendly, confident and assured, clean shaven, well-built, and stood about 6 feet 2 inches tall. I guessed him to be in his mid-30's. How far he was from the closest police station, I had no idea.

We drove a record (for us) 900 km (559 miles) and ended up in Eucla, a small town on the Western Australia/South Australia state border—a border marked by a *huge* fiberglass whale that looked really tacky. While I was expecting a kangaroo as the symbol of the area, whales turned out to be the draw, especially during migrating season. From several vantage points, they can be seen swimming north from Antarctica and along the southern shores of Australia. As tacky as I thought that whale was, it's been added to my journal, and is doing its job to make the place memorable. Nine hundred kilometers is a long way to drive west to east, and it caused us to set our clocks ahead twice each time moving in 45 minute increments. I have no idea why Australians use anything less than an hour, and I didn't ask. I just wanted to know what time it was.

The Eucla Motor Hotel will be our home for the night. Summer in the desert is very unforgiving. The season has reached its peak with the sun high and strong. Warmer temperatures are ahead. Guaranteed. Jeff and I are grateful for a roof over our heads and a soft bed to sleep in. Our safe arrival in Eucla means the car passed the ultimate test and the journey continues.

Day 27, Monday   January 3, 2000

Along the desert drive, we remembered to wave to every car that passed, which wasn't many, and the oncoming cars' passengers invariably waved back. The Ford's holding up well, Jeff and I drank lots of water, took turns driving, obeyed the traffic laws, remembered to stay on the "wrong" side of the road, and made it across safely. The weather was good and kept us relatively comfortable. Not a single 'roo was injured in the making of our three-day journey.

I expected to see several signs announcing Aboriginal communities, but there was only one...that I noticed anyway. The small village of Yalata was home to an art gallery selling original Aboriginal paintings, boomerangs, didgeridoos (a 3 to 10 foot long cylindrical wooden wind instrument), and wood sculptures right from the artists themselves. The town reminded me of the American Indian villages in Arizona and New Mexico. I bought the usual postcards, pins, and magnets to add to my collection.

Aboriginal art is distinctive and beautiful. The more talented artists earn huge commissions for their work. Many paintings are filled with colorful dots, circles, and squares creating truly unique designs. Scenes depict all aspects of their life as native Australians, including stories of The Dreaming or Dreamtime, the Aborigines' tale of creation. Bush tucker, food found in the outback, is also a common theme found in Aboriginal art. Aborigines can survive for months alone in the desert while on "walkabout" by eating witchety grubs (moth larvae), honey ants (ants that store honey in their abdomens), leaves, blossoms, and little known herbs, fruits, and vegetables. A walkabout is similar to our American Indian vision quest, a spiritual journey to awakening; to receive answers from within about life's biggest mysteries. Both journeys are milestones in a person's life and extremely sacred.

There were a few scenic lookouts throughout this last stretch of desert that provided amazing views of the Great Australian Bight, an open bay along Australia's southern coastline. Jeff and I stood looking over the steep rocky cliffs as the cold wind blew, unusually cold for summer. It was a long drop, straight down to the ocean below. There's a point along this stretch of land called The Head of Bight where whales can be seen migrating, often times with their newborn babies, from June through October. That popular lookout sits somewhere between Nullarbor Roadhouse and Yalata. There were no whales to see in early January, so I added this section to the revisit list. Whether the name "Bight" had anything to do with the fact that the jagged coastline looked as if a giant had taken a "bite" right out of the land, I don't know, but it was an association I made to remember the stop. It's believed to be the part of Australia where Antarctica broke away eons ago, though it appears to have broken away yesterday. A closer look at the two separate continents revealed a puzzle-piece-match to one another.

Passing through farm country, Jeff said, "It reminds me of the mid-western wheat country back home; rolling hills, silos, golden sunsets. It's like a Norman Rockwell painting, and could pass as an exact double for Kansas or Oklahoma in the '60's." Sometimes I forgot what country I was in.

The trip was going extremely well until Jeff decided to test the car to see how far it would go on one tank. Rather than fill-up when it was safe to do so, we passed one more petrol station that we normally would have. I'm a "fill it when it gets to a quarter tank" kind of girl, so I was a bit skeptical that the car would make it to the next station, knowing how few and far between they were. Practically on fumes, with the look of "I told you everything's ok" on Jeff's face, we rolled into a small town called Wirulla. I was so relieved to see civilization that I kept my comments to myself. At first, it appeared that all was well, but it wasn't long before there was cause for concern.

The petrol station was closed. Not "Closed" like the other petrol station in the outback was closed—where someone would be walking around the corner any second. It was closed as in, "Lights out, locked up tight, closed." The one and only grocery store next door was closed, too, and not just for the day, it was closed for the "holiday week" the sign read. The owners decided to take a vacation the same time Jeff decided to push the limits of our gas tank. It seemed our luck had finally run out. We walked over to the first house we saw. Jeff knocked, the door opened, and a black and white cat ran out. Two women stood at the doorway.

"Is there another petrol station in town?" I asked.

"Yes, but the owners of both stations are on a trip together. They've gone fishing."

"No way! This can't be happening," I said. Jeff was silent.

"It's an extended holiday for anyone who wants it. The stations will be closed for four more days. Even the local bank is closed five out of seven days a week," the Aussie replied.

All I could think was, "Business is definitely slow in Wirulla."

Neither one of us said a word. It was clear Jeff and I were thinking the same thing. We were *not* going to stay in Wirulla for four days and wait for the fishermen to return. There were places to go, people to see, and things to do. The look on our faces must have inspired the women to come up with a solution. One of them suggested we go next door and ask their neighbor if he could help, so Jeff walked over to the second house, and I went back to the car to wait. As soon as I sat down, I got a visitor.

It was the escaped cat, and he was crying for attention. I opened the car door, the friendly feline jumped in and onto my lap and acted as if he'd known me his entire life. The sun was setting, temperatures were dropping, and I think he just wanted a place to warm up. A pet that sociable deserved a name, so I immediately called him Max. After a few minutes, Max left my lap, crawled over the back seat and onto the blanket in the back of the car. That's where he curled up in a ball and fell fast asleep. It had been cool all day, but with each passing minute, it had turned downright chilly. The Southern Ocean winds were blowing icy air in from Antarctica.

Jeff returned to the car with good news. Lucky for us, two young Aussies, Saul and Melanie, were home. Saul said, "I have a friend who has his own petrol tank with a manual pump. His farm is just a mile down the road. I'll see if he's willing to give you some. We'll be right back." And our rescue team left to find their friend. Twenty minutes later, all three of them returned. Max was still sound asleep in the sun on the blanket in the back of the car, and I didn't want to disturb him, but he had to go. I took his picture, said good-bye, and gently set him down on the cold sidewalk. Max stood there with a dazed look of disbelief as the car pulled away. It was a pitiful scene, and I didn't like it any more than he did.

Jeff and I followed the farmer to his own private petrol station, and I crossed my fingers that there was enough fuel to make it there. We arrived without incident, the tank was filled, Jeff offered $60 AU ($39 US), the average price for a full tank of petrol, but the farmer said, "No, $40 will do." Jeff gave him $50 cash, shook his hand, and said, "Thanks for everything." I felt extreme gratitude for the unconditional kindness and support we've experienced throughout our journey, and fell deeper in love with this beautiful country. *There are so many reasons to love Australia.*

Driving until dark, we found a safe place to park in a small grove of trees alongside the road. We had covered 600 km (373 miles) in seven hours, not including the long pause for petrol. Other cars had pulled over in the same patch of dirt, and it looked like a campground without the amenities. We could have kept going, kangaroos weren't a threat, but it had been a long day. With a bit of rearranging, there was enough room in the back of the car for the two of us to lie down. The stars in the southern sky were amazing. Jeff pointed out strange looking triangular star formations that created kangaroo-like images; shapes with long, narrow snouts between close-knit eyes. The sky was so crisp we could see clouds.

It's the end of our third full day of driving since leaving Perth, and we can now declare that we crossed the Nullarbor Plain and lived to tell about it. I would've bought a bumper sticker to that effect had I seen any for sale. It was quite an accomplishment. Our plans are to leave early enough in the morning to reach Port Augusta, South Australia by noon. From there we'll head north into the heat, again. Jeff and I have yet to truly experience the intensity of the outback, and I am doing my best to mentally prepare. It was hot in Exmouth and Coral Bay, but I have a feeling we haven't seen anything yet.

PART FOUR

South Australia
Mountains, Opals, and a Dry Sea of Sand

"Life is either a daring adventure or nothing at all."
Helen Keller, 1880-1968
Inspirational Author and Lecturer

Day 28, Tuesday   January 4, 2000

After a horrible night in the back of the car, we awoke
groggy and grumpy. It motivated us to get the day going, and
we were back on the road by 5:45 a.m. Jeff volunteered to
drive first, and considering he is not a morning person, it was
a sure sign that he wanted to put the experience behind him,
too. The bags were reorganized and the back seat returned to
its upright position so I could stretch out with the blanket
under my head. In a matter of minutes, I was fast asleep.

Before reaching Port Augusta we made a stop in Kimba,
a small town known as the "Halfway Point Across
Australia." Like Eucla on the Western Australia/Southern
Australia state border, Kimba was marked by a 7 meter high
(23-foot) statue. This time it was a crude rendering of a galah
or pink cockatoo. While in Kimba, we filled the gas tank for
the first time since the farm and got our first cup of coffee of
the day.

Long hours in the car gave us plenty of time to read *Lonely Planet* and check out what's between Port Augusta and Ayers Rock. We saw there was a mountain range, the largest in South Australia, east of the point where the route turned north. The area in question is called the Flinders Ranges, and it looked like our kind of place. The more we read about it and talked to travelers along the way, the more viable an option it became as a worthwhile side trip. With two nights set aside for the park detour, there was still plenty of time to get to Queensland. Besides, it was time to slow things down another notch.

We reached Port Augusta 15 minutes ahead of schedule, and the southern outback was finally behind us. Port Augusta didn't read like much in the travel guide, but it turned out to be a beautiful town. Our good opinions may have had something to do with the fact that we had just emerged from the stark desert. Whatever perceptions were running the show, our short stay was a welcomed change of pace, and that was all that mattered. There were several cafés, a brand new Internet Café, and a short avenue of stores offering a wide variety of food, supplies, clothing and gifts. Jeff and I ate and typed our way through town fairly quickly, and by 2:00 p.m. were on the road again, refreshed, and ready for the short drive into the mountains.

The Flinders Ranges are named after the British explorer Matthew Flinders who, in the mid-1800's, recorded the long stretch (approximately 400 km or 248 miles) of broken and irregular mountain ranges. Wilpena Pound, a natural amphitheater, is the most popular landmark in the area.

It was the Aborigines who first discovered this area thousands of years ago, and it's their side of the story I am most interested in. This will be our introduction to the ancient legends of The Dreaming, one of the many stories of creation, and I'm looking forward to it.

Before officially entering the park, we decided to take a short hike up a hill to the Yourambulla Rock Shelter. There were three shallow rock caves all close to one another and filled with Aboriginal carvings and paintings. It felt really good to stretch my legs after being in the car for three-and-a-half days. The trail gave us panoramic views of the valley and the desert road we had just driven in on.

I was reminded of Utah and Wyoming except the Flinders Ranges are much smaller, due to erosion, and older than the mountains in the western United States. Scientists estimate it was a mere 540 million years ago when this area experienced a sequence of events that caused the earth to buckle and shift, creating the irregular shapes. These days, the terrain remains dry and rocky with a strong desert sun high in the sky. Of course, the native plants were all different than in our western states back home, but I was trying to find something, anything familiar that I could relate to. *I think I'm starting to miss home.*

It was unseasonably cool all day, in the high 70's, which made the walk all the more enjoyable. The average temperature is generally in the high 90's in January, and the summer months are considered off-season to travelers. We lucked out with evening temps predicted to be in the low 60's throughout the next few days. With only half-a-dozen other hikers in the area, we were grateful for our timing. I figured the hike would have been unbearable in the hottest part of the day had it been the norm.

Once back in the car, Jeff and I headed straight for Wilpena Pound Motel, arriving minutes before the office closed. *Lonely Planet* listed this motel as the best place to stay in the park. It was time we added a bit of luxury to our experience and spared no expense. With no reservations, we were able to get a room with our own bath.

Private baths are fast becoming a luxury to us. They are rare in the budget accommodation category, and we are pleasantly surprised to have one in our room. Whether it's a hostel or a motel, many baths are "down the hall and to the right." It isn't always the most welcomed arrangement.

Between car camping the night before and the hike up to the Yourambulla Rock Shelter, I was overdue for a shower, but first things first—food. It was late when we checked in and the kitchen was about to close. The motel's receptionist was kind enough to call the restaurant's manager and inform him that two hungry guests were on their way. As it goes with exceptional Aussie hospitality, the chef kept the kitchen open to be able to serve us.

Looking at the menu, Jeff and I noticed that nearly every animal we had seen in the wild was offered as a meal. Kangaroo, emu, and a few other unidentifiables were listed. As a vegetarian, the choice to venture into the culinary wilds was a non-issue. I honestly don't know if I would have tried the local delicacies had I been more flexible with my diet. What I do know is that it was one of the most unique menus I had ever seen, right up there with finding "alligator tail" on a menu in Florida.

Wilpena Pound Motel in the Flinders Ranges is famous for its food, and people come from miles around to enjoy the exotic meals. Jeff and I, on the other hand, ordered pasta with fresh sautéed vegetables. The chef did an excellent job with the zucchini, carrots, broccoli and green peppers, all the familiar flavors of home, and we were completely satisfied.

On the way back to our room, well after sundown, Jeff and I noticed a dozen kangaroos grazing on the lawn, a relatively small patch of grass, right outside the restaurant. This was the closest we had ever been to this many 'roos, and it was a surreal moment for me. They were anywhere from 2 to 8 feet in height, and I got a close-up look at them all. More intent on eating the grass in the cool night air, they were oblivious to our stares.

As I was watching the wildlife, Jeff's attention was drawn high above us. He said, "Jennifer, look at these stars." Having grown accustomed to seeing certain constellations and patterns in the sky back home, he, once again, noticed that things were a bit different in the southern hemisphere. He said, "There are galaxies beyond the Milky Way that we don't usually see at home, but show up clearly here in the

South." When I looked at Orion's Belt, it appeared to be upside down, and maybe it was. We were in "the land down under" afterall. I put that one in the category of "I'll figure it out later," right next to the lost December day when we arrived, and took a longer look at the stars just as they were. It was a beautiful night.

The shower felt great, a soft bed awaits, my journal notes are all caught up, and I am one happy traveler. We'll need a good night's rest because tomorrow's a big day. We're going to hike the motel's name sake, Wilpena Pound, a large crater-like formation that makes the Flinders Ranges unique. Wilpena Pound is also home of an Aboriginal Dreaming.

Day 29, Wednesday   January 5, 2000

Being on the move for four days, we slept in, knowing we were finally going to stay in the same place two nights in a row. Wilpena Pound was the ideal place to rest, and there was more to do than 48 hours would allow. There were several trails leading up, over, and around the crater-like ridges. Some short, some long depending on skill, time and desire, and for those who don't want to walk, there are four-wheel drive jeep tours, mountain bike rentals, and scenic flights available. On our first time out, we chose the two-hour "bush walk" to Arkaroo Rock, and that was one of the short trails.

It wasn't until I stepped onto the path and into the range that I could fully experience the beauty of the Flinders. From the road, the park looked nice, but I hadn't yet grasped the full essence of the place. The trees created a natural canopy, the shade was inviting, and it was wonderful to have solid ground beneath my feet. Wilpena Pound worked its magic connecting me to the land. At one point, wild goats appeared out of nowhere, easily navigating their way up and over the rocks. The hike was filled with one surprise after another, and it was like being transported to another planet. There was a wide variety of plant and animal life, even the rocks had a color all their own. Jeff and I knew we had stumbled onto an Aussie treasure.

Along the way we saw a thorny devil lizard. It was small and ran super fast. I couldn't get a good look at it, but that particular species was in the park brochure, so I made an educated guess as to what it was. There were more Aboriginal paintings and carvings, distinctly different from those we saw yesterday. Each picture told a story, possibly about initiations, the rite of passage from boyhood to manhood, stories of the Dreamtime secrets forever kept deep within the hearts of Australia's first inhabitants. The Dreaming holds tremendous meaning here.

The creation of Wilpena Pound goes something like this: two massive serpents slithered into a sacred Aboriginal initiation ceremony and surrounded the group. The snakes swallowed all but two men who managed to escape. With stomachs full, the serpents laid down, willed themselves to death, and their bodies formed the walls of Wilpena Pound.

The two-hour bush walk took us along the outer ridges of the low lying mountains. Temperatures remained cool throughout the day and there wasn't another person out there, but we cut the hike short anyway. An hour into the trail, it occurred to us that the adventure was more than we bargained for. Had we continued, the trail would've taken us up and over the highest point of the ridge into the valley below, and then we would have to hike back out. Being a couple of flatlanders from Florida, we really weren't prepared.

After dinner, we made a second attempt at a view from the top of Wilpena Pound by following a trail behind the motel. The hike required a bit of rock climbing, and while the view along the way was worth the effort, we never did get high enough to see the sunset or "the pound." I was going to have to settle with an aerial picture postcard of the area.

Budget and time constraints prevented us from taking a scenic tour by plane or 4WD. There were dozens of pictures I had taken of the places we did manage to reach, but I know once I see the developed photos, they won't do the park justice.

Dozens of kangaroos were scattered throughout the park and inside the campground next to the motel. During the day, they casually hopped among the recreational vehicles, tents, and in-and-out of the trees, all in an attempt to stay in the shade. Beyond the campground, kangaroos blended well into the landscape, often seen sitting out in the open fields. I sensed the 'roos were more relaxed in the Flinders Ranges than the ones cramped under a small eucalyptus tree in the outback. It didn't take a zoology major to see that conditions were more favorable in this part of South Australia.

The park was also home to a wide variety of birds. Gorgeous yellow, green, and black parrots flew through the eucalyptus trees while black-and-white magpies made the most unusual sounds. Four emus, in the flightless bird category, grazed on a patch of grass behind the restaurant. They made the oddest clapping noises with their beaks as they ate. At least I think they were eating. It was a foreign sound to me, and I wasn't sure what that was about nor did I ask the staff to explain.

Once the sun dipped below the trees, fifteen 'roos gathered in that same patch of grass next to the restaurant. I watched as two of the larger ones fought for their own personal space. Two young joeys held an impromptu boxing match. Watching kangaroos in the wild on the travel channel was one thing; standing 20 feet away from the real deal and hearing the smack of a kangaroo punch or kick was another. Their hind leg and tail muscles are massive and extremely powerful. Kangaroos have the ability to balance on their tails as they kick their way through a fight. We knew it was important to keep our distance, but at the same time we wanted to be as close as possible to all the action. As I scanned the group, I noticed one extra-large 'roo slowly lift his head from grazing. He turned, looked me straight in the eye, held me in his sights, time stood still for one brief moment...and then the giant went back to grazing. My own personal encounter with a "big red," and it was *intense*.

At dinner, Jeff and I had the good fortune to meet a few locals who were also dining at the Wilpena Pound Restaurant. They invited us over to their table, and we gladly accepted. Our new friends told us they visited "the pound" as often as they could. They took advantage of the fact that they could fly in on any given weekend. One of the men at the table was a professional pilot and said he enjoyed flying his friends in his own four-seater. I never did figure out where the landing strip was or where they were flying in from. And it wasn't clear whether they came for the scenery or the exotic menu. It could easily have been both. What was clear was how happy they were; completely in the moment, and truly enjoying life.

I wanted to stay a full week, but Wilpena Pound was an unexpected detour along the way to Ayers Rock. It was time to leave if we were to enjoy two full weeks in Queensland. For a country most known for perilous and unforgiving deserts, it's a country filled with extraordinary beauty and life. Further explorations of South Australia will have to wait for a second extended trip abroad.

Jeff and I turned in early, knowing we had a long drive ahead of us. Next stop: Coober Pedy, aka: Mad Max territory. Coober Pedy is where Mel Gibson filmed the 1985 science fiction thriller, *Beyond Thunderdome* with Tina Turner. The town also happens to be base camp to one of the more "colorful" opal-mining fields in Australia.

I am really looking forward to this one.

Day 30, Thursday   January 6, 2000

Jeff and I sat down to breakfast with two goals in mind; to fill up on pancakes and discuss the immediate days ahead. I made my desires known when I suggested we stay "one more day," but it was clear that was not going to happen. The discussion was over as fast as it began. As soon as breakfast was over, we packed up the car, checked out of our room, and headed north. On the way out of the park, we took the time to visit an old abandoned homestead originally settled in the 1800's. One of the best preserved sites in the area was the Kanyaka Homestead (pronounced kah-neeka). Privately owned, it was a pleasant surprise to find that visitors were permitted on the grounds free of charge.

Many of the original stone buildings were still standing, some reduced to rubble, leaving much to the imagination as to what occurred over 100 years ago. Built in 1851 and abandoned in 1888, it was once an active homestead that operated more like a small village. Seventy farmers were known to have lived there, and they did their best to farm the floor of "the pound," but met with unfavorable conditions.

They had better luck raising sheep, and records showed that a herd of over 50,000 were sheared during one season. That was twice the number of sheep sheared at the Warroora Station back at Coral Bay in Western Australia. Overgrazing and drought caused the flock to die out, and the settlers were forced to leave the area. Jeff and I could see several dry creek beds throughout the valley where water once flowed. Still useful to this day, they channel flash flood waters during heavy rains.

Visiting this small portion of the Flinders Ranges gave us a unique opportunity to learn more about the ancient Dreaming, the Australian pioneer spirit, and the plethora of birds, mammals, rocks, trees, bushes, and reptiles. The area is rich in every conceivable way. It could easily be a trip unto itself, a single reason to visit Australia.

The air was cool at the start of our drive, but as we headed north it got hotter and hotter with every passing hour. We were grateful each time a cloud lingered above to block the sun's brutal heat, if only for a few minutes. It was a welcome reprieve each and every time.

We rolled into Coober Pedy at 7:35 p.m. After checking into our motel, we headed to the main part of town in search of pizza. I'll save the room's description for tomorrow's entry. I want more time to experience this unique accommodation, because it is equally as surprising as finding an oasis at the end of the road in Coral Bay.

Now that the trip is at the half-way point, here are a few observations I've made about our drive through Oz:

- *"Peter's Ice Cream" is available everywhere. Even the smallest petrol stations have a freezer full, and we really appreciate it. I get the impression that the ice cream company supplies the signature freezers to all the small business owners and then makes sure the containers are fully stocked at all times.*
  "Good on ya!" I say.

- *The "Aussie Burger" is an all beef patty served with a slice of beetroot and a fried egg. They're in such demand that McDonald's added it to the menu—with a twist, of course— calling it the "Mc Oz"—beetroot, egg, and all.*

- *Burger King is called "Hungry Jack" here. It's the same sign, same colors, different words. They also serve the "Aussie Burger."*

- *"Road trains," while not a food item, are worth mentioning. Our driving skills hadn't really been tested until we learned how to pass one of these on a two-lane highway at 60 mph—that's a narrow two-lane highway with only a yellow stripe down the middle of the road separating us from them. Road trains are semi-trucks with two, three, and sometimes four full-size trailers behind them; aka: semi-trailers. They are huge and they are fast. Jeff taught me how* to "surf" back onto the road after the back draft has done its best to push the car into the desert; scary and thrilling all at the same time.

- Towels, hung in the rear windows of the car, block the sunlight. They do a great job in keeping a few less rays out of the car. We need all the help we can get.

- A six-digit phone number beginning with 13 means it's a national number and works anywhere in the country at the cost of a local phone call. It's one step away from the 1-800 toll-free numbers, which are also available in Australia when calling the airlines, train stations, etc.

- Eucalyptus tree branches stuck into the rear view mirror offer soothing aromatherapy as we drive through the deserts. I give all the credit to Jeff on that one. It was a brilliant idea.

- The Royal Flying Doctor Service (RFDS) is Australia's outback medical service, and these dedicated professionals will fly into the remotest of locations to help anyone in need. Started in 1928 by John Flynn, a Presbyterian Minister, the RFDS continues to expand its territory and improve operations to this day. All throughout our drive, Jeff and I have seen signs by the road that read, "Emergency Landing Strip – RFDS." That is a warning to us and all the other drivers that at any given moment a plane could be coming in for a landing on the highway. Talk about giving way to emergency vehicles. Keep your eyes in the skies drivers! Wherever there are RFDS signs there are usually markings on the pavement and a windsock nearby to help guide the pilot in. Some landing strips are so remote it's hard to tell who the doctors are

*flying in to help. There doesn't seem to be anyone out
there. More times than not, there is little more than a
faint dirt track leading off the main road marking the
direction of a remote cattle or sheep station or maybe
an Aboriginal community miles and miles away.
(I mean kilometers and kilometers.)*

Day 31, Friday   January 7, 2000

The name Coober Pedy comes from the Aboriginal term
"kupa peti." Loosely translated, it means "white fellow's
hole in the ground." Ever since a 14 year-old boy, looking
for gold, discovered the first bits of opal in 1915, Coober
Pedy has been a hot spot for miners. As far as the eye can see
there is sand, kilometers and kilometers of sand. Random
piles, some dug with success, most without, mark where
each miner has staked a claim, and there are thousands of
them.

It is a desert out there, and water is at a premium because
it comes from an underground artesian well called The Great
Artesian Basin. It runs across the entire continent of
Australia. Aussies know how to make it potable which
makes life possible in an otherwise barren land. Strange
looking vehicles cruise up and down Hutchison Street, the
main drag, and it's easy to see why Mel Gibson chose this
town to film *Mad Max III Beyond Thunderdome*. It's a short
trip from fact to fiction. Old movie props remain and are
proudly displayed throughout town. A spaceship on the hill
proves, in my mind anyway, that we have indeed landed on
another planet. It looks as if we could be standing on Mars.

But opals aren't the only riches in town. Word on the
street is that locals dig up "tourist money" as well. Food,
drink, lodging, tours, books, and souvenirs are in high
demand, and the town delivers. There are plenty of opals
for sale, that's for sure, and a whole lot more. It's a rare
breed who settles into this part of Australia. The heat of the

summer is, by far, the hottest yet. A typical day will reach 50 degrees Celsius which is 121 degrees Fahrenheit, but the locals have found a solution to their harsh environment. They build their homes, café's, hotels, pubs, book stores, and churches….underground. Naturally set to a perfect 72 degrees, the underground caves make it possible to live year round in Coober Pedy.

Our motel, Look Out Cave, owned and managed by "Bubby," boasts 19 self-contained rooms, all built in 1993. The hotel is absolutely beautiful. If anyone had told us ahead of time that our room was going to be in a cave in a dusty outback mining town, I would have thought twice before checking in. I had to see it to believe it. I quickly added Coober Pedy as one of the highlights of the trip.

Several tours were advertised in the local brochures and in *Lonely Planet*, offering a chance to see a real opal mining cave. At midday, I headed out, on my own, for "Old Miners Cave," a self-guided walk through a real dig. It turned out to be informative and included plenty of history about the earliest miners and the hardships they endured. The owners left just enough opal exposed so tourists, like me, could see the stone in its natural state. Understanding the concept of "tourist money," I assumed it was more valuable to leave the opal in the walls of the cave and sell tickets, than it was to mine them out and make a one time sale.

While I was sight-seeing and giving the town my share of tourist money, Jeff took care of the car. It was due for an oil change, and Jeff wanted to see if he could straighten out the bumper from Jeroen's accidental meeting with the kangaroo in Exmouth. Every time I looked at the damaged front end, I could hear Jeroen describing the crash: "There was absolutely no warning at all. The 'big red' appeared out of nowhere and then *bam!*"

About the same time Jeff was done with the repairs, I was done with my opal cave tour. We met back at our room to clean up and head into town. I told Jeff all about an opalized lizard skeleton I saw, how it had a blue/green transparency to its bones and teeth, and was unlike anything

I had seen before. As we walked over to the Ford, Jeff showed me the work he had done to fix the bumper. Along with a good sturdy rope and some tools borrowed from a mechanic working nearby, Jeff used his strength and ingenuity to work the bent parts back into place. He did an amazing job. The car was almost as good as new. Repairing the headlight would have to wait until we got to a bigger town where parts were more readily available.

Walking down Hutchison Street, Jeff and I saw two Aborigines standing outside one of the shops. Since our stopover in Koolgardie, on the train ride from Sydney to Perth, we have seen no more than a dozen native Australians. Among those two we saw today, I noticed one was barefoot. The ground was hot enough to fry an egg on. Add in the sharp rocks and course dry sand, I wondered how he could possibly get by with no shoes. But there he was, standing unaffected by the harsh environment. When I looked closer at his feet I could see they were tough like leather, wide and strong, and had probably been "on walkabout" several times over. I wanted to take a picture of the Aborigine and his friend, but I wasn't comfortable asking. And taking a picture without permission was not an option. Maybe they would have agreed to pose, but I erred on the side of maybe not.

After lunch, we went on a hunt for the ultimate Aussie souvenir, an authentic opal ring. In addition to the polished opals generally found in fine jewelry stores everywhere, there was a wide selection of raw opals and fossils. The shell fossils looked like museum pieces, and the shop owners claimed they were millions of years old. The prices ranged between $3 and $20 AU ($1-$13 US) each. There was one in particular that caught my attention. Partially opalized *and* fossilized, it was a snail shell with beautiful colors embedded in stone. It looked like the ocean itself.

Eons ago Coober Pedy was under a deep blue sea full of life. In fact, much of the interior of Australia was under water. Miners and cattle ranchers are constantly finding fossilized sea shells and bones of all shapes and sizes buried in the sand. A good rain may be all it takes to expose the next archeological marvel. Whatever happened in the evolution of things, the massive change in the environment preserved countless sea creatures...and at the same time created beautiful opal gems.

After our fossil discovery, we went to the underground bookstore and café where I leafed through several books about the Aboriginal Dreaming or Dreamtime. It's an entire study unto itself, and I was overwhelmed by the amount of information available. I decided to learn what I could once we got to Ayers Rock, our next destination, and keep things simple. We moved on to another opal shop. This third shop gave us an opportunity to pan for our own opals. Huge piles of discarded fragments, leftover from a miner's dig, were periodically dumped behind the building. In front of the pile of sand was a three-foot high water trough. Just like panning for gold in a riverbed, the idea is to wash away the dirt and reveal the once hidden opal. The colors of the precious stone are intensified in the bright sunlight making it easy to spot. Australians call the process "fossicking." It's a win/win because the excess sand is taken out of the miner's way, while giving tourists a chance to find their own opals.

Jeff and I decided to pass on the opportunity. It was really hot outside and looked like too much work, but we did hear a story from one of the other tourists that two girls had just found an opal worth $1,000 AU ($650 US) in the same heap we were considering fossicking. Despite the promising news, we were content to obtain our opals the easy way, with a credit card. Buying straight from the fields meant a 60% discount over purchasing a ring in a jewelry store back in the 'States. That was good enough for us.

Jeff bought two fossils and two more raw opals for his collection. He remembered to keep the raw ones in water, as Michael from Adelaide had instructed, to protect them from cracking, and I was determined to find the perfect opal ring, a piece of jewelry I could wear everyday to remember the trip.

At each store, the sales clerks took the time to educate us on how to buy a good opal at a good price. Their stories were all consistent and made perfect sense. They clearly understood that an educated customer was more likely to buy. I was impressed with the level of kindness and patience they displayed, knowing what it's like to repeat the same information over and over and *over* again.

I learned that solid opals are best while "doublets" and "triplets" are costume forms of the real deal. A triplet is a thin slice of colorful opal adhered to a crystal quartz capping and a layer of dark opal called "potch." Potch is a non-precious opal and doesn't have the vibrant colors a precious opal has. Potch is plentiful while precious opals are extremely rare.

A doublet is similar to a triplet, but without the quartz capping. The opal color is artificially enhanced by using black cement to glue a thin slice of real opal on to a backing. While the color truly is enhanced, it tends to fade over time as the glue decays. With solid opals, different colors suit different buyers, and choice comes down to personal preference. There are black opals, boulder opals, and white or light opals.

I must have looked at over two hundred rings. By the time I got to the fourth store, I knew exactly what I was looking for and found it. Because opals are fragile and can easily chip or crack, I chose an inlay, a setting that will protect the stone. Enhanced by the halogen lights installed directly over the display cabinets, the stones had the deepest blue/green colors I had ever seen. I chose that particular ring because it symbolized the deep blue/green waters of Turquoise Bay back at the Ningaloo Reef. It also reminded me of what Coober Pedy must have looked like millions of years ago. It instantly become my favorite souvenir easily surpassing the "Cheesy Poofs" we found in Coolgardie and the "Made in Taiwan" beige linen sun hat I bought in

Fremantle. All three are keepers, but only one can be "the best."

We continued to wander around town, amused and sometimes unsettled by what we saw. Due to all the digging, there were signs throughout town telling us to watch our step to avoid falling into a vertical mine shaft, a shaft that might suddenly open up without warning. Motorcycles, outfitted just like in Mel's movie, cruised through town. The riders weren't actors and the cycles weren't props. There seemed to be an unofficial contest going on to see who looked "the baddest."

A brochure describing the local drive-in movie theater showed a picture of a sign posted at the entrance that read, "No Explosives Allowed." I could only guess that a few too many opal miners drove their work vehicles into the theater and a mishap or two occurred when someone flicked a cigarette out the window, or maybe blasting caps were being set off for no good reason. A miner's temper is known to flare as high as the temperatures.

In the few hours we were in town, we saw two trucks clearly marked with the word "Explosives" cruising up and down Hutchison Street. It looked as if they were selling dynamite as casually as if they were selling ice cream to the neighborhood children.

Jeff and I saw an Internet Café across the street and our focus instantly shifted from opals to emails. We were ready to hear news from home. Among the messages from family and friends was the much anticipated email from my client's son, David. The last time I heard from him was three months ago when I received his letter about his farm. He had included his email, phone number and home address so we could reach him once we were in Australia.

David lives in a small town called El Arish (pronounced L-ah-reesh), Queensland along the coastline near the Great Barrier Reef, right about where Boston, Massachusetts sits on the US map. To be more specific, he lives in the rainforest beyond El Arish. An American-born Australian, David bought his farm 27 years ago in 1973. He has dual citizenship in America and Australia, and the last time he was in Florida to visit his "mum" was in 1995, five years ago.

We knew David had no Internet in his home and his correspondence would be sporadic at best because his closest connection was a library several miles away. I had emailed him two weeks ago to confirm we were in the country and on our way. I had also requested directions to his house. With an estimated time of arrival between January 17th and the 21st, there was plenty of time to make further arrangements. It took longer than I expected for David to respond, and I was getting a bit worried each time I checked emails and his wasn't there. I was relieved to finally be able to print the instructions on how to get to his house, but reading them created more confusion than clarity. The directions were extremely complicated, and there was no map for me to get a visual. I thought, "Maybe it will all make sense once we get there." He told us we could arrive any day and any time. He would be there tending to his farm.

Before heading back to our room, we ordered take-away. I chose the usual grilled veggie sub, Jeff ordered a meatball sub, and soon we were back in the cool air of our underground cave. Over dinner, we discussed whether to stay another night or move on. It was unanimous that two nights and one full day in Coober Pedy was plenty. As entertaining as the town was, it was a "been there, done that" experience for me. But despite the explosives and harsh environment, there was an upbeat feeling throughout the community. Maybe it was the challenge they thrived on, and the ability to remain strong and positive in the face of adversity. They could say "no worries" and mean it, because they knew what true hardship was like. Meanwhile, the tourist industry was serving them well, and I figured the thought of striking it rich at any given moment was enough to keep anyone hopeful.

PART FIVE

The Northern Territory
Hidden Secrets of Ayers Rock and Beyond

*"Even a mistake may turn out to be the one thing
necessary to a worthwhile achievement."*
Henry Ford, 1863-1947
Founder of the Ford Motor Company

Day 32, Saturday   January 8, 2000

At 8:00 a.m., and with little fanfare, Jeff and I left our underground cave. There was a bigger item on our agenda, and it was sitting right in the middle of Australia. Originally planned as our destination for New Year's Eve 1999, Ayers Rock was finally in our sights.

It was cloudy all day, making the journey from South Australia into the Northern Territory cool (relatively speaking) and comfortable. We stopped at every town along the way to stretch our legs and buy a snack. Any excuse to pull over for a Peter's ice cream was always a good one.

The closer we got to "The Red Center," home to Ayers Rock, the more tour buses, really BIG tour buses, were traveling alongside us. As remote as Ayers Rock is, people were finding their way in. We arrived at the entrance to Uluru-Kata Tjuta National Park at 5:55 p.m. just in time for sunset. Uluru (oo-lou-roo) is the Aboriginal name for Ayers Rock. Kata Tjuta (cat-uh-jew-tuh) is the Aboriginal name for the second major landmark in the area called Mount Olga, more commonly referred to as The Olgas. While Uluru is one massive monolith, Kata Tjuta is actually a group of monoliths. They are both impressive. All five names are used freely throughout the park, and I made it a point to keep them straight in my head. Unlike the Flinders Ranges, this area is more closely tied to its Aboriginal origins, and the connection travels well beyond the name.

We paid our $30 AU, $15 each ($10 US), which gave us access to the park for five full days. The ride in made us feel welcome, with its wide, smoothly paved roads. We were still in the desert, had been for days, but there was life in this part of the outback, and it was much greener than in Coober Pedy. *Anywhere is greener than Coober Pedy.*

The rolling landscape and wide variety of vegetation and rock formations made the landscape unique and beautiful in its own right. It didn't take long to figure out that Uluru and Kata Tjuta weren't the only monoliths in town. The Dreamtime stories were also plentiful. Unfortunately, Jeff and I learned early on that many of the stories were kept secret, shared only among the initiates during sacred ceremonies. We were going to have to do some digging to understand a fraction of the way Aborigines experienced Uluru-Kata Tjuta National Park – A World Heritage Area.

It's my understanding that Uluru means "meeting place," and many walkabout tracks, also known as "songlines," intersect here. An Aborigine will sing the long trail through the desert, remembering every rock, crevice, plant and tree along a track—landmarks that show him the way. Singing is how they keep their stories alive and stay connected to the land, a land as vibrant and spiritual as the day it was born in The Dreaming. Men have their songs, stories, and rituals, and women have theirs. The men don't always share their secrets with the women, and the women keep some to themselves, as well. Little, if anything, is written down. Wisdom and knowledge is passed from generation to generation in the present moment through song and dance, and as a result, much is lost over time. Ancient stories about the dawn of time during The Dreaming, as well as Aboriginal customs and beliefs, are stored in the memories of the community's best orators. When the last member of a particular community dies, the language and the stories die with them. It's a big concern to those who want to preserve Australia's rich cultural history. Just as a plant or animal species can become extinct, so can a language. Fortunately, cave drawings such as the few we saw at the Flinders Ranges leave clues, but there is plenty of room for misinterpretation.

Talking to the locals, we learned that annual revenues from the park's entrance fees and other concessions were in the million dollar range and probably had something to do with the Aborigines' willingness to share such a sacred place. Tourist dollars offer much needed support to the welfare of the Mutitjulu Community. In 1999, over 400,000 people visited Uluru, and the numbers grow every year. Another local told us that many Aborigines are kept out of the resort to protect tourists from potential begging, the type of begging Jeff and I experienced in the "wild west" gold town of Kalgoorlie. Park management makes every effort to keep the tourist experience a pleasant one.

The Aborigines seem reluctant to share Uluru with outsiders, but at the same time, highly tolerant. A very good example of this is the policy in place that allows anyone and everyone who feels compelled to climb one of the biggest rocks in the world, permission to climb. At the base of Uluru is a request to respect the Aboriginal culture and not climb the rock. Adjacent to that sign is another sign with a severe warning that the climb is a very dangerous undertaking. Your life rests on the choice you make. Occasionally the trail is closed due to extreme weather conditions, but on a good day, the choice is left up to the visitor.

A chain handrail anchored into the rock assists those who insist on climbing, and thousands upon thousands do every year. When a tourist is rescued from the giant rock it's at great expense to the climber's health and to the park's operating budget. Most often it's a heart attack that stops the climber in his/her tracks, due to the excessive heat of the outback and the physical demands of the climb. Dozens have died trying to get a view from the top as they pay the ultimate price of a risky adventure. Yet, the rock remains open and the trail is very busy. The Aboriginal word for tourist is "minga." Directly translated it means "tiny black ant," and that's exactly what a climber looks like on the gigantic monolith.

Uluru is actually much bigger than it appears. More than three quarters of it lies beneath the surface of the earth like an iceberg lies beneath the water line. Another interesting fact about the rock is that the Aborigines have not always been recognized as its rightful owner. Less than two hundred years ago "white man" staked claim on this land very similar to the way land was stolen from the American Indians. The good news is that in 1975 during an historic "give-back" ceremony, the Aborigines were restored as the park's "traditional owners" and given title to the land their ancestors first inhabited thousands of years ago.

The only place back in the 'States that reminds me of this area is Arches National Park in Moab, Utah. While Arches National Park offers remote hiking trails, and campers can go out into the bush for days or weeks at a time if they have enough water and food, in Uluru-Kata Tjuta National Park, the park rangers have a noticeable handle on crowd control and are very good at keeping individuals and large groups moving along the designated trails and roadways. Creating unauthorized "walkabouts" is strictly forbidden.

The Aborigines are doing their best to share their sacred space and preserve their heritage all at the same time. Management of the park is a joint effort between Australian National Parks and Wildlife Service and the traditional owners.

Sunset in the park is world famous for the array of colors that appear on the rock as the sun goes down. We watched from the "cars only" parking lot. A second area was for buses, and both locations were designed to give each visitor a clear view of Uluru as it changed colors in the setting sun. We could see tables being set with white linens, fine china, silverware, and champagne flutes for the first-class crowd. It looked like a lot of fun.

Most evenings, the colors are quite average. But when all the natural elements come together just right, visitors will see the sunset Uluru is famous for. Jeff and I figured we got the average version after reading one of our brochures. "Oranges, reds, crimson and gold, and all shades of purples and blues can be seen as the sky darkens, eventually turning the rock black against a starry sky." Our experience wasn't quite so dramatic. It was still a great sunset, but I wished our timing was better. After the show was over, we got in the car while there was still daylight and took the 5.8 mile lap around the base of the rock. Our next stop was the Aboriginal Cultural Center, but it had already closed by the time we arrived.

Uluru holds the record as being the second largest rock in the world, though it is often mistaken as the largest. Mt. Augustus in Western Australia (almost all the way to Exmouth) is the biggest rock in the world, and is two-and-a-half times the size of Uluru.

The park was surprisingly crowded given it was the peak of summer. Eight days after the New Year's Eve celebration, it was clear we made the right choice to stay in Perth. Had we rushed over by plane as originally intended, it would have been an entirely different experience from the one at Cottesloe Beach and in Fremantle with Jeroen and Ottine. Undoubtedly, countless other people had the same "original" idea we had. It was highly likely that there wasn't a single room or campsite available at any price.

The only camping area in the park was full, and the cost of a hotel room started at $100 AU ($65) and went all the way up to $500 AU ($325). The tourism industry has done a great job in providing every level of comfort to the wide array of travelers visiting from all over the world. With that said, none of those options appealed to us, so we left the park and headed for King's Canyon, another national park that was right "next door" in outback terms—three hours down the road. It was a newfound attraction that wasn't on our original agenda. We learned about it only after arriving in the Northern Territory.

While driving from Uluru to Kings Canyon, we saw Curtin Springs Cattle Station at the half-way point. The sign by the side of the road was our only clue that it was there. Instead of camping for the night at Kings Canyon, we made an instant decision to pull into Curtin Springs and keep our options open to go either way in the morning; back to Uluru or forward to Kings Canyon. Curtin Springs offered the comfort of A/C, and bathroom facilities were in a separate building next to ours. After showering, we caught a late meal before the cooks closed the kitchen. During dinner, Jeff and I discussed our plans for the following day. We hadn't seen Kata Tjuta (The Olgas) yet, and there was still the promise of a spectacular outback sunset flashing colors against Uluru (Ayers Rock). Jeff and I decided to see where inspiration would lead us in the morning.

Day 33, Sunday   January 9, 2000

Yesterday was a big day between our underground cave and Curtin Springs. It was time for a leisurely morning, and by slowing down, we had more time to figure out what we wanted to do. Jeff informed me that a bus full of Japanese tourists pulled into the cattle station late last night. They slept under the stars in sleeping bags side-by-side on the front lawn, 50 yards from our room, and were up and gone by dawn. I missed the whole thing and never would have known they were there if he hadn't told me about it.

Curtin Springs Cattle Station is home to more than just cattle. There are beautiful caged parrots and the usual pairing of emus and kangaroos roaming in fenced pastures. The emus like to stand along the fence near the public areas. They're bigger than expected, taller than six feet. There's a cute young kangaroo, two-feet tall, in a small cage all to itself in the courtyard between the guest quarters. It's hard to tell if it's a pet or if it's wild. Maybe it's a rescued joey that will one day be released into the wild.

There are 15 guinea pigs in a huge wire cage approximately 10 feet wide, 8 feet high, and 20 feet long. I haven't seen any cats or dogs, but they must be around. In the lizard category, we saw a 6-inch gecko in our room. It was a welcome surprise, because we know they are excellent bug catchers. Geckos have the ability to climb walls and ceilings, and can reach the most elusive spider, roach or beetle. The one animal indigenous to Australia that we haven't seen yet and want to see is the koala. I don't know where they hang out, but I hope to find one in the wild before our journey is over.

The kitchen, built from parts of the original homestead, is a real working farm kitchen. It's manned by outback cowboys who cook hot and hardy meals morning, noon and night for the guests, the staff, and the owners. Purely by accident, we have stumbled into our first authentic outback steakhouse, and it could easily be one of the inspirations for the chain of restaurants back home by the same name. The cooks have made us feel welcome and they seem genuinely glad to be here. The "no worries," laid back Aussie attitude is alive and well at Curtin Springs.

A large tiki hut, complete with a thatched umbrella roof over an outdoor table, sits outside the kitchen and offers shade in the outdoor eating area. Beautiful plants and flowers surround the courtyard. Beyond that is a pub, a small convenience store with an interesting assortment of necessities, and a petrol station. Inside the store there's a sign announcing that tent campers can stay on the premises for free, which explains the Japanese group Jeff saw last night. Four-wheel-drive outback tours are also available. The overall atmosphere is pure Australian, and between the homestead's hospitality and proximity to both Uluru and Kings Canyon, this is an ideal place to stay.

At 10:30 a.m., we were on the road heading back to Uluru Kata-Tjuta National Park. It won the vote over Kings Canyon National Park, with our decision to continue the tour where we left off.

The sun had already been up for several hours upon our return to the famous big red rock. The temperature had climbed quickly into the 3-digits making it too hot to walk around the base of the monolith as planned. The heat was so intense I couldn't fathom why anyone would want to climb and risk heat exhaustion or worse, but against the odds, there were people on their way to the top. With outdoor activities scratched off our list for the time being, we headed straight to the Aboriginal Cultural Center. That's where we figured out that our clocks had been wrong for the past 24 hours. Even though the Northern Territory is due north and in the same longitude as South Australia, the residents of the Northern Territory and Queensland don't follow "summer time." Crossing the border required turning our clocks back one hour to get in sync.

Reading and studying the artifacts in the cultural center gave us an opportunity to learn more about the Aborigines and their way of life. There was an authentic Aboriginal campsite set up outside, one typically found in the outback. It was very well done. If we wanted to take our lessons further, Aboriginal tours, private and group, were also available. Tourists could learn more about bush tucker (food found in the outback), animals, and the rock itself—scientifically speaking. At one point, Jeff said to me, "Have you noticed how few Aborigines we've seen?" Once he brought this to my attention, it was clear. The local residents were noticeably missing from the park.

The traditional owners are generally shy and many don't speak English. Our beliefs and customs are quite different from theirs, and may explain why they keep their distance. It turns out, they don't like being photographed. It's a good thing I kept my camera in check in Coober Pedy. In addition to the posted request not to climb Uluru, there are repeated requests throughout the cultural center not to take any pictures of the Aborigines or the rock. They say their ancestors are still living inside Uluru and in the surrounding lands, and there is evidence to this day that supports this belief. Taking pictures of Aborigines or their sacred land is the equivalent of taking part of their soul. With a fragmented soul, it's difficult to move on to the next realm. Some native Australians will make the exception to be photographed as long as their likeness is removed from the picture after they have passed away. It was interesting to see pictures hanging on the wall of the cultural center where faces were covered over, never to be seen again. In a land of camera-happy tourists, it must be difficult for them to deal with this clash of cultures. The Amish in Pennsylvania have a similar request not to be photographed and experience the same challenges to live in a world where their way of life is fundamentally different from their neighbor's.

Despite the request not to take pictures of Uluru, I confess that I did. I justified my actions with the fact that there were pictures of it all over the place. I had seen pictures of the rock since Jeff and I started planning our trip. What's "wrong" with taking a picture of a rock? Risking life and limb while climbing it was one thing, taking a photograph was another. Or was it? The more we learned about the culture and beliefs of the Aborigines, the more Jeff and I sensed we would never fully understand their way of life. There were too many secrets and missing pieces of the puzzle. There were sacred places beyond Uluru and Kata

Tjuta filled with Dreamtime legends and secret names of the Dreamtime ancestors never to be divulged to anyone outside the community. The traditional owners were doing their best to live in our modern world, while keeping theirs intact. Not an easy balance to maintain on any level.

As with any place shrouded in myth and legend, Uluru is home to an "outback curse" that some believe to be as real as the monolith itself. It begins with the simple gesture of picking up small rocks (mini-Ulurus, I call them) from throughout the park, the same way a visitor picks up shells at the beach. It seems innocent enough, I didn't see any signs forbidding the activity, but thousands of people who take these souvenirs claim to have very bad luck once they get home. In a desperate attempt to end the curse they believe has been placed upon them, the rocks are mailed back to their place of origin. It's very similar to the superstition surrounding Pele, the Hawaiian goddess of fire. People who pick up volcanic rocks in Hawaii report the same phenomenon. Ranger stations in these two locations have piles of "returned merchandise" from tourists all over the world. Talk about the power of belief!

Our Aborigine culture lesson was as complete as it was going to get. Time to move on. We decided to check out the second most significant landmark around, Kata Tjuta, also known as Mount Olga or The Olgas. Unlike Uluru, there were trails, one short and one long, leading hikers into the crevices between the cluster of rocks that make up Kata Tjuta. It was like a maze, and there were rules to obey to keep everyone safe. Signs were posted giving instructions on where to hike and *not* hike, and fair warning was given about the dangers of over exposure to the sun.

Weather conditions determined the closing of the longer trail in summer months, and we learned the hard way that our mid-afternoon arrival was poorly timed. Jeff and I were in complete denial about how hot it was. The temperature, already in the 3-digits, was still climbing (as if it could get any hotter), and the 7 km (4 mile) loop was closed. The shorter, 2 km (1 mile) trek was still too much for us, and we were forced to pass on the opportunity. It finally sunk in that if our walk wasn't completed by 10:00 a.m., it was best to wait until early evening or try again another day. Living in the tropics of Florida gave us no advantage. This heat was simply out of our league. We decided to go back to the cultural center and cool off by eating a Peter's ice cream bar. We left the park long before sunset.

We drove away from Uluru-Kata Tjuta National Park for the last time. At one point during the ride out, I looked back and saw a unique and surreal picture across the horizon. I said to Jeff, "Stop the car! I want to take a picture." He immediately pulled over. I jumped out, snapped twice, and jumped back in my seat. The whole event was over in less than a minute. I could only hope the camera captured what looked to me like a once-in-a-lifetime shot. (It turned out to be the cover photo of this book.)

Driving back to the cattle station, there were several more rock formations dotting the land. We learned that Curtin Springs had its own rock mountain called Mount Conner. Scientifically speaking, it's not solid rock like Uluru and Kata Tjuta. Made up of a mixture of sand and rock, Mount Conner sits along the western fringes of the cattle station, is impressive in its own right, and can be reached by 4WD tour jeep.

With Ayers Rock, now known to us as Uluru, checked off the list, we've met two out of three destination goals. But before we head northeast to the Great Barrier Reef, destination number three, we have another national treasure to check out.

Kings Canyon has got our complete and undivided attention.

Day 34, Monday   January 10, 2000

We both slept in until 9:00 am. In keeping with lessons learned at Kata Tjuṯa, Jeff and I knew it was far too late to consider a morning hike into Kings Canyon. Our only goal for the day was reduced to finding the canyon campground, settle in for the night, and try again the following morning.

As tempting as it was, Jeff and I passed on the outback cowboy tradition of drinking a cold beer for breakfast. I can honestly see how it's a reasonable substitute for a hot cup of coffee where the temperatures soar into the three-digits before noon. Had Jeff and I been so inclined, we would have started the day with a buzz, but then we would have ended up extending our stay at Curtin Springs to take a holiday from our holiday. It appeared natural and reasonable for an Aussie to down a cold one first thing. "No worries, mate. Have a g'day," the toast would go. The locals have a healthy balance of work and play and take both very seriously. Too much of one or the other can mean trouble, and they know it.

After two nights at the cattle station, we checked out of our room and drove the hour-and-a-half to King's Canyon, the third of three main attractions in the area; Uluṟu and Kata Tjuṯa being the other two. Standing at the base of the canyon, our strategy session began. When would be the best time of day to climb to the top and back? Early morning before the sun's heat set in or late in the day as the sun set? The canyon loop was a four-hour hike, and we had a lot to learn about desert mountain conditions.

We got back in the car and continued down the road to the campground. Fortunately, there was space available and the pool was a welcome sight. After checking in at the office, we found an empty campsite, a green space among the other campers, and set up our tent. First things first. It was time for a swim. The cool water was a pleasant surprise. Knowing how the sun can heat a pool, it was far from the "bath water" temperatures we were expecting. We alternated between dips in the pool and sitting in the shade of a tree, intermixed with an occasional side trip to the laundry room to keep our clothes moving through the cycles of wash and dry. It was good to get the sand and dirt out of my favorite shorts and tops.

As was our pattern after several days' worth of activities, Jeff and I took a time out. Only when I started to unwind did I realize how wound up I was. *Note to self: do less, be more. Time to slow down.* I declared it was time to have a "nothing day," a chance to catch up with myself and just be. At some point during the lazy afternoon, Jeff and I discussed the possibility of a 4:00 p.m. hike, but the idea was dropped as quickly as it came up. There was a short trail around the floor of the canyon that we considered taking at 7:00 p.m., but did nothing about that one either, and ended up lounging by the pool.

At dusk, a campground ranger walked through camp, answering questions and providing tips on how best to see the canyon. Acting as a concierge of sorts, friendly and generous with his information, he told us he was on his thirteenth week in the park. It was a "working holiday" for him, a perfect mix of work and play. "I'll be up at 'first light' (4:30 a.m.) to take the hike tomorrow morning," he said, "The sun will be hot by 9:00 a.m., and I want to be off the mountain by then." That was the four-hour trail up and into the canyon that Jeff and I were planning to take. "Maybe an early morning hike is the way to go," I suggested. But neither Jeff nor I expressed enthusiasm for the idea.

We've already decided to stay a second night. The air is cool, and we're expecting to sleep well in the tent under the stars.

Day 35, Tuesday   January 11, 2000

Last night was horrible. I think we got about two hours sleep. The campground was filled with the rowdiest group of people ever. All night long there was talking and laughter, people carrying on as if they were the only ones around. With or without the noise, Jeff and I were doomed to a night of discomfort. Despite all efforts to stay out of the direct sunlight, we were cooked and we were miserable. Add in the fact that ants crawled into our tent and inside of our bags— there were plenty of reasons to call the decision to leave Curtin Springs a bad one. A couple of fried, tired, cranky tourists we were, and it was not a pretty sight. "Any and all plans for a morning or evening hike are hereby cancelled," I declared with strong conviction, and then proceeded to pack up our green space. There was no stopping for breakfast, not even coffee. We couldn't get out fast enough. At 8:00 a.m., our only mission was to book ourselves into a reasonably priced hotel and regroup.

After discovering that our one and only air-conditioned sleeping option in Kings Canyon would cost $261 AU ($170 US) a night, the ninety-minute drive back to our favorite cattle station started to look pretty good. For the low cost of $70 AU ($46 US), all the conveniences we wanted were at Curtin Springs. In addition to the assorted collection of animals, gecko included, there were camel rides, horseback rides, helicopter tours, and desert outback tours to consider.

Upon our arrival, the Curtin Springs staff was happy to see us return and said that our room, old familiar #5, was still available. Sleep deprived and feeling the effects of the sun, Jeff and I slept a better part of the day with the air conditioner running full tilt. We woke up long enough to eat lunch, and then went back to the room to relax until dinner was ready. It wasn't until we had fully recovered that we understood what happened to us. The temperatures had reached well over 100 degrees in the "real outback" as they call it here. Jeff and I had no motivation to hike the canyon because we had no energy, and we had no energy because we were experiencing *heat exhaustion* and didn't realize it. I felt as if I had been doped, lulled into a peaceful, but dangerous state of mind. It was time to take the weather a bit more seriously.

Late in the day and off in the distance, a beautiful sunset was taking place, and I wondered if it was one of those great and colorful shows that tourists hope for while sipping champagne in the shadows of Uluru. As the air cooled, I could hear the pet emu making those strange drum noises deep in its throat, the same sound the emus made back at Wilpena Pound. The guinea pigs were enthusiastically munching on their fresh delivery of vegetables and fruit. The parrots were doing their nightly screeching, and I could hear the cattle making all kinds of strange noises deep in the outback. One of the cowboys told us, "The cows call to each other so they know they're not alone." The desert was alive with activity, and I realized we had joined the pattern of the outback. Stay still and quiet during the day and stir when the sun has set. This was the real deal. Curtin Springs may be out of the way, but it's worth every kilometer it takes to get here. Jeff and I may not be privy to the secrets within Uluru, but we have discovered one of the best kept secrets beyond Uluru.

Now to the complaint department: The Law of Duality ensures there is a flipside to life, and there are no exceptions. I'm going to be completely honest and put a rough and tough cattle ranch into perspective. There are basically two major drawbacks about being in the outback. First of all, it's the flies, those few insistent ones that constantly hover in my face and around my food while I eat. They are annoying, and they're giving me flashbacks of our visit to Rottnest Island. The second biggest nuisance on a cattle station is the billions, no trillions, of tiny black ants or "mingas," and I can see why Aborigines use that as a term of endearment for the tourists who love to visit their sacred land. Mingas are everywhere and in everything. There's a reality check if I ever saw one.

I read about the fly issue before leaving the 'States and came prepared. I bought two face nets at the local discount store for a dollar each and packed them away in our duffle bags. Jeff and I were doing our best to do as the locals and go without, but our patience has run out. The cowboys understand our intolerance. Face nets are sold for $7 in the Curtin Springs' convenience store. It's a bargain at any price to get some relief. We look silly wearing the nets, that's for sure, but all vanity has gone out the window. I might as well put a neon sign on my forehead that says "Tourist Here," and I really don't care.

I heard a joke about why Aussies shorten their words. There's a good chance it originated here in the "real outback." If a cowboy speaks too long and too expressively it will give a fly too much time to move in. That explains "g'day" for good morning, "strine" for Australian, "Freo" for Fremantle, "Chrissy" for Christmas, "Oz" for Australia, and the list goes on.

Yesterday at Kings Canyon was the first day we both came to our wit's end with all the buzzing, slapping and swatting. It was time to call in the reinforcements. Being the super prepared packer that I was, I had one more arsenal in my bag to combat the flies and other unforeseeable pests. I brought along a wide-brimmed hat, wider than my new linen one, and a full body net that draped over the hat and down to the ground creating my own peaceful space, sort of like a private tent. I could sit on the grass and read, write in my journal or watch the world go by all in the comfort of a bug-free space outdoors. I didn't care what I looked like. For all I knew, whoever saw me may have been wishing they had a hat tent of their own.

In the final evening hours, I sat next to "Kanga's" cage, the baby kangaroo outside our door. I was thinking about our climb into Kings Canyon.

Will tomorrow be the day we finally make the trek? After three meager attempts, I certainly hope so.

Day 36, Wednesday   January 12, 2000

It's taken us three days to prepare inside and out for our hike into Kings Canyon. Up until this morning, we've been all talk and very little action. No worries. We finally got our act together.

Rather than wake up at 3:00 a.m. to make the long drive, beat the heat and be done with the hike by 9:00 a.m., we decided to sleep in, take our time getting ready, and hike the canyon in the early evening hours. Rushing simply felt wrong. At 12:30 p.m., we filled our water bottles and left the cattle station after lunch. Thirty minutes down the road, we noticed we had left all the water jugs back in our room. Water was far too important to leave behind and there were no stores along the way, there was nothing along the way for that matter, so we turned around, knowing we still had enough daylight to finish the hike. Fortunately, neither one of us made an issue out of whose job it was to pack the water. We both forgot, so we calmly drove back, loaded the water into the car, and started all over again. We left the cattle station for the second time at 1:45 p.m. and arrived at the canyon floor two hours later. The drive was surprisingly cool, due to a rare desert thunderstorm that had moved into the area.

A fog developed and grew thicker the closer we got to the canyon. Our approach up to the trail's entrance was eerie, but we knew the weather was in our favor, and continued onward. Our decision to hike the later part of the day was already paying off. There were no forewarnings about the storm. We hadn't checked the local weather forecasts, not that we knew how, nor did we ask anyone at Curtin Springs what to expect on this particular day. We simply lucked out.

Minutes after our arrival, a mini-van pulled into the parking lot with ten young rowdy campers. Jeff and I assumed we were going to have company along the four-hour hike until we looked at the map. We saw that the trail was a loop and could be hiked clockwise or counter clockwise, though the clockwise loop was recommended.

The group chose the recommended approach. Jeff and I, being the rebels that we were, chose the opposite direction, and off we went.

The interesting thing about Kings Canyon is the way it's formed. Unlike our Grand Canyon which is viewed from the top looking down, Kings Canyon must be climbed first before the canyon is revealed. There is no option to drive up to the rim, but there is an option to fly overhead in a chartered plane or helicopter.

Made mostly of rock, the first part of the trail was relatively easy. It was well marked, and we had the appropriate shoes on. Ankle-supporting hiking boots were recommended, and we listened. Jeff and I each carried a gallon of water in our daypacks along with plenty of snacks to get us through. Thirty minutes into the hike the fog dissipated and we were high enough in elevation to get a fantastic view of the valley below. It was our first long-distance glimpse of the outback, and it was magnificent.

A second tour group was hiking their way down off the ridge and heading toward us. As they passed, they told us how their hike was cut short due to high winds and rain. "It was too cold at the top to stay for very long," one of them said. "Too cold." Now there's a summer outback condition we never expected to hear. Jeff and I agreed that forgetting the water turned out to be a good thing. We may have been driven off as well.

As we climbed higher up the mountain, Jeff spotted a rock wallaby. It blended in so well with the terrain that it was hard to see at first until my eyes adjusted. Known to be shy and elusive, the wallaby is also a marsupial and looks just like a kangaroo. I wasn't expecting to see any type of kangaroo above the desert floor. Watching it hop among the rocks was as surreal as seeing kangaroos on the beach.

When we reached the highest point of the climb, the mountain was flat at the top, making that part of the hike easier than the initial ascent. We were able to get a good look at the canyon before taking the trail down into the first level. Though it didn't come close in comparison to the size of our Grand Canyon, King's Canyon was equally as impressive, because the outback is virtually flat for miles around. Not a single fence or guard rail was installed to mark the canyon rims, and it was critical that we paid attention to where we were going. One false move...I did my best to take the thought out as fast as it came in and stayed clear of the ledge.

The first level of the canyon was worth every day, every mile, and every step it took to get there. Water was trapped in this part of the canyon, enabling palm and eucalyptus gum trees to grow in the crevices below. Lush green native plants filled the spaces in between, creating a strong contrast to the dry outback. There was no mistaking it, we had found what is know as the "Garden of Eden." What we couldn't find was the way in.

Since we were going in the direction opposite to what was recommended, the trail wasn't clearly marked for hikers going that way. Up until that point there were enough posted signs and arrows on the stone floor leading the way. We simply went in the opposite direction of the arrows. Our plan was working...until it wasn't anymore.

As if on cue, a guide suddenly appeared and was sitting on the rim of the canyon. He was from the bus group we saw in the parking lot. While the kids swam in the pools below, their leader had gone ahead to wait for them from a higher vantage point. The Aussie had made the hike countless times before and moved quickly along the path.

When we asked him where the trail was, he pointed straight down. Six inches below his feet was an iron stairway/ladder, similar to a fire escape, anchored into the solid rock wall of the canyon. We couldn't see the ladder from where we were standing and there were no signs from the direction we were going. The guide said, "This is the way to the Garden of Eden."

As we climbed down the series of ladders and stairs descending deep into the canyon, we could hear the birds singing louder and louder. Their songs were mixed with the sounds of the young hikers whooping and hollering in the natural pool below. The echoes were loud and clear.

Thanks to the afternoon storm, the canyon was unusually active for that time of day. Parrots, goldfinch-type birds, and canary-type birds were in the trees fully expressing themselves. The canyon created a natural aviary surrounded by rock, and the rock amplified every note. In addition to the birds, there were tiny black frogs sitting in puddles of water made by the rain. A beautiful little green frog, two inches long, with a bright yellow stripe near its eye, was particularly striking.

Climbing down to the base of the iron stairway, it was a pleasant surprise to find a dirt path on solid ground leading us into the garden. It was an easy walk, and five minutes into the trail, Jeff and I passed the noisy group as they were headed out. One of the young men stopped to give us a tip about the natural pool. He said, "If you swim across to the far side, you'll feel grass under the water. Don't freak out."

The second he started speaking I noticed he had an American accent, and I asked him where he was from. He said he was Canadian, and in that moment I realized how long it had been since we had spoken to anyone from our part of the globe. It was a strange familiarity, after nearly six weeks in Australia, to hear someone, other than ourselves, speak with a North American accent. In the same way the music transported me to another place in time, so did this accent. I got my focus back in time to hear the Canadian say, "When you get to the end of the pool, continue on. Walk over the rocks, sand, and past the trees to another smaller pool beyond. The view is spectacular."

It took another ten minutes to get to the pool in the Garden of Eden. When we arrived, there was yelling at the top of the ridge. I looked up in time to see the group leaving from the place where Jeff and I had stood moments earlier.

Because of the storm and lack of cars in the parking lot, we figured we were the last ones to hike in and there was a good chance we had the canyon to ourselves. Fortunately, the air had warmed to the point where swimming sounded like a good idea. We didn't know there was swimming involved, so we weren't prepared, but it didn't matter. Leaving our clothes in a heap on the rocks (and making the bold assumption there were no other visitors in the park), Jeff and I jumped into the water. I heard a yell from above. It was that same group. Three stragglers hadn't quite "left the building" yet and were cheering us on as we entered the Garden of Eden as only a man and woman should, sans swimsuits. I was grateful for the distance between us and them and the muddy waters stirred up by the rain.

The water felt cool and refreshing. As instructed, Jeff and I swam to the other side, and I felt the grass beneath my feet. Thanks to the warning, I climbed out without freaking out and made it to the other side, avoiding as much of the sliminess as possible. I'm sure I would have thought the grass was a bunch of snakes if the Canadian hadn't told us what to expect.

Barefoot, I made it over the stones and through the trees to the second pool. It was exactly as the Canadian described: another sandy shore followed by another, smaller pool of water. This second pool wasn't visible from where we stood on the rim of the first one. It was highly probable that we would have missed it, and that would have been a great misfortune. Because at the edge of this smaller pool, nature's masterful version of the infinity pool, there was a ledge overlooking a deeper, broader section of the canyon, and the valley below was indeed *spectacular*. It was a part of the park we didn't know existed. Flanked by sheer rock walls and filled with natural overgrowth, it was breathtaking.

Knowing that time was a factor because the sun was beginning to set, we had only been in the Garden of Eden twenty minutes when I felt a sense of urgency to head back up and out of the canyon. I had no idea why, but I said to Jeff, "We have to go." While swimming back through the larger pool, I reminded myself to take a moment to look around and just be. For a few brief seconds, nothing else mattered and nothing else existed, and then it was over all too soon. The sense of urgency returned as I swam to the water's edge.

When I got to the rock wall, I couldn't get out of the pool. It didn't help that I was rushing and still unclear as to what was driving me out. Algae covered the part of the rock below the water line, making it slick and difficult to get a foot hold. There wasn't much to grab onto or step on above or below the water, and the upper ledge was too high to reach from where I was. It was easy getting into the pool because gravity had been in my favor. I wasn't so fortunate getting out, and the sense of urgency grew stronger. Taking another deep breath, I focused on finding the tiniest of ridges and gripped one after the other with the tips of my fingers. Where there's a will there's a way, and I managed to pull myself up onto the ledge. Jeff climbed out after me and had a much easier time of it. Looking back it would've made sense to wait for Jeff and have him help me out, but I was in a panic and I wasn't thinking clearly.

We dried ourselves off, dressed, gathered our things, and got back on the trail. The sky was darkening. We crossed over the bridge to the west ridge and climbed the iron stairs up and out at the opposite side of the canyon from where we entered. The birds' activity and energy was increasing and getting noisier with each passing minute. The parakeets in particular were making quite a ruckus under an overhang, and it sounded as if they were laughing at me.

It started to rain. Jeff and I got soaked, but it didn't matter. The air remained warm, and we were on the move. Painted on the rocks were green arrows that kept us on the trail and going in the right direction, as long as we went the opposite way they were pointing. It was interesting to see how different the western side of the canyon was compared to the eastern side. There were strange dome-shaped rock formations along the way, unlike anything we had seen up to that point.

As we began our descent off the ridge, we watched as the clouds parted on the horizon, exposing the setting sun. A massive orange beam of sunlight suddenly appeared and shot straight into the very spot where we had been swimming. Seconds later, east of the orange beam, a rainbow formed over the canyon's ridge. It grew brighter and stronger with a deep dark pink edge moving closer and closer toward the pool. Then a second rainbow appeared over the first creating a double. They hovered in the sky for ten minutes before disappearing into the returning clouds. "So that's what the sense of urgency was all about," I thought, "We needed to be on the other side of the canyon to see the show."

While the rainbows' stay was short, the colors of the sunset lingered on the horizon. Instead of heading down off the ridge, Jeff and I decided there was enough daylight to climb 50 yards back up the mountain to get another longer look at the setting sun. Orange rays, stretching out for miles, were shooting straight up from the earth and into the clouds. It was one of those sunsets the outback was famous for.

By the time we watched the final colors set, we knew we were pushing our luck with the remaining daylight. We had less than one hour to get back to the car before the sky turned pitch black. Our one comfort came from knowing we had brought flashlights with us, so we could see the trail markings and find our way out, but it was never our intention to be on the mountain after dark.

Thinking we were focused and finally on a mission to hike down with a steady pace, Jeff and I came to a standstill when a tiny marsupial mouse came out from beneath the rocks. The mouse was curious, but cautious, three inches tall, and as cute as could be. It stood only two feet away from us. We knew it was marsupial because the trail brochure described it as such, otherwise it would have looked like any other wild mouse. If I had seen a little baby poke its head out of its mother's pouch, I would have thought I was in a fairytale for sure.

With our 30-second distraction behind us, we headed back to the car. Jeff and I wanted to reach the canyon floor as quickly as possible. The steepest part of the trail was in the last 50 yards, and it was a challenge to finish. This side of the ridge was much steeper than our climb up at the start of the loop. A set of rock stairs had been cut out of the mountain to make the trail manageable, but it was a tough way to end the hike. My legs were shaking and wobbly, and I was relieved when we finally hit the solid wide path leading to the parking lot.

Covering four miles in four hours, including pool time, Jeff and I successfully completed the trail. We never did see another soul once that last group with the guide and the Canadian left the ridge, and there was enough daylight left that we didn't need our flashlights. Bats appeared in the sky offering a glimpse of the nocturnal side of life in and around the canyon. When we finally got back to the car it was 8:00 p.m.

Deep into 'roo and cattle country, Jeff drove with caution so he would have time to break for any sudden crossings. Cows roamed freely in this part of the outback, and we could hear them calling to one another off in the distance. Grazing boundaries were few and far between, and fences were scarce. For all we knew, those cows could've belonged to Curtin Springs Cattle Station.

On the drive home, we came across one lonely brown-and-white bull, standing like a statue in the middle of the road. Jeff came to a stop, honked the horn, and blinked the lights. He thought that would be all the encouragement the bull needed to finish crossing the road, but it didn't budge. Standing in the glare of the headlights, he gave us a clear view of his profile, and with that wide set of horns, it was quite a sight. Before we got out of the car to physically herd the bull across the road, Jeff got the idea to turn the headlights off. It worked. The bull snapped out of its trance and ran off the road into the desert. As Jeff drove the rest of the way home, we watched lightning flash along the horizon, so far away, we couldn't hear the thunder.

There's a whole lot more to Kings Canyon than we were able to see in one day. I added another unique experience to the revisit list.

Day 37, Thursday   January 13, 2000

My legs hurt so much they would hardly move when I tried to get out of bed. I thought I was prepared for a mountain hike. We've been active the whole trip, but whatever muscles were required to climb up and down hills were the weakest ones I had. The walk down is what taxed me the most. As with many good intentions, the one about getting in shape before leaving for Australia remained a good intention. I suppose I could give myself a little more credit. Things had been going well up until this morning.

At breakfast we talked about our experience with the weather and how the forces of nature worked to our advantage. The cool air, refreshing rain, and laser light-show at the end, double rainbow included, made it a day to add to the "best day ever" list. We asked the Curtin Springs staff how many thunderstorms they usually saw throughout the summer months. The cook answered, "We get about six cloudy days a year. Yesterday's storm was a fluke."

The time had finally come to leave Curtin Springs for good. With sore muscles and tired bones, we packed up and headed east and then due north to our next destination of Alice Springs. Also known as "The Alice," the town holds a population of approximately 25,500. We knew it would have everything we needed to replenish our supplies and give us a good dose of civilization. We had been in the triangle of Kings Canyon, Uluṟu and Kata Tjuṯa for five days and six nights. Our pattern dictated that five days in any one place was our limit, and Jeff and I were ready to move on. Besides, the Great Barrier Reef was calling.

The drive from Curtin Springs to Alice Springs took four hours, and that included a side trip to a camel farm to take photographs and enjoy an ice cold bottle of water. We saw our first ostrich in Oz, living on the camel farm, and it signaled the move into new territory. Rolling into town at 1:00 p.m., it was early enough in the day to check into a motel and still have time to drop off the 18 rolls of film to be processed. *Six hundred and forty-eight, that's how many pictures I've taken since arriving in Sydney over a month ago.* I was looking forward to seeing if the camera could translate what we had seen with our own eyes.

Thanks to our trusty *Lonely Planet Travel Guide*, we found a reasonably priced motel, called the Melanka Lodge, at the edge of town. In addition to a nice room, there was a laundromat, pool, and an Internet café called Byte Me. The dog on the logo was cute. We hadn't checked emails since our stay in Coober Pedy, and I was anxious to hear from family and friends back home. Once the car was unloaded, Jeff and I cooled off in our air conditioned room before heading back into 3-digit temps.

Walking through downtown, we noticed that the heart of Alice Springs was only five blocks long. Being the gateway to Uluru or Ayers Rock, I envisioned a much larger town. I was happy to see several photo-processing stores to choose from sitting along the main drag because Jeff and I had plans to stay one night and be on our way once the photos were ready. With less than 4 hours, I divided the rolls between two stores, to guarantee the pictures would be done by morning. The photo clerks in both stores assured me they could get the job done in time.

While I was taking care of the film, Jeff went off to find Chinese take-away. Once both errands were complete, we drove back to our room. We were beyond tired and hungry by the time we ate. After lunch, I thought I would be ready for an afternoon siesta, but the food gave me enough energy to sit in the Byte Me Internet Café for a couple of hours to catch up with emails. I had a lot to write home about, and I was excited to share our most recent adventures.

At 8:30 p.m., Jeff and I indulged in the convenience of watching an in-house movie in our very own room.

Out of the outback and into the lap of luxury. We've got a comfortable bed, soft sheets, our own private bath, air conditioning, and television. It's exactly what the doctor ordered for my sore aching muscles and weary mind.

This is what I call five-star accommodations. Alright, maybe not five, but it's a big step up from where we've been over the past few weeks.

Day 38, Friday   January 14, 2000

We slept so well last night we decided to stay another day in civilization, before heading northeast to the tropical state of Queensland. I liked the idea of working out the muscle soreness with a few more walks around town before another marathon car ride.

When we reach our third and final destination, it will mean we have traveled the same distance as it is between Topeka, Kansas and Boston, Massachusetts. We've allotted the better part of three days because of the nighttime 'roo factor, and the heat of the day will surely wear us down. Every passing kilometer is going to move us deeper into the humidity, closer to the rainforest, and we know all too well how humidity intensifies heat. Queensland sits where New England sits on the map at home, but the conditions are more like Costa Rica.

With our second night secured at the Melanka Lodge, it was time to go into town and pick up the photos. Jeff wanted to lounge awhile longer in the cool air of our motel room and chose to stay back, while I went into town.

When the clerk in the second camera store handed me the large batch of photos, she said with genuine sincerity, "You have some really good pictures here." Two other clerks gathered around and said, "Yeah, we thought they were great." Thousands of photos of Uluru and the outback run through those machines on a daily basis, due to all the tour groups passing through. I couldn't wait to see what they were talking about.

Rather than bring all the pictures back to the room as planned, I took a seat on the first bench I could find and flipped through the 18 batches of photos. It was strange looking at those first few sets I took on the train to Perth and then later on Rottnest Island, almost like looking at another vacation from another time. So much had transpired since then.

The polarizing filter I used on the camera lens helped mute the brightness of the desert sun and deepened the colors of the outback. The photos were definitely keepers, and it was worth the $200 AU ($130 US) I invested in processing. The pictures turned out so well, I returned to that second store to buy another ten rolls, ensuring I would have enough for the remaining two-and-a-half weeks. With film and photos in hand, I headed back to the Melanka Lodge. Jeff sifted through the photos and agreed that they were capturing the trip nicely. Once everything was put away, it was time to head back into town. We wanted to see more of "The Alice."

At 11:30 a.m., the temperature felt hotter than it did in the outback. We couldn't believe it. *Just how hot does it get here?* As often as I recalculated north to south, Celsius to Fahrenheit, and January to summer, it was still a challenge to keep my expectations in proper perspective. "It's supposed to be getting cooler!" my logical mind broadcasted.

While walking through town, I told Jeff about the odd conversation I had with the photo clerks when I was buying more film. It had nothing to do with pictures and everything to do with peeing. One of the clerks was talking to another one about their "pissing contest." I was too curious to ignore what I was hearing and asked one of them to explain. The woman laughed and said, "In the middle of the summer, we hold a contest among the staff to see who can drink the most water without having to go to the bathroom. The air is so dry and hot that the fluids evaporate from our pores faster than we're able to fill our bladders. It isn't about who can hold it the longest, it's more a question of who really needs to go?"

I was finishing my story when we walked into a hat shop called Centre Shade, a name inspired by its location in "The

Red Centre." (Red Centre is spelled both ways, Center and Centre, depending on whether it's of a British or American influence.) The store was filled with authentic Australian hats, the kind I had been looking for since leaving Perth on January 1st. A friend of mine, upon hearing about my trip to the outback, put in a very specific order for an Akubra, a true Aussie cowboy cattle driving "drover" hat. I thought it would be an easy order to fill and gladly said "Yes," but it's taken me awhile to finally find one.

There it was; the last hat in the right size at the right price. A hat badge with a camel in the middle of it completed the order. I was relieved to be able to cross that one off my list of things to do, because time was running out. We were about to leave cowboy country and head into the tropics. I was grateful that the shop owner was extra patient with me, as I took my time making sure I got exactly the right hat. Returns were not an option. At the last second, the owner threw in an extra hat badge for me, because of my accent. I will always remember that.

After we returned to the lodge, Jeff headed for the pool and spent the afternoon sitting in the shade. The water was refreshing, but I chose to stay out of the heat and relax in our room with the air conditioning. I told Jeff, "We'll be back in the elements soon enough. I'm taking advantage of the cool air while we have it." A/C was fast becoming a rare and precious luxury. While in the room, I read the local brochures and learned a few interesting things about Alice Springs.

The classic novel by Nevil Shute, called A Town Like Alice, *published in 1950, is what put Alice Springs on the map. For as small as it is, it's one of the most famous towns in Australia. One of the biggest attractions in "The Alice" is the Henley-on-Todd Regatta, the world's first and only waterless boat race. Yep, waterless. It takes place on the Todd River, a dry river bed just outside of town. Contestants build bottomless boats and then run them from start to finish. There are several creative and hilarious events throughout the day, all in the name of fun and to raise money for a good cause.*

Rotary International, the local chapter in Alice Springs, started the event in the early 1960's, and the race has become an annual event ever since. The regatta takes place in the cooler months of August, September or October depending on the year. Only once did they have to cancel. In 1993 there was a flood, and the dry river bed turned into a wet river bed. Can't have that. Any and all are encouraged to participate in a wide variety of events, and from what I can tell, it's a day to remember.

Relatively speaking, Jeff and I enjoyed a lazy day and it was wonderful. We found a used bookstore right across the street from our home away from home, and, together we bought three books to read in the days ahead.

I know this is going to be the last night in total comfort for a while, so I'm going to read myself to sleep. Who knows how long it will be before we have a situation this good?

Day 39, Saturday   January 15, 2000

As a morning person, getting up at 8:00 a.m. is the equivalent of sleeping in, and this morning we slept in. Afterall, we are on vacation. For breakfast, we ate pears, apples, and peaches bought at a stand across the street. That was one more reason to add Melanka Lodge to our list of favorite places to stay. *Lonely Planet* steered us in the right direction again. The lodge offered comfort, amenities, and location all rolled into one.

With every stitch of clothing washed and neatly packed, Jeff and I loaded the back of the station wagon with the same precision we had done since leaving Perth. We had a system to make it easy for us to get what we needed when we needed it, and it was always a good feeling to get everything back in its place. *I love a fresh start.*

"Next item on the agenda is to get the car fixed," Jeff said. He must have been mulling that one over in his mind while he lounged by the pool yesterday, because he knew exactly what to do. Looking through the local phone book, Jeff found the name and address of a garage that serviced Fords. We headed across town to see if someone could help with the damaged headlight. We used local maps to find our way and discovered how easy it was to navigate through town. The roads were laid out clearly and logically, and the drive over was a breeze. The most unusual thing we saw along the way was a posted speed limit that read, "No Speed Limit." *There's one that will never show up on a roadway in America.*

The mechanic told us that the whole light fixture needed to be replaced, because the housing unit was bent out of shape. That was the bad news. The good news was he thought he had the parts in stock. He said, "These old Fords are quite common in Australia. I know exactly what you need." After a thorough search in the back of the garage, he returned to say, "I'm sorry. I don't have the right headlight afterall." Knowing we were passing through, he said, "No worries. I'll make a few phone calls and see if I can get the parts delivered this morning." I sensed a genuine concern for a speedy resolution to our problem.

No one nearby had what he needed, but he told us his records indicated an order for those exact same headlights was placed a few days ago. A shipment was on its way. With our agreement, he ended up selling us a headlight right out of one of his own vehicles. Used parts and installation came to $100.00 AU ($65 US), the same amount Jeroen allotted for the repair.

"It'll take about an hour," the mechanic told us, "The ideal place to wait is in an air conditioned café two blocks down the road." He pointed us in the direction of food and coffee, and off we went. It was still morning, and the temperature was rising fast. The second we stepped into the café there was immediate relief. We ordered a light breakfast, the second one of the day, admired the fresh flowers on the tables, and were pleasantly surprised to smell real coffee brewing.

The hour went by fast, and the car was ready as promised. But before leaving Alice Springs, we had a nice talk with the mechanic. We told him where we were from, and he surprised us with the fact that he used to live in Florida and knew the state well. When I asked him why he moved back to Australia, he said he missed his family and friends and preferred living in the outback. Maybe they have a saying, "You can take the boy out of the outback, but you can't take the outback out of the boy."

He went on to tell us that Alice Springs had its own version of "Area 51" run by the United States Government. (Area 51 is a top secret military base rumored to house aliens and alien spacecraft on a secret air base in the Nevada desert.) He said, "The site is called Pine Gap, and it's as heavily guarded and secretive as Area 51. No one really knows what goes on in there. Over a thousand U.S. citizens are employed. They're probably listening to us right now," and then he stopped, his eyes searching overhead and around the garage as if checking for wire taps. Jeff and I looked at each other as we put two-and-two together. I told the mechanic, "We've been hearing stories about UFO sightings in the outback, but we didn't take them seriously." The mechanic confessed that the locals weren't too comfortable with all the secrecy surrounding Pine Gap, and the general feeling was that they wanted the United States Government out of the area. I didn't ask why.

With our headlight repaired, supplies replenished, a full tank of gas, and a new story to tell our friends back home, it was time to say good-bye to "Alice." Jeff and I were anxious to get the first leg of our three-day ride to Queensland behind us.

Along the way, we made the fuel stops short because we got such a late start. Jeff did most of the driving, and I studied up on the telegraph stations that were in the area.

The Overland Telegraph Line was built in 1870, so that Australia and England could communicate through overland and undersea cables. Morse Code was used to transmit the messages, and repeater stations using primitive batteries kept communications open. Telegraph stations are a main attraction in this part of Australia, due to their historic significance, and to be honest, there isn't much else out here. Sadly, Australia's history is darkened by the murders that took place around these stations, as Aborigines opposed the encroachment and bad behavior of the British. Many telegraph operators lost their lives in the line of duty (and off-duty) during the late 1800's early 1900's. In retaliation, a higher number of Aborigines were killed.

Along the way, we made the second strangest stop of our journey (Coober Pedy being the first) in a town called Wycliffe Well, aka: "UFO Capitol of Australia." The owner is an artist and expressed his talents through murals of UFOs and aliens. The brochure said the Caravan Park (campground) next door displayed additional drawings, but Jeff and I didn't take the time to see them all. Life-size statues of an alien family landing at the "UFO landing site" were outside the café. Inside, were dozens of articles about alien sightings, and copies of those articles were available for sale. Wycliffe Well claimed to be a hot spot for alien activity and was Australia's version of Roswell, New Mexico, the famous site of an alleged 1947 UFO crash that resulted in an alleged massive government cover up.

We couldn't help notice Wycliffe Well's close proximity to Pine Gap. As we were leaving the alien town, Jeff told me about three white lights he saw high up in the sky while driving between Alice Springs and Wycliffe Well. In broad daylight, he could see lights moving along in an "L" formation. Jeff was familiar with military aircraft, yet had no explanation as to what he saw. "It was all very odd, and I had a strong feeling it was something different," he said. "It was different," he repeated, and left it at that. I had been asleep in the back seat and missed everything.

Fifteen minutes down the road from "Roswell" was Devils Marbles. Devils Marbles are nearly perfect spheres of rock, balanced in, what appears to be, precarious positions, but they are anchored and stable. Formed over time, these huge sand stone boulders erode under the desert sun, rain, and wind. Aborigines say that in the Dreaming a Rainbow Serpent laid her eggs there. The Rainbow Serpent is found in many Dreaming legends and is believed to have made the river beds and mountains in northern Australia. It also governs life's most precious resource, water.

The area reminded me of the Flintstones. Both comical and fascinating, Devils Marbles looked as if it could have been the real life set of the famous cartoon. Jeff and I took some fun photos and got back in the car to continue on to our evening's destination, Tennant Creek. Termite mounds appeared along the way, giving us additional changes in scenery. The mounds were basically narrow piles of dirt, two to three feet high. I was able to identify them because there were matching pictures in the travel guide.

A few roaming clouds offered periodic relief from the intense desert heat, and we rolled into Tennant Creek at 6:45 p.m. It was a good day's drive, and "Mum's Taxi" was holding up well. We found the local YHA Backpackers Lodge and checked in. The town reminded me of a scaled down version of Coolgardie, with its saloon-style buildings. The minute we arrived I knew we were in for a treat.

YHA Backpackers Lodge was within walking distance of a steakhouse on the main street. The restaurant was nothing like the cowboy kitchen at the Curtin Springs Cattle Station, but just as authentic when it came to an outback steakhouse, and more of what I expected one to look like. It was dark inside. There were hardwood floors, tall ceilings, poor lighting, and the bar was the center of attention. There were plenty of customers, too, signaling to us that the food was going to be delicious. I enjoyed a large serving of homemade leek and sweet potato soup, complete with freshly baked bread, and Jeff ate a steak big enough for the both of us. He said it was one of the best he had ever eaten in his life.

While in the restaurant, the mystery of "singlets" was revealed. Quite often signs were posted on restaurant walls reading, "No Singlets," but we didn't know what they meant. My theory was that it had something to do with dining alone, so when I finally asked the waitress what a "singlet" was, thinking it had something to do with taking a whole table to oneself when a barstool was available, she pointed to me and said, "It's what you're wearing sweetie." I felt my face flush with embarrassment with the newfound knowledge that I was breaking an outback rule, and I was mortified. Ever since landing in Sydney, I had done my best to learn the customs and manners of a country that had welcomed me as their guest, and there I was being disrespectful. Our server saw the look on my face and quickly explained that the message was primarily aimed at men. A singlet is a tank top, and restaurants want their male customers to wear shirts with sleeves. It's similar to the "no shirt, no shoes, no service" policy often seen in restaurants and shops back home. I was grateful they didn't kick me out. All my singlets have spaghetti straps, and I had been wearing one every day since we headed north.

After dinner, we walked back to our room, took showers in the community bathrooms down the hall, and turned in for an early night's sleep.

"I'm going to wear a top over my singlet from now on," I silently vowed. "I don't want to go through that again."

Day 40, Sunday   January 16, 2000

We drove 700 km (434 miles) today. That was our second longest drive to date. It was also the hottest day I have ever experienced in my life.

In a car with no air conditioning, I question our decision to take on the Northern Territory and Queensland in the summer, but truth be told, I wouldn't have it any other way.

It's the thrill of the challenge that keeps us going. Jeff has done most of the driving, and I really appreciate it. I am still a bit nervous about driving on the left side of the road, and those road trains are as big and fast up North as they are in the South.

The used books we found back in Alice Springs are getting dog-eared. I've really enjoyed being able to stretch out on the back seat during the long drives, feel the wind in my hair, and read the day away. There was a moment on the last stretch of highway we crossed, when the air got so hot it was difficult to breathe. Rather than fight against the elements, I decided to minimize the struggle. For ten seconds at a time, I paused at the exhale before taking in another full breath. Time shifted down a notch, and I was content to lie still and watch my hair blow in all directions.

I've heard people talk about what it's like to nearly drown and then return from the brink of death. They describe the event as a strangely peaceful one, once they give in and surrender to the finality of it all. In the extreme heat of the day, nearly suffocating in 3-digit temperatures, I got an odd sense of what it may have been like for them. I never felt as if my life was in danger. I was still breathing when I wanted to, always enough air to stay conscious. But it was surreal.

From what we could tell, the highway between Tennant Creek, Northern Territory and Townsville, Queensland on the east coast was called the Flinders Highway, but there seemed to be discrepancies depending on which travel guide we read.

Matthew Flinders was a busy guy. One could say he really got around. Not only is there a mountain range named after him (the Flinders Ranges), there's also another Flinders Highway in South Australia—not to be confused with the Flinders Highway in the north. They are miles apart from one another.

Sometime during the day, we crossed the Northern Territory/Queensland border and pulled into Mount Isa (pronounced mount eye-za) at 5:15 p.m., early enough to take our time in finding a good hotel. We had been spoiled back in Alice Springs, and we wanted another upgrade.

"The Isa," as the locals know it, is an active mining town in the northwest corner of Queensland. It's also the birthplace of the famous pro-golfer, Greg Norman. With a population of approximately 21,000, it's similar in size to "The Alice" though the two cities look entirely different. Mount Isa appears to have far more than 21,000 residents, while Alice Springs looks as if there are fewer in number than reported. Both are considered major cities.

Jeff and I have learned to ask a lot of questions before checking into a motel or hostel having learned the hard way that things are not always as they seem. Questions such as, "Do you have private rooms? A double bed? Are the showers in the room or down the hall?" were always on the list. Once we had a satisfactory answer, then and only then did we look at the room. We often found a suitable place to stay within the first or second attempt, but it took three tries to find a winner in Mount Isa. It was the Mount Isa Outback Motor Inn, and the room came complete with two bug-eating geckos. What a friendly and hard working species they are.

After washing off the day's dirt and grime in the luxury of our own private bath in our beautiful room, Jeff and I walked over to the motel's restaurant. It was a short distance across the parking lot from the main building to the dining room. Gazing up at the sky, we saw the *biggest* bats we had ever seen in our lives. They must have had a 2-foot wingspan. It was dusk, and we could see dozens of them flying at treetop level. The ones that were directly overhead gave a perfect bat silhouette. All I kept thinking was, "I am so glad we're sleeping inside tonight."

The interior of the restaurant looked strangely familiar to us. And then it dawned on me, "They're playing country western!" I said. That's when we noticed license plates from all fifty states and the nation's capital, Washington, D.C., hanging on the walls. The Mount Isa Outback Motor Inn restaurant carried an American theme, and we really got a kick out of it. In that moment, I developed a new awareness and appreciation for all the ethnic restaurants back home. I finally realized how much comfort those restaurants must bring to our foreign visitors and immigrants. "Maybe this is how Aussies feel when they step into an Outback Steakhouse," I thought. *Now there's a turnaround.*

The restaurant did a great job serving traditional American food, and I enjoyed another bowl of homemade vegetable soup with a side of freshly baked bread. It was absolutely delicious, and exactly what I needed— nourishment for the body *and* soul.

When Jeff returned from a late night walk by the pool, he said, "There are two gigantic frogs outside and they're really cool looking." If it wasn't for the gigantic bats, I might have gone out to take a look.

PART SIX

Queensland
Paradise, Koalas, and the
Great Barrier Reef

"Faith never knows where it is being led,
but it knows and loves the One who is leading."
Oswald Chambers, 1874-1917
Scottish Minister

Day 41, Monday   January 17, 2000

We woke up at 7:00 a.m. to check the map to see how far it
was to get to David's farm in El Arish. According to our
calculations it was thirteen hours away. If we really wanted
to, we could arrive at his front step before midnight. That
was an *ah-ha* moment. I thought, "We're close. We're really,
really close."

   David wasn't expecting us for another four days, so there
was no reason to rush. It would behoove us to enjoy the
sights along the way. Surely there were places to go and
people to meet between Mount Isa and El Arish. The
bustling coastal city of Townsville was due east of Mount Isa
and marked the end of the Flinders Highway. It was also the

point where we would turn left to head up the coast to David's.

We considered making Townsville our goal of the day until we did the math and saw it was 903 km (561 miles) and would take eleven hours. That was too far and too rushed, so we agreed it was best to divide the drive in half and make two easy days out of it. With another leisurely morning placed on our agenda, we became Mount Isa tourists for half a day so we could see what an outback mining town had to offer.

Mount Isa sits alongside Highway 66, another name for the Flinders Highway. That one main thoroughfare connecting the desert outback with the tropics of Queensland carries several different names, but it's "Highway 66" that has my attention. U.S. Route 66, one of the most famous roads in America, was made popular by the 1950's and '60's television show "Route 66" and a song by the same name. The highway starts in Chicago, Illinois, and takes travelers all the way to Los Angeles, California. It's been slowly replaced by the Interstate Highway system and takes a bit of detective work to find it today. Could it be that the American restaurant we found last night was inspired by this connection?

There were several attractions we wanted to take advantage of before leaving town, but first things first. We checked out of our room, headed downtown in search of breakfast, and along the way discussed our options for the morning. We noticed how drastically the landscape had changed over the past two days. There were hills and valleys and more green than we had seen in a very long time.

There was no mistaking that mining was the core industry in Mount Isa. A huge industrial plant sat on the edge of town, where lead, iron, and silver, recently harvested from the rich landscape, were processed. While we ate our toast and cereal, the waitress told us that blasting occurred on a regular basis. "You can't miss it," she said. "At precisely

7:50 a.m. and 7:50 p.m., every twelve hours around the clock, the miners set off huge explosions. The evening blasts are *the best*. Everything shakes."

In addition to the rich ore minerals, fossils were significant to the area. There's an exhibit called Riversleigh Fossils Interpretive Center, and we made it the first item on our agenda. Because the coffee at the restaurant was on the weak side, we stopped at McDonald's on the way to the museum. McD's was one place we could always count on for a strong cup, and if a town was big enough to have a McD's, we were sure to find it. The second we walked through the doors, I was shocked to see a familiar face behind the counter. I said, "I know you!" It turned out to be our server from the night before, and I thought, "What a hard worker she is."

The Riversleigh Fossils Interpretive Center turned out to be a small exhibit, but it delivered big time. Filled with life-size models of creatures discovered in stone, the center had recorded over two hundred species of animals never known before on earth and unique only to the island continent of Australia. The species that fascinated me the most were the marsupial lions and rhinos. The idea that lions and rhinos carried their young like kangaroos do today was stranger than strange. They walked the land millions of years ago and were long extinct, but through the marvels of earth and science their stories could be told. The message throughout the exhibit was that Archaeological digs continue to this day, and it's quite possible that more fascinating species will be discovered as technology advances.

After our walk through the interpretive center, we headed downtown to see what was there. I found a stationery shop and remembered my father's birthday was coming up in three weeks. I wasn't going to be home in time to mail it from the 'States, so I decided to mail a card from Mount Isa. "He'll enjoy adding the Australian postmark and stamp to his collection," I thought. Not knowing how long a letter would take to get out of the outback and into the 'States, I figured I would stay on the safe side if I mailed it right away. The card should reach its destination in plenty of time.

The local post office was right around the corner from the card shop, and the deed was done in a matter of minutes. I've always known our United States postage was a better deal than the world's average. After factoring in the exchange rate, postage was in fact much higher in Australia than at home. When I was a postal clerk I used to hear complaints about the cost of stamps being too high. Those customers simply didn't know how good they had it. I tried to educate them, but a mind made up is a mind made up.

There was surely more to this town than an eighteen hour visit could possibly reveal, but we were anxious to get to the coast, and Townsville won out. We were about to complete our sea-to-sea circuit, crossing Australia from one end to the other, and were on the home stretch.

"On the road again," as the Willy Nelson song goes, played in my head. I noticed that the two-lane highway was becoming narrower and the speeds were increasing with every passing kilometer—not the safest of combinations. At times, there was barely enough room for two cars to pass. I fully expected the road to widen as we got closer to the coast of Queensland, but the opposite was happening. Every time we saw a road train coming, and they could often be seen a mile away with as many as three trailers in tow, Jeff would pull off to the side of the road, come to a complete stop, and give way, as if it was an emergency vehicle on route to an accident. Road trains commanded a wide birth, always carrying the tacit message, "Get out of the way. I'm comin' through!"

The closer we got to the Pacific coastline, the greener and more beautiful the countryside became. Creeks and river beds actually had water in them, and I grew more excited with every passing hour at the thought of exploring the rainforest and snorkeling the Great Barrier Reef. When we reached the town of Richmond somewhere between Mount Isa and Townsville, another "middle-of-nowhere" kind of place, we found it odd that there were only a few cars traveling in that stretch of the Flinders Highway. I was sure there would be more traffic.

We were looking forward to Richmond because it was described as having "The best fossil museum in Australia." A title like that deserved attention, and we headed straight for the main attraction. Our expectations were met on Kronosaurus Korner. There was a huge life-sized statue of a water dinosaur called Kronosaurus queenlandicus on the museum's front lawn. It looked like a giant alligator, and the head alone was twelve feet long.

The original Kronosaurus queenlandicus was discovered in the mid 1920's by the owner of an outback cattle station called "Army Downs." The owner was able to get word to a team of paleontologists at Harvard University who, upon hearing the news, took great interest in the project. They traveled half way around the world (no small feat in the 1920's) and took on the pain-staking work of excavating the 42-foot creature. The dinosaur was evidence that this vast area surrounding Richmond, millions of acres, was once part of Australia's inland sea and completely submerged under water over 100 million years ago. Other station owners have found prehistoric treasures as well.

Fossicking, the Coober Pedy sport of sifting through sand in search of fossils and gems, was advertised as the thing to do while visiting Richmond. Unfortunately, we were unable to participate in any of the local activities because the museum was closed. Most everything in Oz closed at 5:00 p.m. sharp, so we should've known better than to assume otherwise. It was 5:25 when we got to the door. The huge Kronosaurus on the front lawn had the same appearance as the giant whale in Eucla, Western Australia and the giant galah (pink cockatoo) we saw in Kimba, South Australia. All three were a bit rough around the edges, and I got the feeling the same artist was commissioned to create each one, possibly securing the work as he or she drove a similar route to the one we just did. I may have chuckled at the craftsmanship, not that I could possibly have done any better, but those landmarks were doing their job to get our attention. In the land of advertising, *attention* is everything.

During a short planning session in front of the locked museum doors, Jeff and I considered staying in Richmond, so we could see the exhibit first thing in the morning. But our attempts at finding a place to stay proved futile. Either we didn't know where to look or Richmond could use a few more hotels, because it didn't have much to offer. Car camping was not an option.

Breaking safety rule number one, we drove the last ninety minutes in the dark before reaching our next destination. It was a good thing Jeff drove slowly because we saw two kangaroos cross the road and through the light of our high beams. It was always a thrill to see a "big red" in the wild, hopping the way they do. All I could think was, "I really want to bring my sister to Australia one day. She has got to see this!"

We arrived in Hughenden, Queensland at 9:10 p.m. and found a funky motel where the desk clerk passed our question-and-answer session. The motel was cool, clean, and inexpensive—always a winning combination.

Those final minutes on the road brought us so close to the South Pacific Ocean that I could feel and smell the sea air. We had 600 km (373 miles) between us and David's farm, and as I read the directions to his house, I once again tried to make sense out of it. The doubter inside continued to question our ability to find him without further assistance.

The email read, "Turn at the second dirt road and park the car in the first clearing you see to the left of the road. Walk through the creek and up the stone steps leading to my house." I'm not used to this. I want to see road names, mile markers, gas stations listed. Those are real landmarks. I keep telling myself that David knows what he's doing, and the directions will make perfect sense once we're there. My worry over finding David is compounded by the fact that he has no email at his house, no cell phone and, while he does have a house phone, he has no answering machine of any kind. He is often out in the fields working, so contacting him directly, catching him at home, is nearly impossible. The rest of the trip has gone along so smoothly, I'm doing my best to convince myself that we'll find him.

All thoughts turned to the Great Barrier Reef and my heart started pounding. The reef was too big for me to comprehend. I was nervous and excited all at the same time. This had always been someone else's trip, one I only heard about on the nature channels or read about in school. The Great Barrier Reef is one of the Seven Wonders of the World. "That's a really big deal," I said out loud to no one in particular.

I was beginning to sense that we had saved the best for last.

Day 42, Tuesday   January 18, 2000

There's less than two weeks left in our trip. All of a sudden time is speeding up.

The road was as narrow as narrow gets on the last portion of the Flinders Highway before reaching the coast. Several times we were forced to pull over for oversized vehicles. One in particular was a massive flatbed truck carrying a monstrous earthmover. I made up the story that it was on its way to a quarry in Mount Isa. Maybe it was. The giant machine dwarfed everything in sight within a half mile radius. In addition to the monster machine, there were vehicles in odd shapes and sizes carrying anything from roof trusses to odd looking machinery. Each transport vehicle had a lead car ahead of it to give warning that something big was coming down the road. The silent, but oh so clear, message was always, "Get out of the way...*now!*" and off to the side of the road we went.

In addition to odd looking vehicles, we continued to see odd looking wildlife. Bustards (bush turkeys), like the one we saw in Western Australia, are in Queensland, too. They are gorgeous birds that stand three feet tall, and watching them fly is a thrill. How they can ever get off the ground is a mystery to me and a seeming defiance of gravitational flight laws.

The air continued to remain cool until noon, long past the usual 9:00 a.m. burst of heat that we'd grown accustomed to. It made the drive a pleasant one. Maybe the sea breezes had something to do with it. I don't know. We were expecting continued heat waves. Every kilometer was taking us out of the outback and into the tropics of Queensland.

Ninety minutes from the Pacific Ocean coastline, we passed through an old gold mining town called Charters Towers. Founded in 1870, it was a tropical version of Coolgardie, Western Australia and equally as impressive with its large commerce buildings and rich history. City Hall sat on the main thoroughfare. Palm trees were growing in large planters on the porch, and the building was painted a faint pink, reminding me of Key West, Florida. I felt another pang of homesickness and wanted to stay awhile. Another town added to the revisit list.

We arrived in Townsville, Queensland (estimated population 125,000) after a gorgeous drive through deep green mountains. The Ningaloo Reef and Uluru were long behind us in every sense of the word.

As we looked out onto the Pacific Ocean, it was clear we were in an entirely different portion of Australia unlike anywhere else we had seen to date. The cool ocean air created a mist that began moving in on the nearby mountains, similar to the fog effect seen in San Francisco, only it was a lot warmer. Reaching Townsville meant we had safely and successfully navigated the entire length of Australia, covering the same distance as if we had driven from Los Angeles to New York City—and then some. Because of the massive interior desert that makes up most of this island continent, the journey was far from being a straight line. I felt a huge sense of relief, coupled with an equally large sense of accomplishment. We were back in civilization with the choice to travel by railway, plane or taxi, but we planned to keep the old Ford until the very end. "Mum's Taxi" was proving to be a true road warrior. I thought, "It will be a pleasure to pass her along to the next traveler."

Upon our arrival in Townsville, Jeff and I had full intentions to immediately turn left and head north up the coast to David's. We were anxious to reach our final destination even though we would have been two days early. While Jeff drove, I started reading about Townsville in *Lonely Planet*. We were still within city limits when I made a quick case for us to stay in town a night or two. There was so much there to see. I didn't want to rush it.

While I was listing all the reasons to stay, Jeff, still focused on heading north, unknowingly took a wrong turn and ended up driving deeper into the city instead of towards David's hometown of El Arish. Right about the time we had decided on Townsville, to tour the Living Reef Aquarium and catch a movie at the connecting IMAX movie theater, we figured out we were lost in the big city. Jeff kept going, making a turn here and a turn there, while I tried to find a reference point on the map and navigate the rest of the way to our destination. I looked up to get another street name, and there it was, the movie and aquarium complex, as big as day, right in front of us. I said, "Wow! That was easy."

Jeff parked the car and we headed straight for the movie theater. The last showing of *The Living Sea* was half over, but the ticket guy must have sensed our disappointment and said, "I can take you in the back way for free, and you can watch the rest of the movie." I still don't know if it was our accent that was opening all those doors or if it was simply genuine Aussie hospitality. Whatever was going on, it was alright by me.

IMAX, with its massive screen, surround sound, and audio/video technology brought the snorkeling experience we were about to go on closer than ever before. There were several SCUBA divers on screen, weaving their way through the reefs off the coast of the Palau Islands, due north of Australia's continent. It was a great introduction to our upcoming reef adventure.

The Living Reef Aquarium was open for another ninety minutes, giving me and Jeff enough time to take a walk around. Already, we could tell that our stopover was a wise decision. The brochure boasted that The Living Reef Aquarium was "the best living reef exhibit in the world." With the world's largest natural living reef, the Great Barrier Reef, at their doorstep, I figured the marine biologists must know what they're doing. I was impressed. Whatever it took to keep the water perfectly balanced to keep the reef alive was beyond my scope of understanding. Any marine biologist worth his or her salt would probably say, "It's simply good science."

Jeff and I had time to see the sharks and the sea turtles, and I got a good up-close-and-personal full-on look at a tiger shark in the tank. The memories of our swim with the manta rays the day after Christmas and the catamaran sail in Shark Bay at Monkey Mia came flooding back.

The aquarium was built on the water's edge the same way the National Aquarium in Baltimore, Maryland sits on the Inner Harbor. Next to the Townsville aquarium was a large dock lined with ferries positioned and ready to cruise over to a place called Magnetic Island. I had never heard of the island before and didn't notice it in our well-worn travel guide. While in the aquarium's gift shop I found a book on the shelf titled *Magnetic Island* and began to browse. That's when I read the four magic words, "Koala Capital of Australia." Koalas! We had yet to see a koala, captive or free, and decided that a trip to Australia was in no way complete without seeing one in the wild.

I talked to the saleswoman who said, "There are thousands of wild koalas that live on the island. They're very easy to spot." That was all the confirmation I needed to hear. As far as I was concerned the next twenty-four hours were set. We were going koala hunting...with my camera, of course. Fortunately, Jeff wanted to go as much as I did, and within minutes we hatched a plan.

With a name like "Magnetic Island," the most common question has to be, "How did the island get its name?" Other than the fact that Jeff and I were drawn to its shores as if by a magnetic pull, I knew there had to be a story behind this one, and there was. In 1770, Captain Cook sailed through this area and reported that his compasses "went funny." He decided there must have been a magnetic pull on the island, and the name stuck. There is much debate among the locals whether this is true or not, but it's obviously one that works for the tourists, me included.

We learned that many of the locals who worked in Townsville lived on Magnetic Island. It's only a twenty minute commute by ferry. Jeff and I decided to eat dinner on the mainland before heading over. A pizza parlor, similar to a small "mom and pop joint" back home, was the closest and most convenient restaurant we found. We were on a mission to eat and get over to the island as quickly as possible. The owner of the restaurant and our server made a few suggestions on where to stay, and off we went.

We packed enough clothes and toiletries in our daypacks to spend the night, leaving the rest of our stuff under a blanket and locked tight in the car. The awaiting ferry was a short walk from the parking lot, and while the ferry did accommodate cars, we were assured by the locals there was no need for a vehicle on such a short visit.

Right on time, the boat motored out into the channel. The closer we got to the island, the more we could tell that it would be, at minimum, a two night's stay. In addition to being the "Koala Capital of Australia," Magnetic Island was also called "Australia's Finest Island." We knew we had stumbled onto a gem, and we were going to thoroughly check things out.

As the boat cruised in closer to shore, the sky grew dark. The choppy waters, thick fog, misty rain, and a jungle filled with steep rocky cliffs gave it all the makings of an opening scene in a Hollywood movie. The rich green landscape was so thick it was hard to believe I was in the same country where Alice Springs and Coober Pedy were located. Palm trees grew densely on the hillsides. Large bats, appearing bigger than the ones we saw in Mount Isa, flew high in the air, and strange bird calls came from deep inside the eucalyptus forest.

Despite the rough surf, the ferry docked promptly at 7:30 p.m. with the precision only a captain with years of experience could demonstrate. Minutes after the boat's gates opened, the newest arrival of tourists and commuters walked off the dock and up into the main village. Strange looking egret-type birds wandered around the outdoor cafés, and I had the distinct feeling that we had just entered *Jurassic Park.*

Without a car, and too late to hunt for a hotel by means of public transportation, we took the advice given by our pizza parlor guides that the Traveler's Backpackers Lodge, located steps from the ferry, was the place to stay. A private room with our own shower was available for $40 AU ($26 US) each, since it was off-season. The room was large enough to accommodate eight guests, but with so many vacancies, we had the room to ourselves. Once we got settled, Jeff found the pool.

We enjoyed a moonlight swim and watched the bats, known as "flying foxes," soar through the sky above us. The palm trees around the pool framed the skyline. We'd been swimming for ten minutes when the "flying rodents" (another colorful name for bats) started to buzz our heads. Jeff and I made a game out of ducking under the water a split second before they made their final swoop.

Back in the tropics, Jeff and I are in our element. It has been a long wait to get to Queensland, but we have finally arrived. The water is warm, the air is surprisingly cool, and koalas are all around us. Tomorrow is going to be great.

Day 43, Wednesday   January 19, 2000

We slept and slept and slept. After being on the move for the past four days, it was time to slow down. The room turned out to be nice and comfortable, and we are happy with the arrangements.

There is something about being able to keep our stuff in our own room all day that makes a visit more enjoyable, more relaxed. The way we've been moving across Australia, it has become a luxury to be able stay in one place for two or more nights in a row.

We may be doing well in the decision-making department, but our relationship is beginning to show signs of stress. I'm noticing that Jeff is getting distant and quieter with each passing day. I know I have my quirks, but something is amiss, and now I am growing distant, too. For the most part, we have a peaceful and respectful relationship, but we have become more like roommates then boyfriend/girlfriend. We've experienced not a single outburst of anger, but that doesn't mean there aren't issues. We both know we have two more weeks together, side-by-side, so we're keeping the peace.

Jeff hasn't told me why he's upset, but it's clear he is. Maybe it isn't me at all. Maybe he's stressed about being so far from home for so long, and he's ready to go. I could guess all day long, and in the end, only Jeff knows what he's thinking. I haven't asked him what's wrong because he'll tell me when he's ready. That's been my experience anyway.

We know each other well. Before this trip, we had been living together for three-and-a-half years. We've talked about marriage, but any conversations about the future of our relationship, such as buying a house or any long range plans, usually end as quickly as they begin. Not good, not bad, nor right or wrong. I'm just noticing. What I love about our relationship is that we live in the moment. Being with Jeff has taught me to enjoy today, and that in itself is a gift.

For the most part, considering we have been together 24/7 for 43 consecutive days, 44 when I count the travel time to get here, we are good. That alone is a miracle in any relationship. This isn't our first trip together, but it's the first one longer than a week. The surest way to get to know a person is to travel with him or her. Even three days can be enough to see what lies beyond the honeymoon phase, because travel is stressful. There are no two ways about it. Stress brings out the best and the worst in a person every single time, guaranteed.

Fortunately, Jeff and I have come to an agreement with all the decisions we have had to make when it comes to where to go, where to stay, what to eat, and how we are going to get to our next destination. The biggest decision, to buy the Ford, also came easily, and we are sharing all expenses 50/50 the same way we do at home.

On our 43rd day in Oz, on "Australia's Finest Island," it's now clear to me that we are beginning to separate emotionally. I can feel it and, at the same time, I'm not doing anything about it. I believe it started for Jeff back on Christmas Day. Something shifted in him, I don't know what it was, but when he got quiet and distant he never fully came back to his old self. We've had only a few tense moments between then and now, and they were mild. But here on Magnetic Island, it's intensifying. Our relationship has definitely changed. We are two friends traveling together pretending nothing is wrong, and we still have 12 days left.

When we made the choice to stay two nights at the lodge, we bought time to relax. The nearby Internet café made checking email easy, and after breakfast I logged on while Jeff went back to the room to sleep the rest of the morning. As soon as I finished emailing, I sat outside the café and enjoyed the view of Picnic Bay, the same bay the ferry passed through on its way to the dock. When we arrived last night, I hadn't noticed the banyan trees—too dark, I suppose. The natural canopy made a memorable impression in the light of day. It's taken me awhile to get my bearings, but I figured out we are on the south end of the island. Knowing there is more to see than we have time for, I added Magnetic Island to the "revisit list." "I'll need at least a week for further explorations," I thought.

Jeff woke up at the same time I returned to the room. Shuttle bus schedules in hand, I sat down on the bed to read up on how the public transportation system worked. Buses ran every twenty minutes and went to all the places we wanted to go. The waitress on the mainland was right, there was no need for a car. Our first stop was at Horseshoe Bay to check into the possibility of renting a couple of kayaks. We decided to view the island by sea.

Several cafés dotted the shoreline along Horseshoe Bay, and small brightly-colored parrots filled the trees. They were rainbow lorikeets (pronounced laura-keet), and their entire bodies were splashed with blue, red, yellow and green feathers. A second breed was also striking. They were red tailed black cockatoos; not something I was accustomed to seeing in the wild, and they were gorgeous. But as hard as I looked, I couldn't see a single koala.

We took a short walk down to the beach, and I found a few unique shells to add to my collection. Running on the sand along the water's edge were one-inch soldier crabs. I remembered seeing this species on one of the nature channels. The crabs ran fast, in groups of hundreds, and behaved as if they were in a complete panic. Individually, they looked like miniature brown tanks with legs flying in all directions. Whenever we got too close for comfort, they would tilt on one side and dig fast and furiously into the sand, running in a tight circle, legs still flying in all directions, all in an effort to find safety. It was like a herd of miniature shovels disappearing into the beach. Hysterical little creatures.

On land, Magnetic Island is a paradise. Swimming its shores? That's another story. The waters along the northern Queensland coastline, during the summer months, are extremely dangerous. Yes, sharks are a problem, but it's the

*deadly box jellyfish floating off shore that are the real threat
to life, and few swimmers will risk getting stung in the open
waters. One dose of venom from this sea creature can be
lethal to a human being and agonizingly painful, at best.*

Jeff and I took advantage of the protected swimming area
Horseshoe Bay had set up to keep the jellyfish out and the
swimmers inside a sting-free zone. Similar to what can be
found in a campground lake back home, netting was placed
in the water with clearly defined markers indicating where
the boundaries were. We knew exactly where it was safe to
swim and where trouble could ensue should we venture
beyond the borders. It was tempting for me to jump in
anywhere I pleased because the water was inviting
everywhere I looked, but I heeded the warnings and kept to
the safe areas. When the subject of a kayak tour returned, I
suggested to Jeff that we cancel due to "Not enough hours in
the day." But if I am to be completely honest, it was the box
jellyfish that took the fun out of it for me.

At 5:00 p.m., still on the hunt for the elusive koala, we
left the beach to venture deeper into the island. It was a short
bus ride to a popular hiking trail called Forts Walk, a path
leading up to "the forts."

*"The forts" are hilltop concrete lookout stations built
during World War II to ensure that United States and
Australian military ships, loaded with supplies, arrived safe
from enemy attack. Years later, the gun emplacements,
command post and observation post were opened to the
public transforming the site into an ideal place for hikers to
enjoy a bird's eye view of Magnetic Island and the
surrounding ocean and bays.*

It was a bit of a climb to get to the top from where the
bus left us off, 2 km (1.24 miles) to be exact, but along the
way we figured out that the main attraction was not so much
the forts, nor the view they provided. It was the koalas! We
finally spotted our first one sitting in a eucalyptus tree. The

koala was completely camouflaged within the tree's branches, and, just like the kangaroos in the desert, hard to detect. That first koala was all by itself doing what koalas do best, sleep. It was so adorable and looked exactly like all the pictures I had ever seen prior to the trip. The brochures describe koalas as one of the laziest creatures on the planet, clearly demonstrated by the fact that they sleep two-thirds of the day. When they are awake they move v – e – r – y s – l – o – w – l – y.

The next koala sighting came five minutes later when we found two young ones in the same tree. And then we saw another and another until we spotted six, all in the same place. One-by-one the koalas slowly came into focus. We kept count all the way to the top of the hill, and by the time we got to the forts, we saw a total of fourteen, which meant there was probably ten times that amount within camera range.

Once at the forts, we found a koala, sitting in a tree, ten feet from the concrete structure. That was the closest one yet. I could see its eyes blink and its jaw move ever so slowly as it chewed on the eucalyptus leaves. Jeff was much better at spotting koalas than I was, until one of the other tourists we met on the trail gave me a valuable tip. She said, "Look for their white bottoms." Well, she was right. I got as good as Jeff once I knew what I was looking for. Every time I saw something white there was a koala attached to it.

As late as it was at the start of the hike, Jeff and I were able to complete the loop before sunset. We watched a nearly full moon rise up over the mountains, and like clockwork, the bats came out. While we waited to take the bus back to the lodge at the south end of the island, a wayward koala, walking on the ground looking for another tree to climb, gave us a good look and then kept on going. So cute.

As the sun went down, the forest became restless and the sounds intensified. Jeff and I heard strange noises coming from the hills. When the bus arrived, we got on, and I immediately asked the driver to explain the odd sounds. He said, "That's the male koala making guttural burps to attract the female." "Interesting," I thought, "Never would've figured that one out."

There must have been millions of birds screeching, calling out to one another, and doing whatever birds do before they settle in for the night. One species in particular stood out. I asked the driver a second question, "What is making that 'oo-oo-ah-ah' sound? It reminds me of the monkeys in a Tarzan movie." He answered, "That's a kookaburra bird. The reason it sounds like a Tarzan movie is because a sound crew decided it would be fun to record the language of an Australian jungle and dub it into an African jungle movie sound track." *I love a good inside story.*

Back in our room, Jeff and I made plans for the days ahead. With twelve days left in Australia it was time to discuss our exit strategy: how and when to sell the car and how that would fit in with our visit to David's. Townsville was a much larger city than expected and only two hours from El Arish. Surely there would be a buyer in the area, and maybe David knew someone who could use a reliable car. By selling in the North, we could take the train south to Sydney, the equivalent of traveling from New York City to Savannah, Georgia.

The same way I reserved our tentative flights from Perth to Alice Springs, I made tentative railway reservations from Townsville to Sydney. The thought of getting one more train ride in was appealing to us. It meant we could end the trip the same way it began with the added bonus of shortening our drive time. We'd had enough of the wide open road.

This train reservation out of Townsville is my last attempt at planning anything beyond two days in advance. Every time I think I know what will happen next, I find out how wrong I am and a much better scenario would be revealed. To keep my sanity and stress level down, I will remain open to any and all ideas that will present themselves in the days ahead. I say "I" because Jeff doesn't appear to be nearly as concerned with the details as I am.

At the end of the day, we were both worn out. Once again, we got too much sun and did too much walking, but it was worth it. Seeing the koalas was a highlight of the trip I will always remember, and Magnetic Island was absolutely beautiful. The mountains, boulders, beaches, trees, plants, kookaburras, flying foxes, koalas, parrots, lush green fields and valleys, and the friendly locals have made our stay exceptional.

Day 44, Thursday   January 20, 2000

I woke up with the same sense of urgency I felt in the Garden of Eden. I said to Jeff, "We've got to go." Our time in Australia was slipping away all too fast.

Seeing the koalas yesterday gave me a sense of fulfillment that our stay on Magnetic Island was over. Jeff agreed. We checked out of the Travelers Backpacker, skipped the morning cup of coffee, and were on the ferry by 10:00 a.m. The ride back to the mainland was calming to me.

I will never know for sure what caused our hurried return to Townsville, and it doesn't matter. I could guess all day long at the reasons why, and still never know. That's the thing about hunches, the only thing that matters is how life looks on the other side of those inspired actions.

After breakfast and emails, we returned to the Living Reef Aquarium and IMAX Theater to watch the movie *Egypt*. I may have felt rushed to leave the island, but I was in no hurry to leave Townsville. We took our good 'ol time, meandering through the reef exhibits before catching the next big screen movie. Once we had our fill of city life, we got in the car and headed north. At 2:15 p.m., Highway 1 became our ticket to a scenic drive up the tropical coast of Queensland.

Highway 1 connects all the major cities in Australia (Sydney, Canberra, Perth, Darwin, Melbourne, Adelaide, Brisbane and Townsville) and runs the entire circumference of the island continent, making it one of the longest national highways in the world. It's 24,000 km (14,900 miles) long. Certain sections throughout the country are difficult to find, because over the years the road has been given different names, but it's there.

I've traveled across Australia twice now, and I have a new goal—to circumnavigate Oz, taking Highway 1 all the way around. There's a short stretch of this historic drive within the state of Tasmania on the island of Tasmania, south of Sydney, right about where Florida sits on our map back home. Of course, it will have to be included if I am to say, "I drove the entire length of Highway 1."

Jeff and I knew we didn't have far to go today, certainly not the great lengths we were used to, so we took advantage of the scenic route. We turned a two-hour drive into five, due to countless stops along the way and a slower pace. It put us into El Arish just in time for dinner.

I thought Magnetic Island was as tropical as it could get, but we hadn't seen anything yet. The farther north we drove the more I was reminded of Hawaii. It made sense. We were in the rainforest, after all. The northeast portion of Highway 1 is called the "Great Green Way," and it absolutely lives up to its name. The landscape was a gorgeous deep, dark green, and the variety of plants was equally as impressive. Jeff said it reminded him of Pennsylvania in the summer.

Florida may be tropical, but it's definitely not a rainforest. We don't experience saturating rains like they do here December through April. North Queensland must get hundreds of inches each season to make everything grow so rich and dense. I expected El Arish to look like Hawaii, knowing it was in the rainforest, but hearing it compared to Pennsylvania? I didn't see that one coming.

There's a small sign by the side of the road marking the border of El Arish, and had I blinked, I would've missed it. Following David's directions to the letter, we were in and through downtown El Arish in a matter of minutes. The town was only three blocks long. One turn off the main drag took us straight up and into the forest. Seeing that we were about to leave the town as quickly as we arrived, Jeff turned the car around and headed back to give us a longer look at the neighborhood. There was an historic tavern, a few city blocks of small cottage homes surrounded by lush green lawns, and flowers blooming all around. The old abandoned railway station added another dose of charm. The town was picture perfect. I could see why David chose El Arish as a place to call home.

Focusing back on David's directions, we headed up the hill and, of course, the clues started to make sense. We parked the car right where he told us to, in a clearing off to the side of the road. It turned out we couldn't have driven much farther if we wanted to. There was a shallow creek running across and over the private drive. David thought it was best if we didn't try to cross the stream with our low-riding station wagon, though he admitted to driving his own car through the water on a regular basis.

Jeff and I headed down the lane.

A split second before Jeff was about to step into the creek, a 3-foot long black snake came out of nowhere. At mid-slither, the snake stopped, lifted one-third of its body off the ground like a cobra and set its sights on Jeff's calf only two feet away. I froze. Totally unaware of the danger he was in, Jeff kept walking as the snake settled back down and continued along into the tall growth of the forest. In a matter of seconds, Jeff moved out of harm's way before I ever had a chance to warn him.

Jeff's actually a fan of snakes and had been reading about the indigenous reptiles over the past few weeks. He said, "It's the plain looking ones that tend to be the dangerous snakes and the colorful ones that are the least threatening. That's just the opposite throughout North America."

I didn't get a good look at the snake that almost bit Jeff, but because it took on an attack position and appeared to be all one color, we assumed it was venomous. That was our introduction to David's place, and I asked the ultimate question, "What *else* is out there?"

Twenty yards later, we found the next set of clues that matched David's. It was a free-standing open air carport, but there was no car, and we assumed David wasn't home. With our failed attempts to contact him directly to give him our exact date of arrival, we knew we were taking our chances in finding him right away. We had made the agreement that we would probably arrive on Friday, but were clear to say that we may be a day ahead or a day late of that goal. As it turned out, even with the side trip to Magnetic Island, we managed to arrive early.

Still no house in sight, we continued on to the next clue: a set of rock steps buried into a hill. Green ferns and lush ground cover made it nearly impossible to detect the path leading up to the house. I felt as if we were on a treasure hunt, excited with each matching clue. I had every reason to believe we were on the right track, but my mind brought up questions like, "Could this be someone else's property? Are we really in the right place?" All I knew for sure was that we were going deeper into the forest and there was a snake out there that wanted us out. It probably had plenty of cousins, too.

We carefully took one step at a time. Half way up the steep rocky steps we could finally see a clearing, and through the clearing a house appeared. It was David's, and all doubts to the contrary vanished.

Right away, I thought it was a tree house, because it was built on stilts high up off the ground. I felt as if I had stepped into one of my favorite childhood movies, *The Swiss Family Robinson*, only things were a tad more civilized. While the house wasn't actually built into the trees, it was built among the trees, made entirely of wood, and therefore, was a tree house for all intents and purposes. It was wonderfully rustic, a true "green" space, and I could tell David put a lot of attention to detail into the planning and construction of his home. The foundation was exceptionally strong with huge pilings dug deep into the earth. There were three solid walls with the fourth side, the front of the house, open to the elements. We called out to see if he was home, despite the absence of a car, but there was no answer.

In David's last email, he gave us permission to go in and make ourselves comfortable, in case he wasn't there to greet us when we arrived. Standing at the top of the stairs, Jeff and I saw a young woman sleeping in the open air front porch on a day bed/couch. How she was able to sleep in that intense heat was a mystery to me. It may have been 6:00 p.m., but it was as hot as the midday sun in August. No, it was hotter. We called to her in a whisper so as not to startle her, but no response. Taking a seat in the open air living room, it was best for us to wait quietly until she woke up on her own.

Her name was Melon. She was a traveling WWOOFer who had read David's WWOOF ad in Cairns (pronounced cans, as in "tin can"), a city north of El Arish. WWOOF stands for Willing Workers On Organic Farms. It's a worldwide organization that offers creative alternatives to work and travel. In exchange for a room and three meals a day, Melon had agreed to work four hours a day tending to David's organic fruit trees and vegetable crops. She said, "David and I started early in the fields this morning to get as much done before the heat set in." She was exhausted from the morning's work. I could tell she was earning her keep.

"David went to the nearby town of Innisfail to do some shopping and visit his favorite library where he checks his emails. He should be back soon." Melon said. The three of us sat on the porch talking about where we were from and how we ended up at David's, of all places. The conversation was interrupted when a baby cassowary, four feet tall, came strutting through the front yard. David told us in his emails about this unique bird living wild on the farm, and I was thrilled to see it so soon into our visit. These birds are known to be shy, and there were no guarantees one would show itself. Our first hour in the rainforest revealed how alive this part of the world is, and I had a feeling we were in for a few more surprises.

Cassowaries are an endangered species, a flightless bird that is often compared to emus and ostriches, only smaller. Cassowaries are different in color and have a distinct horn-like crest on their heads. While an emu and ostrich are basically brown with a few variations, a cassowary has beautiful black feathers on its torso and a bright blue neck with red coloring at the base.

David was home by 7:30 p.m., and it was good to finally meet him. He said, "Thirty minutes ago I read the email you sent yesterday announcing your arrival. I left the library as soon as I could."

The moment I met our host, I saw the family resemblance. I know his mom, Betty, and had already met his two brothers and sister when they each flew in to Florida for their respective visits. Betty, a client of mine, lives on her own and is in her 80's.

A typical schedule would show I made two visits to her home each week. As Betty's bookkeeper, I balanced the checkbook, organized her financial statements, took her to various attorneys to update her wills and trust, and during tax time, I would gather the necessary documents to send to the CPA. Whenever Betty asked for assistance beyond those functions, I was happy to help in any way I could. Extra errands included grocery shopping, laundry, and taking her to a doctor's appointment whenever the distance was farther than she was willing to drive. She was always good company and had a wonderful sense of humor.

David asked for a full update to hear how his "mum" was *really* doing. He knew her well enough to know she often said things were "fine" when they may have been quite challenging. I told him she was taking good care of herself, remained 80% independent, and could still drive around town.

"She says 'hi' and sends her love," I told David, and then delivered the hug his mom wished she could give on her own.

Initial greetings completed, David proudly told us the story of how he *and* his custom-built home survived the 1986 Category 3 tropical cyclone known as Cyclone Winifred. (What are called cyclones in Australia are called hurricanes in America.) Winds were in excess of 100 mph. David said, "I watched the house flex as much as two inches during the worst of the storm." As he told his story, I got a mental picture of him clinging to one of the vertical beams attached to his bedroom loft. Only he knew if he was willing to *ride out* another one.

After a delicious veggie stir fry and brown rice dinner that David prepared for the four of us, we talked well into the night about his mom, the crops, and how he made the rainforest his home after growing up in southeast Pennsylvania. David explained that solar panels provided lighting throughout the house and bottled gas fueled the hot water heater, stove top burners and oven. He didn't have a refrigerator. "It draws too much power," he said. While there was indoor plumbing for a kitchen sink and hot shower, the toilet was located in an outhouse east of the main house.

It had been a long time since Jeff and I sat down to a home-cooked meal and enjoyed a good long conversation with friends. At the end of the evening, David said we'd be most comfortable on the futon in the living room, as opposed to the guest bedroom. I think it had something to do with the night breezes. He climbed the ladder up into his loft, Melon took her place on the porch, and looking high above the rafters, I could see bats flying *inside* the tree house. David assured me they would keep to themselves.

Day 45, Friday   January 21, 2000

The natural air flowing through David's house made it so cool I had to put a sweater on in order to stay warm. Our first night sleeping in the rainforest went well, and the drop in temperature was a pleasant surprise. Right after breakfast, Melon and David took off to work on the fruit trees, while Jeff and I stayed back to take a day of rest.

We talked about what David said at dinner about the hundreds of rare and exotic trees growing throughout his property. Many of the seedlings came from Borneo, an island north of Australia, and David planted every tree himself. Because of his extensive research, David has written and published numerous articles and is considered an expert on exotic fruit trees.

In 1973, when David was 27 years old, he bought the land. The fields were originally filled with sugar cane and bananas, and back in the 1920's up until World War II, previous owners used horses to plow and harvest. The old farm house is located near the main road, on a portion of land that was divided and sold to another buyer.

The horses are long gone, and a tractor has taken their place. David's favorite childhood toy was a tractor with a manure spreader behind it, and now he owns the real thing. "It's the same make and model of the toy I used to play with," David told us, "and was a sign that I found my home." (That certainly lends proof to the popular saying, "The only difference between men and boys is the size of their toys!")

What David's accomplished over the years to build his own home and plant all new crops is truly remarkable. The care and attention he gives the land is evident. The trees are mature, and our proud American-bred farmer is reaping a good harvest.

At mid-day, Jeff and I drove 15 minutes down the road into Tully, as per David's instructions, and found a nice, big, clean laundromat to do our laundry. Oddly enough, Tully reminded me of a typical Colorado ski town in summer, because of the way it was situated at the base of a mountain. The one main difference being that Tully would never ever see snow.

El Arish and Tully are positioned where Boston, Massachusetts would be in the USA. It may be in the northeast, but it's nothing like New England when it comes to temperature. I am still chanting, "North is South and South is North."

Despite the cool evening, the day was the hottest and muggiest yet. Oppressive is the only way to describe it. My body moved in slow motion, as if shifting down a few gears to conserve whatever energy I had. I felt doped without the dope. Like David's home, the laundromat was open to the elements and had no air conditioning. As soon as the clothes were in the wash, Jeff and I set out to find a restaurant or bar to sit in where we could keep cool while the machine went through its cycles.

Once the laundry was done, we decided to go back to the farm and take a swim in one of the three creeks on David's property. We saw the first one on the way in when we first arrived. David showed us a second creek when he took us on a short bush walk before dinner last night, and the third remained a mystery. In planning our afternoon hike, I had totally forgotten about the snake that greeted us upon our arrival. *Out of sight, out of mind, I suppose.* David never mentioned that poisonous snakes were a concern, but I assumed he'd had a few run-ins with them.

Returning to the second creek, Jeff and I discovered it was deeper than we first thought. "Seven feet," David later confirmed. The water was so clear, the rocks at the bottom were as visible as if they were only 7 inches deep.

For mid-summer, the water was surprisingly cool and refreshing, and I was in awe that David had his own private swimming hole. He said, "An afternoon dip is essential this time of year. The WWOOFers and I swim every chance we get."

Unlike in the outback where the photo film developers in Alice Springs said they could drink water all day long and never have to go to the bathroom, the opposite occurred in the rainforest. David said, "In the heat of the summer I pee far more than I drink because my skin is literally 'drinking' water all day long through every pore on my body." It was fascinating to me that the two extremes could occur in the same country, possibly in the same state.

After our swim, Jeff and I went back to the house and waited for David and Melon to return from their day's work. As soon as they got back, David took us on a walk, this time deeper into the fields to see more crops and meet Lotho, his pet donkey. Lotho lived a comfortable life, and appeared content and well fed. Nearby, taro was growing. David explained that it was his cash crop, his bread and butter. He said, "There's a strong demand for organic taro, and my customers can count on me to deliver as much as they need."

This root vegetable is the main ingredient in poi, a Polynesian staple commonly served at Hawaiian luaus. From what I've heard, poi is like Vegemite, in that it tastes terrible to the outsider, but the locals love it. David's current crop stands well over 6 feet tall, and looks like a thick green field of corn without the corn, of course. It's the healthiest bunch of vegetables I have ever seen.

We continued our walk through a grove of trees. At one point, David reached up and picked a handful of fruit from the "mamey" (pronounced *mah*-may) tree. *Now there's an exotic name if I ever heard one.* Eating the fruit of a mamey tree was a first for me. It was delicious and tasted unlike anything I had ever tried before, so different I had no flavor reference to compare it with.

In the livestock department, and in addition to Lotho the donkey, David was the proud owner of four chickens. They strutted, all day long, throughout the property. Not a fence in sight. David explained, "Chickens are native to the rainforest. Their instinct to scratch at the dirt is the way they find insects and seeds in the dense ground cover."

A few weeks ago David had five chickens, but when one turned up missing, he assumed it was eaten by a python. "Snakes that big can swallow a chicken whole with absolutely no problem," David said. "It happens. I lose a hen every so often, but that's nature. I would rather they roam free than keep them cooped up in a cage all day."

Nighttime was another story. I was glad to hear that the domesticated birds slept inside a secure hutch, a small house of their own a few yards past the outhouse. On the rare occasion that David finds a python before the python finds a chicken, he'll stuff the giant reptile into a sack, carry it deep into the forest, as far away as possible, and release it.

Each morning, right after the chickens were let out of the hen house, they would take turns laying eggs in a single nest; a wooden box filled with straw located under David's house. Two chickens could fit in at a time, if they chose to share the space, and each time an egg was laid, the hen cackled at the top of her lungs as if to say, "Come and get 'em!" or maybe it was more a cry of, "Ouch! That really hurts!" All of David's chickens were productive and gave him more eggs than he could consume on his own. He often sold the extras in town, and never did he kill the chickens. With the exception of eating eggs, David was a strict vegetarian.

That evening, I assisted our gracious host in the kitchen and we cooked a pesto dish together. David added all kinds of veggies including leaves off some unknown plant growing on the front porch. It reminded me of spinach. He explained that it was a nutrient-dense food and had everything a person needed nutritionally. After dinner I was much more relaxed in my new surroundings than the previous night. I glanced around to see what made David's house a home.

I saw his mom's gold Christmas card that I helped her select at the card store two months earlier. It was next to a dozen other Christmas cards lined up side-by-side across a string tied between two wooden beams. He said, "I used the

Christmas money mum sent me to buy this Australian Dictionary." It was a volume three inches thick. David's a self-proclaimed wordsmith and, in my opinion, a wealth of information. One of his hobbies was learning new and uncommon words in the English language. At age 53, the farm kept him physically fit, and he exercised his brain, too.

I enjoyed talking to him about his mom, his brothers and sisters. I learned that his father had passed away when David was one year old. The family lived "in the country," as David says, near Philadelphia, and he agreed with Jeff that El Arish reminded him of home. I noticed that after 30 years in Australia, David had not lost his American accent. Other than a few slang words and the fact that he was an Australian citizen, he was still all American to me. How he ended up so far from home remained a mystery. I didn't ask and he didn't tell. It simply never came up in the conversation.

After dinner, David shared an exotic fruit called a durian, which he grew on his farm. At a jaw dropping price of $40 AU ($26 US) per fruit, it's among the rarest of natural foods in the world. The seeds came from Borneo.

A durian is the size of a cantaloupe with three to four sections in it. Its shell is a light greenish-yellow color, spiky, and looks a lot like a puffer fish all puffed out.

The oddest part about the durian, I discovered, was not the outside, but the edible part inside. It mimicked the color, texture, and flavor of cooked chicken breast, and was actually quite tasty. I know, the joke is usually about a strange piece of meat tasting "just like chicken," but this time it was a fruit that came from a nearby tree. If I hadn't seen the dish prepared, I was sure David had one less chicken in the yard.

David handled the oppressive heat with ease having been acclimatized for three decades. Jeff and I, a couple of novices, were having a hard time adjusting. Other than the first cool night, swimming in the spring, and eating lunch in an air conditioned restaurant, we've been sweaty and miserable ever since we arrived. It didn't cool down on our second night in the jungle, and the flies and mosquitoes were out in full force. Oddly enough, there were no buzzing insects earlier in the day, so I'm guessing the heat must have been too much for them, too.

To get relief from all the swatting and arm waving, I went to bed early. Because the bugs were especially active at night and David's home was open to the elements, without any screening other than a net over the beds, he offered us his caravan to sleep in. The caravan was a one person motor home permanently parked behind the tree house. It took on the role of "guest house" whenever necessary.

While David showed us our room in the caravan, I felt a cool breeze blow in through the screened windows. "There's a three-inch spider that lives in here," David said, "It's a 'housekeeping' spider and completely harmless." We took his word for it. I was more relieved to be free of the flies and mosquitoes than I was afraid of spiders, and Jeff held the same sentiment.

The light of the full moon is shining in through the window and right in my eyes. It's so bright I don't know if I'll get to sleep, spider or no spider. This is one very strange place.

Day 46, Saturday   January 22, 2000

Sometime during the night, I saw the housekeeping spider, in broad moonlight, clinging to the wall of the caravan. The arachnid was stationed four inches from my right foot. David's assurances that the spider was harmless were taken to heart, and before drifting back to sleep each time, I filled my head with visions of the eight-legged creature busily "house cleaning" all other bugs out of existence. It worked. I got a better night's sleep than the night before. Jeff, from the way he looked in the morning, didn't fare so well. He said the moonlight kept him awake most of the night.

Skipping breakfast, David, Melon, Jeff and I left the farm early in the morning and headed to the local bus station. Melon was on her way to Magnetic Island via Greyhound Australia. The bus's side panel was painted with the same racing greyhound logo we often saw in the 'States. It was another familiar "face" in a land called Oz.

Jeff and I enjoyed telling Melon all we knew about Magnetic Island. For the first time, we were able to share our experiences with another traveler. Melon caught our enthusiasm for a beautiful island filled with koalas and couldn't wait to get there. I didn't ask if she had another work/stay arrangement lined up, but I got the feeling her next stop was going to be a real vacation for her.

With Melon heading south and the farm taken care of, David's schedule was clear. The three of us had serious business to take care of, and we were on a mission. It was time to reach our third and final planned destination in "the land down under." It was time to snorkel a small, yet sure to be memorable, portion of The Great Barrier Reef.

Yesterday, David made reservations for us to take a chartered boat out to "the reef" as the locals call it. It was only $33 AU ($21 US) each. Jeff and I paid David's way. It was the least we could do to express our appreciation for all of his hospitality over the past few days. Like many locals in any other town with a great tourist attraction, David hadn't taken advantage of the sights close to home. He said, "I haven't been out to the reef in over three years. I'm just as excited to be going as you are!"

From Mission Beach, which is right up the road from El Arish, it was a two-and-a-half hour boat ride out. It's only an hour out to the reef from Cairns, the city north of El Arish, but the drive up would've cancelled out any time saved on the water.

The charter company David arranged for us was Friendship Cruises, and Captain Perry Harvey was in charge. Fifty-two people were on board, making the charter a small one when compared to others we had seen. Flyers throughout Tully advertised massive three-deck cruisers able to transport two to three hundred people at a time out to the reef. Jeff and I discussed this option with David, but after he gave us the inside story about the occasional tourist who was accidentally left out on the reef due to an incorrect head count at the end of the day, we cancelled that idea. Between the fast currents, exhaustion, and the challenges of an open water search, often times, those missing swimmers were never found. I felt confident that smaller numbers meant greater odds we would all make it back to shore safe and sound.

The Great Barrier Reef is massive. It extends more than 2000 km (1240 miles) down the eastern coastline of Queensland and is made up of over 2500 individual reefs and 250 islands that were once part of the mainland. It covers an area larger than Pennsylvania, New York and New England combined, and is the largest mass of living organisms on our planet. In addition to being one of the Seven Wonders of the World, the reef was the first place listed as an Australian World Heritage Area. Scientists continue to go to great lengths to preserve this part of the world, and we learned that not all reefs are the same. Some are grey and lifeless while others are pristine and filled with activity.

It was a long ride out before the engines stopped, and we were finally drifting above the reef, or so they said. The view looked like any other ocean view, and I waited patiently for proof that I was indeed at The Great Barrier Reef. With years of experience, our captain knew exactly where the permanent mooring was. He tied the boat securely to the buoyed line that was attached to a fixed anchor buried in the sand a safe distance away from the coral. It was a way to ensure the reef was protected from damage caused by a poorly thrown anchor, a boat adrift on its way to a collision with the reef at low tide and/or an anchor that had loosened its grip, on its way to snagging the reef.

Captain Harvey promised to take us to one of the more beautiful and active reefs in the area, and he delivered. For the first twenty minutes, there was no evidence that we were anywhere special. But then slowly, as if by magic, the tide turned, the waters pulled back, and the reef began to show itself below the surface of the water. A small island of pure white sand appeared out of nowhere, as if being raised on an underwater platform from the ocean's depths. Minute-by-minute the island grew from it's initial crown of 5 yards across to 50 yards, making it big enough for our entire group to walk on.

Before we all jumped in, the captain put on a show as he threw chunks of bread out into the water. Hundreds of fish, between 6 inches and 3 feet in length, swam in from the north, south, east and west. They appeared to be regulars.

Ten minutes into the feeding frenzy, as if on cue, a huge, massive, wide body, bigger than a shark, "Queensland" grouper (pronounced grow-per) cruised into sight. It must have been 6 feet long and 4 feet wide. Up until that moment, I didn't know fish like that could get so big. One of the Aussie crew members said, *"That grow-per they-are is a guude 700 pay-ounds."*

Once the show was over and not a shark in sight, the captain signaled all the snorkelers to jump into the cool water of the Pacific Ocean. The second I got my mask snug on my face, I looked down into the water and immediately saw how different, how spectacular, how much more impressive this portion of The Great Barrier Reef was over all the other reefs we had experienced over the past six weeks. While every reef was beautiful in its own right, and each one made a lasting impression, Jeff and I agreed that snorkeling the west coast first was the way to go. We had indeed saved the best for last.

After we floated around awhile, admiring the view, David, Jeff, and I decided to swim over to the small island and check it out. The current was against us, and I was tired by the time I reached the sandy beach. It took a lot longer than expected, too, but it was worth the effort. The island looked exactly like a "stranded on a desert island" commercial, except the single palm tree was missing. The sand was as white as white gets, and the island was perfectly round. There were 2-foot crests, breaking onto the island, so clear they looked like green glass waves. I was taken in by nature's beauty and felt extreme gratitude for all the forces that came together—seen and unseen—that made the experience possible.

After an hour of snorkeling, beach walking, then snorkeling again, it was time to return to the boat. A skiff was available to take people over from the small island, for those who didn't want to swim back. David and I knew there was more snorkeling ahead and wanted to conserve our energy, so we opted for the free ride. Jeff chose to swim and met up with us on the boat. He asked, "Why did you take the skiff? The current was in our favor." Jeff described how the reef kept getting more and more beautiful the lower the tide got. He drifted his way back to the boat, and I felt pangs of regret for a misguided decision to take the easy way.

After fresh deli sandwiches, cold drinks, and a rest, everyone returned to the water for a second swim. The tide continued to recede, offering a wider variety of coral and fish than before. It was easy to lose track of space and time while snorkeling above the most impressive reef in the world. Because the current was brisk, It was important to pay close attention to my surroundings and keep tabs on Jeff and David, my snorkel buddies. I also kept a close watch on the boat, a valuable lesson I learned in Coral Bay.

We were given another hour in the water before climbing back on board for the second time. Once everyone was accounted for, the captain detached the line from the permanent anchor and motored 15 minutes to another section of the reef. This second location gave us a third chance to swim above the reef, and was equally as impressive as the first—with one added bonus: there were 5-foot wide clams lying on the ocean's floor 20 feet down.

The giant clam is the largest of its species and native to the shallow coral reefs of the South Pacific. They can weigh more than 400 pounds, measure as much as 6 feet across, and live to be 100 years old or more.

They looked like fake props placed by a Hollywood studio. One of the crew members tried to pull a fast one and told us, "Keep your distance. Those giant clams are known to grab a swimmer's arm or leg and not let go." Aussies like to have fun with tourists and often tell tall tales. The truth is, a giant clam is a filter feeder and has no interest in humans. It only closes its shell out of defense, to protect itself. I suppose it could grab hold of a person, but it's not likely, and many of the clams in that area were so old and so big, they would be hard pressed to close their shells at all.

Jeff pointed out some blue brain coral that looked exactly like, well, blue brains, and then we saw two schools of white flying fish. The first school jumped out of the water, stretched their fins, and glided through the air for a few seconds before returning to the sea. (They're capable of flying 30-40 seconds on a single bound.) The next school of flying fish leaped four times, like feathered skipping stones, in and out of the water, all in a row, as high as 3 feet above the waterline each time. It was one of the coolest things I have ever seen.

Once everyone was back on the boat and, again, accounted for, we enjoyed a smooth ride back to the mainland. I was pleasantly tired and thrilled with my first time out to the Great Barrier Reef. Semi-retired, Captain Perry Harvey clearly enjoyed his chosen role in life and was a pleasure to talk to. He said, "For years I've brought people out to the reef and educated them about this fragile environment. I am doing what I love to do. It's a privilege to be here."

Jeff and I could see a large island off in the distance. David said, "That's Dunk Island. It's a well known luxury resort. People fly in from all over the world to go there."

Unfortunately, we knew we wouldn't be seeing that one. "So many islands, so little time," I thought.

With our feet on dry land, David took us to his friend's restaurant on Mission Beach called The Shrubbery. The restaurant's name was inspired by the movie *Monty Python and the Holy Grail.* We enjoyed delicious smoothies and carrot juice before heading back to "the country," as David calls his home. The day was getting late, and the three of us wanted to get going while the sun was still shining. Expecting to be done earlier in the day, Jeff and I had left our flashlight back at the house, and I was feeling nervous about walking through the woods in the dark.

We made it back okay, and once we were settled in, David made fried breadfruit and steamed broccoli for dinner. The breadfruit tasted like pancakes and went well with the broccoli. Eating a wide variety of local, organically grown produce has been refreshing.

Thoughts of what to do with the car began weighing heavy on my mind, and I asked David if he would be willing to sell the car for us. He could keep a share of the money for his efforts and then wire us the rest. David explained that selling a car in Queensland was not the same as in the other states and there would be costs. There was advertising, of course, but then the car would have to be inspected and repairs made if not up to specs. A "road worthy certificate" would be issued once all was in order. Then there were the details of the final delivery to be sorted out. It might not be a local buyer. The whole thing sounded complicated and hardly worth David's time. Jeff and I decided to sleep on it.

The evening's temperature was cooler than the night before, and there were fewer bugs as a result. David said, "It's unseasonably cool. Your timing has been really good. Tropical storms are quite common this time of year, and it could just as easily be pouring rain with gale force winds right now."

Since Jeff didn't sleep well in the caravan, we're sleeping in the spare bedroom inside the house. At least for tonight, the guest room is the best of our four options.

Day 47, Sunday   January 23, 2000

I slept well, but the flies and mosquitoes started swarming early, and my patience wore thin. This was our fourth day in the rainforest, and it occurred to us that we are not cut out for living in the bush. Jeff and I decided it would be best if we moved on. Between all the bats, bugs, heat, and unknowns lurking in the woods, I was in a state of overwhelm, and I think Jeff was, too. What was completely normal for David had become a challenge for us. It was time for a dose of normalcy. As beautiful as the rainforest was, it was equally as harsh, especially in the summer months. *Living "off the grid" in Queensland is intense.*

David was busy with his morning chores when Jeff and I decided to take a short hike to the swimming hole. It was an attempt to cool down, escape from the bugs, wake up, and figure out what to do next. We talked about leaving right away, as in "making a run for it" after a quick "thanks and good-bye" to David, but instead we decided to stay and have breakfast with our host and try to relax. It wasn't anything personal. David made us feel welcome and tried to make our stay as comfortable as possible. It's just that we were freaking-out and we didn't know how to tell him.

When we got back to the house, David was in the middle of making fried breadfruit, again, using the other half of the football-sized fruit from the night before. It smelled really good. He added a banana to the pan, the makings of a delicious meal.

David, noticing that Jeff could benefit from a strong cup of coffee, put a pot on the stove after we were done with breakfast. I drank peppermint tea, and the three of us ended up sitting on the front porch discussing our options for the day.

David may or may not have picked up on the exact level of our distress, and we should've just told him that we were a bunch of wimps and couldn't handle the rainforest, but he took care of us in a way that expressed he knew what we were going through. Oddly enough, a breeze blew in at 10:00 a.m. and took the edge off the heat. A cold compress held against my eyes and forehead helped, too. It was a very difficult morning.

Looking at David's calendar on the wall, I figured out that I had my days mixed up, maybe from the heat or maybe from being on vacation for so long. Whatever it was, I discovered that our flight out of Sydney was on Tuesday, not Sunday as expected. With two days more than I thought we had, Jeff and I decided there was enough time to drive further north into Port Douglas, a town we wanted to see, but thought we couldn't. My mood brightened with the news. Port Douglas is described as one of Australia's "hottest vacation destinations," and it was time we found out why.

David's healing potions worked to calm us down, and the three of us sat around the house talking until noon. Crisis averted. Since breakfast was light, it wasn't long before we were talking about eating again. I guess that meant we were feeling better, too. I helped David prepare another organic meal of rice and veggies, and during lunch, we discussed the possibility of a four-hour hike through the forest. David had a favorite trail near Mission Beach he wanted to take us on, but Jeff and I decided against it because we weren't feeling that spry. My vote was more along the lines of a day of rest and relaxation somewhere other than David's place.

We talked about all three of us driving north to Cairns, but in the end, Jeff and I realized we wanted to explore northern Queensland by ourselves. David understood. At 2:15 p.m., Jeff and I were headed for Port Douglas, a two-and-a-half hour drive up the road, which was a hop-and-a-skip compared to the trips we had made across the outback. Knowing the reef came in closer to Port Douglas than at Mission Beach, we decided to take a second trip out while we're there.

Before leaving El Arish, I used David's house phone to call the railway station and firm up our travel plans for our return to Sydney. Some interesting options have presented themselves since leaving Townsville.

With a new exit strategy in the works, we plan to take the train out of Tully rather than drive back south to Townsville. Tully is the small town where we did our laundry when we first arrived. Before the train reaches Sydney, Jeff and I will disembark in Brisbane, the capital of Queensland.

Once in Brisbane, we'll take a two-day layover so we can tour the city on our own. On the third day, we'll board the train one more time for our final journey into Sydney. That last leg will take less than a day.

Passing through Cairns we saw signs every few miles calling the city "The Gateway to the Reef." The reef came in considerably closer to shore there than anywhere else along the Queensland coast and was only an hour's boat ride out. Couple that with an international airport, one of the busiest in the country, and we could see how Cairns earned its second title of "The Tourist Capital of Tropical North Queensland." Jeff and I made a point to stay in town long enough to shop for snacks, postcards, and magnets. The locals were gracious and genuinely friendly confirming the claim posted in *Lonely Planet* that "Australian hospitality is at its finest in Cairns." Tourist money keeps the town alive and well. When in the people business, it sure helps to like people.

North of Cairns, the Great Green Way became a winding, twisting road that hugged the coastline. With every turn, the elevation increased and the beauty surrounding us intensified. The greens got greener, and the plants grew denser. Temperatures rose (since we were driving north), and the warm air blowing through the open windows of the old Ford offered little relief.

Summer in Pennsylvania may be green and a good comparison to El Arish, according to Jeff and David, but there was no way it was as green as Port Douglas. There were times when I thought I was driving straight into a postcard, it was so gorgeous. The brochures we picked up in Cairns, said Port Douglas was the only place on earth where one World Heritage Area met another World Heritage Area, where "the rainforest meets the sea." Jeff and I, knowing we'll be taking a second snorkel trip out to the reef, are looking forward to the swim with as much anticipation as the first time.

High tourist season in Port Douglas is between June and November. Jeff and I were confident our luck would hold up and there would be a room available in our price range. We arrived with plenty of time to find a place to stay, check in, and tour the downtown area before shops closed up at 5:00 p.m. Again, *Lonely Planet* led us to an affordable, no-frills motel, called The Coconut Grove Motel, located right on the main drag. It was easy to find. The name of the motel and the town's ambiance triggered memories of the year I lived in Miami, Florida in the mid-eighties, long before I met Jeff.

After a short discussion with the desk clerk, she told us there were several rooms available, and we had a variety to choose from. We also found out she could handle our snorkel reservations as well. The accommodations passed our Q&A with flying colors, and the clerk handed us our room key and our snorkel tickets in one fell swoop. It was almost too easy.

We had heard that the charter boats in Port Douglas were bigger than the ones in Mission Beach, so we were careful to choose a boat with less than fifty snorkelers and *only* snorkelers. Mixing too many SCUBA divers and snorkelers together seemed a bit chaotic to me. I wanted to be sure the crew had an easy head count and would know absolutely positively if I was back on the boat or not before I had time to get into too much trouble. *And that's what I call "snorkel insurance."*

Our final instruction for the night was this, "Be ready and waiting out front tomorrow morning when the shuttle bus arrives. It will pick you up at ten past eight and take you to the docks."

Our room is nice, and there are no bugs, bats, or snakes. A cool breeze is flowing out of the air conditioner, and there's just the right amount of motor humming white noise to put me to sleep.

Day 48, Monday   January 24, 2000

Two months before Jeff and I left on our trip, Port Douglas was one of the few places that was recommended as a "must see." Our neighbors had been there and were quick to tell us how much they enjoyed their stay in the quaint seaside village. Arriving at Port Douglas, I felt as if we had reached the end of the road, though, according to the map, it was possible to travel further up the coast. The only reason we hadn't put Port Douglas on the short list was because we knew how far out of the way it was, and we didn't know if we'd have time to fit it into the trip.

Port Douglas is as far north up the Australian eastern shoreline as Portland, Maine is on America's eastern shore. What began as a tiny fishing village has evolved over the years into an international travel destination, and it's a favorite among Aussies as well. When Sydney residents vacation here, it's like New Yorkers vacationing in Coconut Grove, Miami, Florida, only on a much smaller scale and far more laid back. While Port Douglas looks and feels as if it's on an island, because there's water all around, it's actually situated on a peninsula that juts out into the Pacific Ocean. The town is overflowing with beauty, character, art and charm, and I have quickly fallen in love with the place. Apparently, so have countless others. Every level of accommodation is available, from campgrounds to luxury spas and golf courses. The big resorts are charging as much *as $430 AU ($280 US) per night and the golf courses are world class. The town is changing fast and reminds me of the small towns in Florida before the big trophy homes came in and changed the landscape. It's the way Florida used to be.*

Jeff and I made sure we got up early enough to have a leisurely breakfast and get a good hot meal before a long day at sea. The first restaurant we came to was closed at 7:00 a.m., but the opening staff/surfer dude was very accommodating. In pure Aussie fashion, he said, "The restaurant doesn't open until noon, but I can make a fresh pot of coffee for you." Since it was off-season, the streets were empty and nothing else was open at that hour. We walked back to our room, coffee in hand, and ate some of the fruit David gave us before we left his place. *We are so well taken care of.*

Our shuttle bus arrived on time, and we were soon on our way to board the *Wavelength*. It only took 20 passengers out to the reef. As a snorkel-only cruise, our day was sure to be relaxed. We knew we had made the right choice as soon as we saw the boat, and I was grateful for the clerk's recommendation. She knew exactly what we were looking for.

At the marina, there were two massive boats still tied to the dock. Each boat transported as many as 350 snorkelers and divers out to the reef, and they were filling fast. All I could think was, "That is a lot of people to keep track of in open waters."

It was an enjoyable cruise, and from dock to reef it only took ninety minutes to reach our destination. I had heard it would take an hour and assumed the extra half hour may have taken us to a reef that was worth the extra distance or maybe the tide was against us. With several individual reefs to choose from, our captain probably kept his routine varied. Overnight trips, with time to cruise farther from shore, would allow for additional reef choices.

Our first snorkel was easy and beautiful. I brought along a disposable underwater camera to do my best to get quality pictures of the coral and fish and capture the color of the sea.

Visibility under water was exceptionally good, and the conditions were ideal.

We moved on to a second location where the guide gave us an underwater marine tour. He pointed out rare fish, coral, and various marine life. It was well done, and I appreciated the extra information at that point. Three retired couples were on board, and they had never ever snorkeled before. The crew assured them they would be fine, and all three couples did well. The reef came up within inches of the waterline, so there was no need to dive down to get a closer look. Everyone took advantage of the long foam tubular floatation aids (called "noodles") that were provided for us. I used them often in the pools back in Florida. Never did I think I'd snorkel the Great Barrier Reef with one. Those colorful tubes made it easy for us to float along and gaze at the reef below. There didn't seem to be much of a current, and it was the easiest, most enjoyable swim in open waters I have ever experienced.

The crew reminded us that it was *critically* important to the survival of the reef that we did not touch it in any way. It was a living, breathing, fragile environment, and where it's disturbed, that part of the reef dies. We could see where areas had been kicked or run over by a boat, and it was a constant reminder to keep a safe distance away for the reef's sake. Our guides took great pride in their World Heritage Area and were understandably protective of their livelihood.

The water was clear, and we could see where the ocean floor dropped substantially at the edge of one of the coral heads. It was an eerie sight, and each time I drifted too far over the dark depths of the ocean, I would quickly kick my way back over to the reef again. My first thought was "sharks," but we were told that sharks were not as much of a threat on the east coast as they were on the west. That was one message I was relieved to hear. The guide said, "On the west coast, it's a bit more dodgy," and I knew exactly what he was talking about.

For our third and final swim of the day, the crew gave us a choice of more coral or more fish. As a group, we voted to see more fish. The guide said, "We'll take you to a reef with heaps of fish." (That's 'strine for "a lot")

The first sign of marine life to show up was a school of 6-inch long squid, and then a barracuda swam into the scene. Jeff told me how he went face-to-face with the gnarly fish and got so close he could see its teeth. "The barracuda stared right back at me and never moved an inch," Jeff said. Realizing the 'cuda was a bit too close for comfort, Jeff backed off and said it was exciting and frightening all at the same time. That was his moment with *"danger." I can hear Steve Irwin saying it now.*

I noticed that the pattern we experienced with the ever increasing beauty and complexity of each reef swim from the west coast to the east coast remained intact. This last swim was like the "grand finale" in a fireworks display as we made our way through an explosion of colors brought on by thousands of fish. Red, yellow, blue, orange and purple marine life, all darting throughout the coral beds, put on a spectacular show I will always remember. Our reef journey through Oz was complete in every imaginable way.

Relaxing by the motel's pool, Jeff and I talked about our day at sea. We were still getting along well, but behaved more like old acquaintances; distant, but kind to one another. *There's a proverbial elephant in the room and neither one of us is willing to acknowledge it.*

Day 49, Tuesday   January 25, 2000

Our stay in Port Douglas was over as fast as it began, but the 36 hours we carved out for "one of Australia's hottest destinations" was worth the extra effort to get there. At 10:00 a.m., we checked out of the Coconut Grove Motel and took a walk down the main drag in search of breakfast. This time, it was later in the day, off-season lessons learned.

We found a cute little café that served real coffee and a delicious bowl of oatmeal or "porridge" as they call it here. Afterwards, we walked next door to check emails. Jeff stayed on the computer while I wandered the four blocks through town do some window shopping. Thanks to oppressive heat and the threat of cyclones, the town was barren. Fortunately for us, the weather remained in our favor with not a single storm on the radar. It was definitely hot, but manageable as long as we had a dose of air conditioning once in awhile.

While shopping, I found a beautiful little Buddha necklace, the only one there. It was a copper Buddha strung on a thin black string, and it looked as if it had been hanging on the outdoor display for years. It quickly became one of my favorite souvenirs because it represented peace and calm, always a welcome reminder.

In the short time we were in Port Douglas, we didn't see a single crocodile. There were signs posted all over the place, especially along the water's edge, warning swimmers of the potential danger to life and limb. Crocs were clearly a threat. From the safety of our car and the reef shuttle bus, I was half expecting to see a crocodile lounging by the side of the road or crossing the road like the alligators do in Florida. In hindsight, that was one Australian species I was glad I didn't see in the wild.

There are basically two types of crocs, "freshies" and "salties." Now there's a great pair of nicknames. Freshies live in the fresh water creeks and rivers, and salties live primarily in the salt water, but are known to cross over into fresh water and swim with the freshies. While freshies are not a threat to human life due to their size (freshies reach an average of 9 feet in length, while salties average 16 feet and can grow as big as 20 feet in length), they can still pack a mean bite. In any case, it's best to heed all warnings because salties can be lurking anywhere. They're the ones to watch out for because a saltie will go after anything that moves; cats, dogs, small children and even adults—all are

*considered prey. There are warnings to campers not to set
up tents too close to shore (campers have been dragged to
their deaths from their sleeping bags and into the marsh),
and instructions are given on how to store food and supplies
to keep the attraction-factor down to a minimum. I thought
our alligators back home were bad.*

We left Port Douglas shortly after 2:00 p.m. to return
south to El Arish. Jeff and I made plans beforehand to spend
the evening with David, and he was expecting us. On the
way back, we stopped in Cairns to take one last look around
and then headed for one of David's favorite places called
"Golden Hole" named after an old gold mine. David's
directions were to turn at Josephine Falls and follow the road
in to the park. He said, "It's a beautiful area with a crystal
clear river to swim in. There are also picnic tables and toilets
available for your convenience." "No roughing it there," I
thought.

Off-season had its perks. There wasn't a single car in the
parking lot when we arrived, and we had the park to
ourselves. The grounds were well manicured, the tall trees
offered welcome shade, and the water was cool and inviting.
Jeff and I decided to take a swim.

Floating along at the deepest part of the river, I could see
the bottom. It must have been 20 feet to the rocks below, and
fish and turtles were swimming all around. I thought about
going back to the car to get the snorkel gear to take a closer
look, but we didn't have time. With another hour to go, it
was important that we kept moving, because we promised
David we would be back early enough to take him out to
dinner before nightfall. If we were going to spend the night
in the tree house, we would need plenty of daylight to see
our way through the woods. I was still thinking about those
snakes.

On the ride back to El Arish, a light rain fell, and we saw
several intense rainbows off in the distance. Coupled with
the deep dark green of the Great Green Way, nature created a
surreal and magical landscape.

While driving the last 5 km (3.1 miles) into town, Jeff and I talked seriously about our options for the night and decided to stay in a hotel instead of going back to David's. "The country" proved too rustic for us, and we'd had enough of wild critters roaming in the night. Given the current state of our relationship, I could only assume that Jeff felt the same way I did about keeping things as normal and comfortable as possible.

Somehow, we found the Eco Village. I say "somehow" because I wasn't sure if we saw a sign by the road, if I read it in the travel guide, or if we were led in the same way we were led into Townsville. However it happened I was glad for it.

Eco Village was a relatively new accommodation with individual bungalows. Ours had a king-sized bed, and we were steps from Mission Beach. There was a rock pool with a spa calling us to jump in, and the cost was only $79 AU ($51 US) per night. The room was huge, a real luxury, so we made a decision to unload the car and conduct a mass reorganization of our belongings first thing in the morning. As soon as we were settled in, we called David. The three of us made arrangements to meet at a restaurant called Coconuts, also on Mission Beach and a short distance from our bungalow. David drove into town while Jeff and I walked along the shoreline.

We could *not* find the restaurant. The dense forest growth between the beach and the restaurant gave us zero visibility, and we couldn't see any signs of civilization from where we were. The directions the hotel clerk gave us were not as clear as David's instructions were to his house. We needed a clue such as "turn off the beach ten paces from the fallen log."

Wandering up and down the shoreline for twenty minutes, ready to give up, back track, and take the road in, we finally narrowed in on our target. David was patiently waiting at one of the outdoor tables when Jeff and I finally stepped through the jungle and onto the restaurant's parking lot.

Coconuts served a great meal, and when it was time to leave, David drove us back to our bungalow. It was in our room at Eco Village where Jeff and I revealed "Exit Strategy: Plan B." Plan A was to drive south to Townsville and sell the car there. Jeff said to David, "Would you like to be the new owner of "Mum's Taxi," a very reliable, previously-owned red 1983 Ford Falcon station wagon? Jennifer and I want to give you the car as a gesture of appreciation for all you have done for us. Can you use a second car?" David thought about it for a few seconds, probably running the numbers in his head knowing it would cost him to transfer the title....and to our relief he said, "Yes! I'll be happy to take the Ford." We didn't have a Plan C, so it was a good thing he was in agreement. It was clearly a win/win all the way around.

Jeff and I now have one less thing to think about and there will be no more long drives. David will have a backup vehicle or extra cash in his pocket should he choose to sell the car after we leave in two days.

It was Jeff's idea to donate the car to a good cause and to a good friend. Knowing how much rental cars were, especially one-way rentals (picking up the car in one city and dropping it off in another), we had gotten more than our money's worth out of the old Ford. As Jeff said, "David can really use a second vehicle." I was in full agreement and said, "Yes, that's a great idea."

But I have a confession to make.

The practical and thrifty side got the better of me, and I made a feeble attempt at selling the car on my own. Despite the list of obstacles David gave us, I wanted to give it a try and see if I could recoup my expenses. I was also going back on my word to give the car away.

Right after leaving David's house two days ago to head for Port Douglas, I put a "for sale" sign in the car window. I thought if I could find a buyer, David could take over from there. I listed my email address, the price, and a brief statement that the car was "very reliable." I noticed Jeff wanted nothing to do with it, and I could only imagine how disappointed he was in me. My motive: I was going home to a nearly empty bank account and my faith was waning. Worry was building around how I was going to pay my bills. There was an IRA, an Individual Retirement Account, from all those years with the Postal Service, but it was off-limits, untouchable, as far as I was concerned. I knew it was going to take a week or two before money started rolling in once I got back to work. Selling the car would give me extra cash to go home with, assuming we could make a profit at the end of the deal.

Beyond the email address, the only other way anyone was going to contact me about buying the car was if they happened to see me standing next to it. It was no surprise when not a single inquiry came in, and I realized that donating the car was the only thing to do. By the time we left Port Douglas, the sign was out of the window, and I decided my financial situation would work itself out.

I have taken trust to a whole new level on this trip. It's time I took it home with me as well.

Day 50, Wednesday   January 26, 2000

It *poured* last night. The sky opened up and dumped massive amounts of water into the rainforest, 10 to 12 inches, at least. Jeff said he could hear the storm approaching from off in the distance as it rolled in from the sea. I slept through the night, but I also slept through an earthquake once, so I'm obviously a sound sleeper. We'll never know what our experience would have been like at David's, but I am sure it would have been memorable.

Lucky for us, Eco Village provided room service. Jeff and I indulged and ordered the "tropical breakfast," a basket full of fresh fruit, coffee, juice, and two bowls of whole grain cereal. It was a luxury having food delivered to our room, and I was grateful we followed our hunch to splurge on a real hotel. Apparently, I was able to put my financial worries aside for the time being.

The rain continued on through the morning. Despite the weather, we stuck with our plans to unload the car anyway. Running between the car, the room and the laundry facilities, all within 50 feet of one another, we made as few trips as possible. Two hours later, the laundry was done, the skies cleared, and David arrived.

Last night during dinner at Coconuts, the three of us made plans for a "bush forest hike" on David's favorite trail, the one he wanted to take us on before we drove north to Port Douglas. He was passionate about this trail, brought it up numerous times, so Jeff and I agreed to go. This was our last full day in the area. Our train leaves in the morning.

David also invited us to his house after the hike for a potluck dinner with several of his friends, in honor of our last night in El Arish. Everyone was to bring a vegetarian dish, and it sounded like a wonderful time. Since we'd already be at David's late into the night, I suggested we stay over.

With bags repacked and picnic sandwiches delivered from the kitchen, we checked out of our room at Eco Village and headed for the car. I thought, "Surely the skies must be empty by now."

David's nature tour started the moment we left our hotel room. Right outside the door was an intricate sunbird's nest tucked deep within a bush, a bush we had walked past a dozen times since we arrived, and we never noticed. The nest was well camouflaged and hanging from a branch, chest high, by a collection of spider webs that the sunbird had collected to secure its home to the plant. It was a unique nest building technique. David's knowledge of the rainforest impressed us from the moment we met him, and he continued to impress us with each interesting tidbit he shared. He spoke with such passion and enthusiasm that I knew our hike was going to be good.

The forest in question was only a few miles down the road. Jeff wanted to drive, so we took the Ford. Minutes later, we were at the base of the trail. "Why is the path so wide?" I asked David. He explained that it was originally a dirt road, long since converted to a walking path.

We didn't get to enjoy the wide open spaces for long, because 50 yards into the trail, David took a sharp 90 degree turn straight into the jungle. Jeff and I hesitated for a second, looked at each other, and then followed behind, stepping high over the tall ground cover. David said, as he pushed back the overgrowth and moved dead branches out of the way, "This is my own track. I've been clearing it for years. I get a little bit done each time I come here." And I was thinking, "Track? What track? I don't see a track."

Between the dense forest growth, the fallen trees, and the "lawyer vine," it was a difficult hike; one of the most difficult I have ever been on. It was the lawyer vine that made it especially miserable. That nasty plant was a thorny, prickly rope, and it hung from every tree in the forest. It kept catching onto my clothes and on my skin, making the walk painful and annoying. I could see that Jeff and David were having the same difficulties. An image popped in my head of an Australian hiker laughing as he or she came up with the name "lawyer vine." *Aussies really have a unique sense of humor.*

On the upside, many of the other plants were interesting and impressive. I remember seeing a rare fan palm that was simply beautiful. And there were more than tropical plants deep in the forest. A full grown cassowary, the same type of bird on David's farm, crossed the path ahead of us. David said it was rare to see one in the wild, and it was the first time he had ever seen one along that particular path.

It's been a roller coaster ride of emotions through the tropics of Queensland over the past eight days, ever since arriving in Townsville. One minute I love it, the next not so much, and then I love it again. But this is where things went very, very wrong.

There I was, standing ankle deep in forest ground cover on David's own personal track when I felt an odd sensation on both feet. I looked down and was shocked by the sight of six black leeches latched onto my toes.

Completely grossed out by those blood-sucking worms, I wanted to run, run all the way back to the car as quickly as possible, but first, I had to get them off. Disgusted, I bent down and removed the half-inch long freeloaders, one by one. Each time I pulled, my toe bled profusely.

If I had any clue that there were leeches in the woods, I would have worn sneakers. I was following David's lead. He showed up in sandals, so I figured it was appropriate footwear. "Why didn't he warn me?" I thought. Snakes, spiders, flies, lizards, bats and mosquitoes I could tolerate to some extent. Leeches were in a category all their own.

The fun was over as far as I was concerned. I asked David and Jeff if they were okay with turning around and ending the hike. They let me have my way, and we were back in the parking lot after two-and-a-half hours, ninety minutes short of the planned four-hour hike. I could tell they would have liked to stay, but the leeches ruined it for me.

We drove back to Eco Village where we had left David's car. David went his way and we went ours, because we all had things to do to prepare for the farewell party. Jeff and I headed for the shops of Mission Beach to check our emails, get an afternoon snack, and look for some veggie treats to add to the potluck dinner.

I absolutely love Mission Beach. The more I see, the more I want to stay. The casual and laid back atmosphere is inviting. The food is delicious, healthy and light, and the town sits at the water's edge. A great combination, and definitely my kind of place. If I could live anywhere I pleased, I would live in Mission Beach.

It had been awhile since Jeff and I checked emails. With plenty of time before dinner to get caught up, I sat down to send the usual updates to friends and family back home. It was my mum's birthday, as they say in 'strine, so I sent her a message via my sister, Lisa. Two weeks ago, when I needed to mail a card, I was a bit distracted with the whole drive through the outback thing, so I sent a "Happy Birthday" with the help of the Internet. Time was on my side. It may have been January 26th in Australia, but it was still January 25th in the 'States, the day *before* my mum's birthday.

What a great invention. I know the Internet has been around for decades, but in the short time I've been using it, I can see how it's changing my life for the better. I remember the day, years before I had a computer of my own, when I went to the library to check my mail via the World Wide Web. I realized, "This is it. The digital age is here. The day of the handwritten letter and paper financial statements are going the way of the dodo bird." Having worked for the Postal Service for sixteen years, I have seen my share of changes in automation and delivery, but this one single change, the Internet, is going to really shake things up. For years, the decision makers in Washington have been talking about delivering five days a week instead of six to adjust to the continued decline in mail volume. Whether it will ever become a reality is anyone's guess. I believe it's important to do what's best for the greater good: whatever that looks like, and there's only one thing certain in life: change.

Jeff and I bought brie and a nice loaf of bread to add to the potluck dinner. We arrived right on time at 5:00 p.m. It wasn't long before the other four guests, all organic farmers, arrived as well. They each brought samples from their fields.

I had never heard of the fruits and vegetables that were presented in their natural states and cooked in a wide variety of dishes. I didn't write the names down either, but I did remember David's friends.

There was Kerry, a "kiwi" from New Zealand. She was in her fifties, 5' 2" with grey hair, living a physically demanding life as an organic farmer, and loving every minute of it. Her property was twenty miles away. She said, "I take a tractor to get to my house," as if it was as common as driving a car.

Eric was 45 years old, single, and rented a house in Mission Beach. He said he commuted twenty minutes everyday to his 50 acres, so he could tend to his fruit trees. With "only" 50 acres, he called it a hobby. The other couple joining us for dinner was Andrew and Marie-Noelle. I guessed them to be in their forties. Marie-Noelle was French-Canadian, and Andrew was born and raised in Queensland. I'm not exactly sure where Eric was from, but he was definitely an Aussie through and through.

Andrew and Marie-Noelle said they met thirteen years ago in Thailand, and together they owned 950 acres of rainforest, a huge chunk of land that bordered the National Park. They were a good looking couple. Both healthy and strong. Marie-Noelle had long dark brown hair, and Andrew kept his long blonde hair pulled tight in a ponytail.

Everyone has their own unique story about how things happen in their lives, how they are able to do this and that, but I didn't get the details on how this couple was able to claim 950 acres as their own or what Eric did for a living beyond farming. Of course, I was interested. Inquiring minds want to know. But instead of asking, I let the conversation flow around the crops, the odd variety of fruit, what it was like to live in Australia, and shared travel stories. At one point, Marie-Noelle described her home. She said, "The house has no walls, but we do have a bread-maker!" "The woman's got her priorities," I thought.

Marie-Noelle lives a very interesting life. She travels to New York City where she works for a year as a physical therapist, and then takes the following year off to come back to the rainforest. She has triple citizenship in the United States, Canada and Australia. As she was speaking, I felt such envy for a life I could only begin to imagine. I started thinking of ways I could live a similar lifestyle.

There were so many questions I wanted to ask Marie-Noelle (and didn't), but the story of one of her trips to Thailand revealed her personality and approach to life.

Weeks before she was to board the plane, she had meticulously packed one small perfect bag with what she considered "essential items only." She had put a lot of thought into her preparations, but when she arrived in Thailand, her bag was nowhere to be seen. All she had with her was her purse. When she realized the bag was gone for good, she decided to make the best of a bad situation and went shopping. She bought clothes, a few toiletries, a tooth brush and a small backpack to put it all in. She said, "My entire wardrobe consisted of two shirts and a skirt. It was liberating to get by with so little, and it made all that packing I had done beforehand seem so ridiculous." All I could think about was our car full of stuff, all that luggage, and how embarrassed I would be if she knew. I thought, "Any second now David is going to make a big joke about it," but he never did. It probably never crossed his mind. I was inspired from that point on to be just like Marie-Noelle in lifestyle and in travel.

Our last evening with David and his friends was life-changing. Not only did I meet new people, I had been introduced to a whole new world. Taking my career from beyond the confines of the four walls of the Postal Service to working self-employed among my community as a freelance bookkeeper was one thing. Thanks to Marie-Noelle, I saw the possibility of living part-time in the 'States and part-time in a foreign country. I began to think about how I could use the Internet to take my work with me wherever I went.

PART SEVEN

Full Circle Back to Sydney in New South Wales

"If we all did the things we are capable of doing,
we would literally astound ourselves."
Thomas Alva Edison, 1847-1931
Inventor and Scientist

Day 51, Thursday   January 27, 2000

Of all the sleeping options David had to offer, Jeff and I chose to take the couch/day bed on the front porch. Yesterday's rainstorm cooled the air, which meant fewer bugs, and it was actually quite pleasant.

It was our last day in the rainforest. Jeff and I had a morning train to catch to Brisbane, the capital city of Queensland, but David had one more surprise in store for us. With only two-and-half hours before departure, Jeff and I were invited to take a third and final tour of the farm, a five-minute hike to David's own private waterfall. David hadn't mentioned a word about it up until that moment, and the whole way over, he kept apologizing, "It's not a very big waterfall. Not nearly as big as the ones Queensland is famous for."

When we got to a clearing in the forest, I looked up. I was expecting a waterfall 10 feet high, maximum, because of the way he downplayed it, but David's private waterfall was 60 feet off the forest floor and dropped down a steep rock wall. A 4-foot deep rock pool at the base of the falls offered a cool alternative to the rising temperatures. Jeff kicked off his sandals, peeled off his t-shirt, and jumped in wearing only his shorts. I chose to sit along the edge of the pool with my feet dangling in the water, and David half-sat half-leaned up against a large rock. We told jokes, talked about the dinner the night before and how cool David's friends were, and then did our best to solve the world's problems in ten minutes or less. I told David, "I am so glad we stayed long enough to see this. You should've mentioned it sooner. It's beautiful."

Thirty minutes later, it was time to head back to the tree house, settle the business of the car, and focus on our departure. Sitting at the dining room table, I passed the necessary paperwork over to David, and Mum's Taxi was one step closer to getting a new owner. As I walked out onto the front porch and looked over the railing into David's front lawn, I saw the same young cassowary we had seen a week earlier step out of the woods, as if to say his good-byes. Jeff and I hadn't seen the bird since it greeted us the day we arrived, which made this second appearance especially meaningful. David took no notice as the cassowary lowered its head and chased the chickens into the bush. I expected a concerned look on David's face because minutes earlier, he had told us that the livestock count had, again, been reduced by one. A hen disappeared while Jeff and I were in Port Douglas, and I could tell David was saddened by his loss. He said he didn't know exactly what happened, only that she was missing. "Maybe there's a chance she'll show up," I said, but David replied, "I don't think so."

We continued on down the steps, into the thick forest, across the creek where the snake hangs out, and over to the Ford. Jeff got behind the wheel, I rode shotgun, and David took a seat in the back. Of course, David had to go along. He had to drive his "new" car home.

Our first stop was at the local travel agent's office in Tully. The woman who booked our reservation told us to pick up the train tickets there before proceeding to the Tully train station, but when we got to the agent's office, the tickets weren't available. The woman said, "I wasn't able to issue them. Check with the Queensland Railway ticket office at the train station." Lucky for us, all was in order when we arrived, and our boarding passes were awaiting pick-up. The bags were then checked with the exception of one carry-on daypack for each of us to be taken on board and stashed in our cabin.

With pass in hand and cabin number at the ready, Jeff led the way onto the train. Non-ticketed passengers were permitted onboard to look around, so David went with us. We were all pleasantly surprised to see that the berth was twice the size of the "closet" on the first train's journey from Sydney to Perth. It looked comfortable, as well. Jeff and I put the bags on the bed, stayed long enough for a thorough look around, which took all of 60 seconds, and then the three of us walked single-file off the train and back to the car to say our good-byes. All I kept wondering was, "Will I ever see David again? Is this really it?" We had only met a week ago, but it was as if we were old friends.

Handing David the keys to the Ford, I took one last look at the old girl and gave her a pat on the hood. It felt great being able to give away a car and to get a glimpse into the world of philanthropy. Up until that moment, my largest donation was $100 to an environmental group six months ago. David, still in disbelief, had few words as Jeff and I gave him a big hug, wished him well, and thanked him for everything. The last thing David said was, "Tell my mum I said 'Hi,' and give her a big hug for me."

Back on board the train, Jeff and I somehow caught on to the fact that we had been placed in first-class, while our tickets clearly read "coach." When the conductor came by to collect the tickets I explained our situation, how we were fully expecting coach and got first-class instead. The last thing Jeff and I wanted was to hear a knock on the door and a voice on the other side telling us there had been a mistake. We could be left with no cabin at all. An overnight train ride from Tully to Brisbane, the distance from Boston, Massachusetts to Wilmington, North Carolina, was a long way to travel in the passenger-only carriage, sitting straight up in a section built much like a bus.

Jeff and I offered to pay the upgrade, if that was how we needed to keep our space, but the conductor didn't know what to do. He said he would look into it further, but several hours into the ride, we never did hear back from him. Jeff and I decided to take a chance and assumed all was well. Feeling like I'd been given a golden ticket, I wondered if it was one of those "miracles" people talked about after giving away something of value with no strings attached. *Some things will forever remain a mystery.*

I relaxed into the thought of no more driving and that the trip was coming to an end. Jeff and I were still getting along well considering the awkward silences. "After being in Australia for seven weeks, the remaining five days and five nights are going to be easy," I silently declared. We knew where we were going, how we were going to get there, and how long we would be in each city. There were few remaining decisions to make before our flight out on Tuesday.

Between the gentle rocking motion of the carriage and the sounds of the wheels on the track, I was reminded of how much I loved the train ride to Perth. I vowed, once again, to travel by rail more often.

I have mixed emotions about leaving. I'm ready to go home, but there's a part of me that really wants to stay. One thing is for sure, I will miss this country very much.

Day 52, Friday   January 28, 2000

First-class room service was right on time. The coffee and biscuits we ordered last night were delivered outside our cabin door at 6:30 a.m. sharp. *I can definitely get used to this.*

Six-thirty may sound early to the average person on vacation, but it was late to me. For some reason, I got up at first light, which meant it was 4:30 a.m., long before breakfast arrived. Despite the early start, I felt better than I had in days.

The cabin was nice and roomy. Sequestered in our own private space for most of the trip, Jeff and I left the berth for only three reasons: to eat in the dining car, to use the bathroom facilities, and to step off the train whenever it made a stop to load and unload passengers at the various stations along the way. The view from the cabin window was beautiful, and I was content to sit and watch the world go by, again. The Queensland countryside was green and gorgeous. I loved every minute and didn't want it to end. Sadly, the ride was over as fast as it began when the train pulled into Brisbane at 4:10 p.m. Time to move on. *Repeated mental note: Must ride trains more often.*

Once in Brisbane, I called a youth hostel and arranged for a pick-up. Using our YHA Directory, Jeff and I found a hostel that provided shuttle service to and from the train station. It was a smooth transition from Point A to Point B, but we made one critical error. Standing at the threshold of our assigned room with all of our stuff in tow, we realized we had made a big mistake. It was all because we let our guard down, forgot to ask the basic screening questions, and the room wasn't what we expected. The beds were bunk beds, and the hostel was exceptionally noisy. Not a good combination. Our final nights abroad have caused us to become more discerning than ever. We simply wanted more comfort.

The desk clerk kindly gave us a refund, and Jeff called a cab for a ride to the Explorers Inn, a hotel recommended by

Lonely Planet. Located two blocks from the train station and in the heart of downtown Brisbane, it was right where we wanted to be all along. Once we were settled in, I saw it as a good use of our time and effort to make the move from one accommodation to the next.

The day had been filled with enough activity by early evening that, rather than explore the city, we decided to take in a movie. Since we were car-less and car-free, it was important to find activities close by. An independent movie theater, the Dendy, was half a block from the hotel making our decision on which theater to choose an easy one. The hotel clerk said, "The film selections lean toward underground documentaries, but one of the movies showing tonight is the American film, *Being John Malkovich.* The other is a Cuban music documentary. It's very good." Jeff and I were in the mood for something familiar and chose the first one mentioned. I have a feeling we were both missing home more than we cared to admit.

Day 53, Saturday   January 29, 2000

Only three more days in Australia, and I don't want to go home.

What a roller coaster. One minute I want more, the next I want to leave. I started the day off with the "If only's." "If only I had enough money to travel back and forth between countries like Marie-Noelle does." "If only I had that kind of freedom."

Our current plans included two full days in downtown Brisbane to wander around and get to know the city. Reading about the state capital, I learned that the state of Queensland is two-and-a-half times the size of Texas, and Brisbane is the third largest city in Australia right behind Melbourne and Sydney. As I read those facts, I decided to crunch some numbers, since that's my thing, and I discovered a few more interesting comparisons. The entire population of Australia is estimated to be around 19 million. That's less than the population of Texas alone (roughly 20 million), and to put things into deeper perspective; 8 million people live in *New York City*. The population of the United States? Approximately 281 million. Most of Australia's residents live along the east and west coasts, with a majority of them in the southeast states of Victoria and New South Wales. Having traveled through the outback, it was clear why few lived inland.

As I wrapped my mind around the numbers, we kept the rest of the day on the simple side. The farthest we ventured out around Brisbane was to see the Myer Centre. It's a huge outdoor shopping center with a six-story mall indoors, complete with a mini-roller coaster on the sixth level. Walking through the shops, I noticed I was on sensory overload and a bit overwhelmed after being in the desert and the rainforest for the past several weeks. The sidewalks were filled with musicians and talents of all kinds, and we decided to sit down and be the observers. Doing any more than that was too much effort.

Along the row of shops, we found a reasonably priced photo developer and had the remaining nine rolls developed so we could see all of the pictures before flying home. They were ready within an hour, and I was very happy with the results, especially the shots of David and his farm. I planned to put together a small photo album for his mom so she would have current pictures of her son. She'd never been to El Arish, and given her age, it was unlikely she would ever go. There were two dozen pictures in all. Pictures of David's tree house, his waterfall, the crops, flowers, Lotho the donkey, the chickens, the cassowary, and of course, David.

Rather than eat out for the second night in a row, Jeff and I decided to get "take-away" from the hotel's restaurant on the lower level and then carry our meals to our room. It was the usual steamed veggies and rice for me, and a hamburger and fries for Jeff. After dinner, we watched two more American movies, this time via videos provided by the hotel.

Having slept in this morning, I stayed up later than usual to finish reading one of the books I picked up in Alice Springs.

Jeff and I are still getting along, but our relationship as boyfriend/girlfriend is strained. Sadly, the "honeymoon" was over a long time ago. There were a lot of good times over the past two months, but we continue to drift apart even though we are together night and day.

Day 54, Sunday   January 30, 2000

On our last full day in Brisbane, we repeated what we did yesterday and went to the mall and walked around town. We could have traveled beyond the city center to see more of the area, but we were tired, tired of traveling, and tired of seeing something new and different. I bought two more books to read, and we watched the Robin Williams movie *Bicentennial Man* in our room. It was another video rental provided by the hotel.

For dinner, we ate sushi and veggie rolls, and went to bed early. Tomorrow, we head south. Only one full day left in Oz.

Day 55, Monday   January 31, 2000

On a mission, we woke up at 4:40 a.m. to take the early train to Sydney. It was the XPT, sleek, aerodynamic, fast, and modern in design, a train very different from the first two we rode.

Since this was only a day trip, we booked regular coach seats, which meant no cabin and no lying down to stretch our legs. Unfortunately, we learned the hard way that when riding a train for more than three hours at a time, it's a must to be able to move about. Sitting fourteen hours in seats made for buses and airplanes was other than ideal. We had inquired about a lounge car before we boarded, to give us the freedom to walk around, but there were none available. All we had access to were our assigned seats and an extra buffet car that served "take-away" only. We brought our meals back to our cramped quarters and dealt with the situation.

The countryside between Brisbane and Sydney was absolutely gorgeous. There were bananas growing in every conceivable space throughout the rolling landscape. I enjoyed the view the whole way down, as we crossed the state border from Queensland into New South Wales. Heading south through the Gold Coast meant the temperatures were dropping with every passing mile. When not reading, I stared out the window daydreaming, scheming of ways I could come back.

At 9:40 p.m., the train pulled into the exact same platform as the one Jeff and I departed from 55 days ago. A lifetime had happened since then.

Because that first night at the Pacific International Inn, two months ago, was such a pleasant experience, Jeff and I decided to stay there on our last night as well. Since the hotel was only two blocks away, Jeff and I borrowed a luggage cart from the train station, piled it high with all of our stuff, rolled the cart down the hill to the hotel, and checked in. The trolley (as they call it here) was returned to the train station before anyone noticed it was missing. *I think.* At least no one said anything. Our luggage count was exactly the same as when we arrived, but the total volume and weight had increased, due to the multitude of souvenirs and photos we gathered along the way.

It's late. I've got to try and get some sleep. I'm overtired and anxious to be flying out tomorrow morning.

Departure, Tuesday   February 1, 2000

We woke up dangerously late at 9:00 a.m., and given my recent history, I have no idea how I slept in that long. We needed to be up and on our way to the airport by 10:00. Somehow we managed to pack, check out, and eat breakfast in less than an hour. Surprisingly, the waitress said she remembered us from our visit nearly two months ago. "Must be the accent," I thought.

Since we were already in downtown Sydney, there was no need to call a taxi service. All that was required was to walk outside the front doors of the hotel and hail a cab, but we didn't have to do that either. The moment we stepped out to the curb a taxi pulled up to let a passenger out. Within seconds, we were on our way to the airport.

Our Qantas flight home made its first connection in Fiji before continuing on to Los Angeles. Noticing this route on the itinerary that we received in October, I said to Jeff, "I want a vacation from the vacation." He agreed, and before leaving Florida, Jeff and I requested a four night, five day layover in Fiji. Fortunately, there were no fees or charges for the extended stay, and we added five days of rest and relaxation onto our trip.

"Hotels and meals are very inexpensive this time of year. Pennies on the dollar, and there are lots of vacancies," the travel agent said, "No need to book any arrangements in advance." With that bit of information, Jeff and I decided to take our "no-plan" plan to the islands and choose our accommodations once we landed at the Nadi International Airport.

Lounging by a pool, staying in one place for five days straight, sleeping when we want, swimming when we want, and doing virtually nothing was exactly what the travel doctor ordered.

Jeff and I knew, all too well, we would be back to work and back to our daily routines soon enough.

CONCLUSION

"Be who you are and say how you feel
because those who mind don't matter
and those who matter don't mind."

Dr. Seuss, 1904-1991
Author and Illustrator

The American dollar goes a long way in Fiji, and once we landed, we found an authentic island hideaway called Tabua Sands Beach Resort for only $45 US per night. It was one of a dozen options listed in the airport on the accommodations board, and to us, it had the prettiest picture.

We took an island taxi, which was an experience in itself, because we were dropped off at the wrong resort. The driver took off before we realized his mistake, and we had to call for another ride. The hour-and-a-half transfer to the resort ended up taking three hours, and it was 10:00 p.m. when we finally reached our proper destination. Fortunately, the front desk clerks were gracious, friendly, and seemed genuinely glad to see us despite the late arrival. A baggage handler escorted us to our own private bungalow on the beach.

For the most part, as planned, all we did was eat, sleep, and swim in the pool. Jeff and I spoke only about the day's current events, and I noticed that we never mentioned our relationship, nor did we speak about future plans together.

While in the Los Angeles airport waiting for our connecting flight back to Florida, Jeff calmly said to me, "I don't think I want to be with you anymore." I was sitting to his left, looking straight ahead watching the planes taxi down the runway when he spoke those ten life changing words. With a slight pause I replied just as calmly, "Okay." Jeff was the first to say what we were both thinking.

I came home with enough money to buy food and pay a few bills, until the first few paychecks started to roll in. As promised, my jobs were waiting for me when I returned. I was so relieved. All five clients were glad to see me again, and the predominant theme of every conversation was, "How was the trip?! Tell us all about it!"

When I caught my breath long enough to open the huge pile of mail waiting for me, there was a letter from an attorney handling the estate of my godmother, a woman I hardly knew. She was an old friend of my father's. Mildred and I wrote sporadically, at best, and I hadn't seen her since my high school graduation decades ago. The letter from her attorney explained how she had remembered me in her will, and inside the envelope was a check for one thousand dollars. That was enough to cover my bills for a month, and more than what I had hoped to get out of the sale of the Ford. Again, I thought, "Did donating the car to our farmer friend have anything to do with the unexpected gift or is this check somehow tied to the good feeling I had about giving the car away? Did my 'smarter self,' my intuition 'know' this money was coming?" *I may never know for sure how it all works, but I now understand how important it is for me to trust my intuition, because it is right one-hundred percent of the time.*

Jeff and I tried to mend our relationship, once we had time to rest and settle back into our routine, but three months later he moved out. After four years and two very intense months, the relationship had run its course. Fifty-five days in Australia revealed our future together. We would be happiest if we took separate paths.

Australia left me wanting more—more time in the rainforest, on the reef, exploring the lush green countryside of New South Wales and Queensland, and first-class train rides across the Nullarbor Plain. I want to go back to the Flinders Ranges, Uluru, Kata Tjuta, and Kings Canyon to learn more about the Dreaming, walkabouts, and songlines…the ways of the Aborigines. The revisit list is long, and there is much I have yet to discover for the very first time.

While America will always be home, the child in me will always be dreaming of *Oz*.

Epilogue

After Jeff and I parted ways, I took a journey inward and participated in a series of self-development and self-improvement seminars. I remained inspired by Marie-Noelle's freedom to roam about the world and began searching for a new career. I also had a strong desire to share my life with a man I truly loved, a man who loved me back. That was a tall order, one that required serious introspection, but eight moves and two states later, I got answers and "I got better," as the Monty Python line goes.

In 2001, I began to take my writing seriously, and in 2004, I met my future husband; all the while building upon the three foundational life lessons I learned in Australia.

1. Trust my intuition, my heart, and the ideas that come to mind. They are my inner GPS, my personal global positioning system.

2. Take inspired action, no matter how illogical it seems, because my "smarter self" sees the big picture.

3. When I do what is best for me it is best for the whole.

In January 2009, eighteen months into writing and editing *An American in Oz*, my husband, Patrick, asked me with the most sincere curiosity, "Why *did* you write this book?" It was such a big question, I couldn't answer him at first. I needed to give it some thought, and the following day, I came up with three reasons why:

Reason #1 – Because I am a writer and writers write. That's like asking, "Why does a singer sing?" It's what we do.

Reason #2 – Because I have a story to tell, and it was time I told it. In the recent epic movie, *Australia*, the message throughout was this, "At the end of our lives, when it's all said and done, all we really have left is our story." *An American in Oz* is my story.

Reason #3 – I was finally *ready*.

Ever since I sent the first emails home from halfway around the world with details I had logged in my journal, my friends and family have said to me, "You should write a book." Whenever I talked to anyone at length about my trip to Australia, I heard the same thing, "You should write a book." I've learned over the years that when people make suggestions that fit in with what I'm naturally interested in (writing), it's a clear indication that I might be able to make a living doing what I love.

It took me seven years to take the small travel journal, quite literally, out of the closet. Up until that fateful day in 2007 when I began rereading my notes, much of the trip had become a vague and distant memory. I couldn't have drawn the map placed at the beginning of this book if my life depended on it. It was a bigger trip than I was willing to admit, and I had a lot of "stuff" to look at. (All that luggage really did represent something.) Fortunately, the more I read the more memories came flooding back, one triggering the next and then the next, until all the pieces of the puzzle came together to paint a vivid picture. I finally saw what an extraordinary two months it was. Writing *An American in Oz*, the same way the original journal was written, at the end of the day recounting the day's events, took me back to Australia. It is my hope that I can offer a glimpse of this wonderful country to the reader as well.

Patrick and I are planning our own trip to Oz. At the moment, it's in the category of "someday," and we are confident it will become clear when it is time to go. We may take the book's journey from beginning to end, or maybe we'll travel a different path all our own. Whatever happens and wherever we go, I look forward to the day when the two of us, together, are watching one of those magnificent sunsets in the outback or witnessing something so unusual, so different from home, that I turn to my husband and say, "We are definitely *not* in Kansas anymore."

Jennifer Monahan
Author and Adventurer

Appendix A

States, Territories, and Capital Cities

<u>Six States</u>
New South Wales (NSW)
Victoria (VIC)
Queensland (QLD)
Western Australia (WA)
South Australia (SA)
Tasmania (TAS)

<u>Two Major Territories</u>
Australian Capital Territory (ACT)
Northern Territory (NT)

<u>Capital Cities of the States & Territories</u>
Sydney, NSW
Melbourne, VIC
Brisbane, QLD
Perth, WA
Adelaide, SA
Canberra, ACT – the Nation's Capital
Hobart, TAS
Darwin, NT

Appendix B

Post-Trip Itinerary

Day 1 – Pacific International Inn, Sydney, NSW
Day 2 – Indian Pacific Railway, train to Perth, WA
Day 3 – Indian Pacific Railway, train to Perth, WA
Day 4 – Indian Pacific Railway, train to Perth, WA
Day 5 – Britannia YHA, Perth, WA
Day 6 – Britannia YHA, Perth, WA
Day 7 – Rottnest Lodge, Rottnest Island, WA
Day 8 – Rottnest Lodge, Rottnest Island, WA
Day 9 – Metro Inn, Perth, WA
Day 10 – Metro Inn, Perth, WA
Day 11 – Metro Inn, Perth, WA
Day 12 – Potshot Resort, Exmouth, WA
Day 13 – Yardie Creek Campground, Cape Range National
Park, WA
Day 14 – Ned's Camp, Cape Range National Park, WA
Day 15 – Ningaloo Reef Resort, Coral Bay, WA
Day 16 – Ningaloo Reef Resort, Coral Bay, WA
Day 17 – Ningaloo Reef Resort, Coral Bay, WA
Day 18 – Ningaloo Reef Resort, Coral Bay, WA
Day 19 – Exmouth Cape Tourist Village, Exmouth, WA
Day 20 – Denham Seaside Tourist Village, Denham, WA
Day 21 – Denham Seaside Tourist Village, Denham, WA
Day 22 – Priory Lodge, Port Denison, WA
Day 23 – YHA Coolibah Hostel, Perth, WA
Day 24 – YHA Coolibah Hostel, Perth, WA
Day 25 – Goldrush Lodge, Coolgardie, WA
Day 26 – Eucla Motor Hotel, Eucla, WA
Day 27 – Car camped along the Great Eastern Highway
Day 28 – Wilpena Pound Motel, The Flinders Ranges, SA
Day 29 – Wilpena Pound Motel, The Flinders Ranges, SA

Day 30 – Look Out Cave, Coober Pedy, SA
Day 31 – Look Out Cave, Coober Pedy, SA
Day 32 – Curtin Springs Cattle Station, NT
Day 33 – Curtin Springs Cattle Station, NT
Day 34 – Kings Canyon Campground, NT
Day 35 – Curtin Springs Cattle Station, NT
Day 36 – Curtin Springs Cattle Station, NT
Day 37 – Melanka Lodge, Alice Springs, NT
Day 38 – Melanka Lodge, Alice Springs, NT
Day 39 – Tennant Creek Youth Hostel, Tennant Creek, NT
Day 40 – Mount Isa Outback Motor Inn, Mount Isa, QLD
Day 41 – A motel in Hughenden, QLD (name unknown)
Day 42 – Travelers Backpacker Lodge, Magnetic Island, QLD
Day 43 – Travelers Backpacker Lodge, Magnetic Island, QLD
Day 44 – Treefarm, private residence, El Arish, QLD
Day 45 – Treefarm, private residence, El Arish, QLD
Day 46 – Treefarm, private residence, El Arish, QLD
Day 47 – Coconut Grove Budget Accommodations, Port Douglas, QLD
Day 48 – Coconut Grove Budget Accommodations, Port Douglas, QLD
Day 49 – Eco Village, Mission Beach, QLD
Day 50 – Treefarm, private residence, El Arish, QLD
Day 51 – Train to Brisbane, Queensland Railway
Day 52 – Explorers Inn, Brisbane, QLD
Day 53 – Explorers Inn, Brisbane, QLD
Day 54 – Explorers Inn, Brisbane, QLD
Day 55 – Pacific International Inn, Sydney, NSW
Departure – morning flight to Fiji

Appendix C

List of Accommodations

Pacific International Inn, Sydney
717-723 George St, Sydney, NSW
(Now called The Great Southern Hotel)
www.greatsouthernhotel.com.au

Indian Pacific Railway – Train from Sydney to Perth
http://www.gsr.com.au/our-trains/indian-pacific/the-journey.php

Britannia YHA, Perth – 253 William St, Perth 6003, WA
http://www.perthbritannia.com/

Rottnest Lodge – Rottnest Island, Western Australia
http://www.rottnestlodge.com.au/

Metro Inn, Perth – 61 Canning Highway, Perth, WA
http://www.metrohotels.com.au/perth-hotels/metro-hotel-on-canning-13

Potshot Resort – Murat Rd, Exmouth, WA
http://www.potshotresort.com/

Yardie Creek Campground – In the Cape Range National Park,
38 kilometers south of the Milyering Visitor Centre along
Yardie Creek Road, Western Australia
http://www.exmouthwa.com.au/pages/cape-range-national-park/

Ned's Camp - In the Cape Range National Park near Milyering
Visitor Centre
http://www.dec.wa.gov.au/hotproperty/property/national-parks/cape-range-national-park.html

Ningaloo Reef Resort – 1 Robinson Street, Coral Bay, WA
http://www.ningalooreefresort.com.au/site/

Exmouth Cape Tourist Village
Truscott Crescent, Exmouth, WA
http://www.wheretostay.net/listing.htm?ql=60900370

Denham Seaside Tourist Village
Knight Terrace, Denham, WA
http://www.sharkbayfun.com/

Priory Lodge
6 St Dominics Road, Port Denison, WA
http://members.iinet.net.au/~jaguar/ads/priorylodgedongara.html

YHA Coolibah Hostel
194 Brisbane Street, Northbridge, Perth, WA
http://www.hostels.com/hostels/perth/coolibah-lodge/1924

The Goldrush Lodge aka: The Railway Lodge
75 Bayley St, Coolgardie, WA
http://www.aussieweb.com.au/details.aspx?id=1831265

Eucla Motor Hotel – Eyre Hwy, Eucla, WA
http://www.nullarbornet.com.au/towns/eucla.html

Wilpena Pound Motel, The Flinders Ranges
Wilpena Road, Via Hawker, SA
http://www.wilpenapound.com.au/

Look Out Cave
Lot 1141 McKenzie Close, Coober Pedy, SA
http://www.cooberpedy.sa.gov.au/site/page.cfm?u=234&c=305

Curtin Springs Cattle Station – On the Lasseter Hwy, 85km east of
the entrance to Uluru-Kata Tjuta National Park, NT
http://www.curtinsprings.com/

Kings Canyon Campground
3.5 hours north of Ayers Rock and 3.5 hours west of Alice Springs
in the center of the continent. Kings Canyon Campground is
situated 7 km from the Canyon, NT
http://www.kingscanyonresort.com.au/campground/

Melanka Lodge
94 Todd Street, Alice Springs, NT
http://www.addhotel.com/Australia/Alice_Springs/Melanka_
Lodge.htm

Tennant Creek Youth Hostel
Corner of Windley St and Leichhardt St, Tennant Creek, NT
http://www.hostels.com/hostels/tennant-creek/tourist's-rest-vip-
tennant-creek-youth.../1903

Mount Isa Outback Motor Inn
45 West Street, Mount Isa, QLD
(Now the Mount Isa Outback Motel)
http://outbackmotel.com.au/

Travelers Backpacker Lodge
1 The Esplanade, Magnetic Island, QLD (No longer there)

David Chandlee
Treefarm, El Arish, QLD 4855
phone + 617 4068 5263
http://www.countryenglishtreefarm.com

Coconut Grove
56 Macrossan Street, Port Douglas, QLD
(It's changed quite a bit since 2000!)
http://www.coconutgroveportdouglas.com.au/

Eco Village
Clump Point Road, Mission Beach, Queensland
http://www.ecovillage.com.au/

Train to Brisbane and Sydney
Queensland Railway
http://www.qr.com.au/

Explorers Inn
63 Turbot Street, Brisbane, QLD http://www.explorers.com.au/

Acknowledgments

It takes a village to create a book. This publication was made possible through the support of family, friends, and business associates who showed up brilliantly with their time, resources, and talents. I definitely had "heaps" of help.

Deep appreciation goes to:

The One who Loves, Supports and Sustains us all – thank you for answering my call for You to be in charge of my day and in charge of my thoughts.

My parents, Meredith and Eleanor – thank you for your love and support, and for always seeing the best in me from the moment I was born.

My husband, Patrick – thank you for sharing life's journey with me. Your love, patience and trust gave me the strength and courage to finish this book and find joy in marriage.

My identical twin sister, Lisa – you are me and I am you, as close as two human beings can possibly get. You help keep me grounded and encourage me to be myself. When I asked if you would read over the early manuscripts, you said, "Yes," and made the book better.

Editor Extraordinaire, Robert Fulton, Jr. PhD – thank you for taking on this project, and thank you for making me laugh. The comic relief was needed as much as the lessons in grammar were. (Did I write that right?)

My dear friend, Santiana Jean-Baptiste – you encouraged me to show up, to write my life stories and share them with others. I was terrified the day I promised you I would write a book, because I knew you would hold me accountable.

David Chandlee, my American/Australian friend – for your insights, knowledge of Australia, and the contributions both in time and expertise that you made to this book, thank you.

Retired Postmaster, Robert Pijanowski – you are a true leader. You encouraged me to go back to college after a nine year "recess." While we thought it would help move me up the ranks in the Postal Service, it was instrumental in moving me *out* of the Postal Service.

My niece-in-law, Breanne Monahan – if it wasn't for you, this book would still be locked away in a "safe place." Thank you for typing the original words from the scribbled pages of my travel journal, all 22,803 of them. You took on the challenge when I wasn't willing to do it myself.

Jeff – Together, we found what's best by choosing our own individual paths. It took me seven years to revisit this trip, and I am a better person for having taken the journey …twice.

My ebook mentor, Ellen Violette – thank you for all the coaching, encouragement and expert advice you've so generously shared over the years. You know what it takes to get here. www.theebookcoach.com

My publishing mentor, Stephanie Gunning – thank you for teaching me the hidden rules of the publishing industry and the business of books. You made it real for me. www.stephaniegunning.com

My friend, Audrey Ziegler – thank you for creating the travel route graphics on the map inside this book and especially for always believing in me. You're a true friend.

Bill Singer – the laptop you gave me when my old one crashed was a godsend. Thank you.

My proofreaders checking the final drafts: Lisa Calvert, Patrick Monahan, Chris Posti, Gary Greenfield, Katie Graves, Grace Moore and David Chandlee, thank you for your keen and discerning reading skills.

Everyone at Infinity Publishing who brought this book to life, especially John Harnish, thank you for all you do.

All the Aussies – thank you for sharing your life and introducing me to your country. I had an amazing time, and I look forward to my return.

…and to the countless others at home and away who made this journey possible inside and out, I am eternally grateful to each and every one of you.

*"Don't ask yourself what the world needs.
Ask yourself what makes you come alive, and then go and do
that. Because what the world needs are people who have
come alive."*

Dr. Howard Thurman, 1899-1991
Author, Philosopher, Educator,
Theologian, and Civil Rights Leader

INTRODUCING:
The Science of Knowing™

Dedicated to the Pursuit and *Attainment* of Happiness

A Curriculum for L.I.F.E.*

E-courses available by logging on to:
www.thescienceofknowing.com

No grades, no tests, no pre-requisites
Because every answer is already inside you.

*"At our deepest level, we are all the same. We are all in
search of lasting and profound joy. The answers lie within.
It's a journey with great rewards."*

Jennifer Monahan, Founder

*<u>L</u>earning <u>I</u>n the <u>F</u>ield of <u>E</u>xperience

About the Author

Jennifer Monahan grew up in Washington, D.C. and the suburbs of Maryland. Her love of traveling started early when, at the age of twelve, she flew on her own to Aspen, Colorado to visit a sixth grade friend who was vacationing there with family. That single journey opened up a whole new world.

Jennifer's travels have taken her to forty-four of the fifty United States. In her adult life, she has lived in Maryland, Utah, Wyoming, Alaska, Florida, North Carolina, and Pennsylvania. Trips abroad include Canada, the Bahamas, Taiwan, New Zealand, Solomon Islands, South Korea, Great Britain, Mexico, Australia and Fiji. The author currently resides in Pennsylvania with her husband, three step-sons, and two very cool cats.

An American in Oz is her first book.

For more information visit: www.anamericaninoz.com
www.jennifermonahan.com

281